ADVAITASIDDHI—A CRITICAL STUDY

SRI GARIB DASS ORIENTAL SERIES NO. 103

Advaitasiddhi
A Critical Study

K. MAHESWARAN NAIR

SRI SATGURU PUBLICATIONS
A Division of
INDIAN BOOKS CENTRE
DELHI—INDIA

Published by :
SRI SATGURU PUBLICATIONS
A Division of
INDIAN BOOKS CENTRE
Indological & Oriental Publishers
40/5, Shakti Nagar
Delhi—110007
(INDIA)

First Edition—Delhi 1990

ISBN. 81-7030—229-3

Printed in India :
Sainion Printary, Delhi-110032.

Contents

Foreword

'Advaitasiddhi' is one of the most difficult abstruse book in the philosophical world. Sri Nair must be congratulated for the hazardous task of going through this entire text step by step and critically analysing the stand point of Madhusūdana Sarasvati set against the background of the staunch antagonists of the advaitavādins. He has left no stones unturned to present his contention with as much conviction as possible. I must admit that his presentation has demonstrated his technical mastery of his field of specialisation and first-hand knowledge of the 'Advaitasiddhi' as well as its allied works. The presentation of the text itself is highly satisfactory, the application of research methodology is sound and the chapter-division is refreshing and instructive.

Divided in as many as twelve chapters the work gives a short but coherent picture of the siddhi literature of the advaitavedānta school which is very interesting, important and informative. In the second part which is entitled as 'Textual Examination' Sri Nair has exhibited his brilliance in presenting the views of Madhusūdana faithfully as delineated in the text of the 'Advaitasiddhi'.

The material presented here deserves careful consideration. Sri Nair has scientifically marshalled the material and brought to light this abstruse text clearly and logically.

Calcutta
1.12.1989

Dr. ASOKE CHATTERJEE SASTRI
Professor and Head of the
Department of Sanskrit,
University of Calcutta.

Preface

Advaitasiddhi is the magnum opus of Madhusūdana—sarasvati who was one of the greatest stalwarts of the philosophy of *Advaita.* The book is a verbatim reply to *Nyāyāmṛta*, the masterpiece of Vyāsatīrtha, the great champion of the philosophy of *Dvaita. Nyāyāmṛta* and *Advaitasiddhi* together constitute the fountain-head of neo-*Vedānta*; both marvel as the best specimens of the controversy between *dvaitins* and *advaitins*.

What is intended in the present book is a modest attempt in the study of *Advaitasiddhi.* In the study of *Advaitasiddhi* one has to pass through certain hurdles. In the first place, there is the absence of a complete translation of the text in English. Secondly, since *Advaitasiddhi* is written employing throughout the method of *Navya Nyāya*, an acquaintance with the same has to be acquired before embarking upon the study of *Advaitasiddhi.* Thirdly, since *Advaitasiddhi* is a verbatim retort to *Nyāyāmṛta* the study of the latter is a pre-requisite. I have tried my best to get over these difficulties. The incomplete English translation of *Advaitasiddhi* by Pandit Ganganath Jha, though it contains only the first twentysix topics out of the total of one hundred and twelve, was of immense help to me. I have taken pains to compare the work with *Nyāyāmṛta* as and when found necessary.

The study is divided into three parts each comprising of four chapters. The first part is general. The first chapter deals with the author, his date, life and works. The second chapter is devoted to give an account of the *siddhi* literature of the *Advaita* school. The third chapter presents a brief history of the controversy between *dvaitins* and *advaitins.* The fourth chapter refers to the nature, contents and commentaries of *Advaitasiddhi.* The second part is a textual examination of *Advaitasiddhi* which has four *paricchedas.* The fifth chapter examines the first *pariccheda* of *advaitasiddhi* distributed in sixtythree topics. The sixth chapter examines the second *pariccheda* having thirtyfive topics. The seventh chapter examines the third *pariccheda* in eight topics. The eighth chapter examines the fourth *pariccheda* in six topics. The third part is completely devoted to observations and conclusion. The ninth chapter comprises of general observations on *Advaitasiddhi.* The tenth chapter consists of observations on the schematism of *Advaita* as evidenced by *Advaitasiddhi.* The eleventh chapter contains philosophical and other observations. The twelfth chapter is the conclusion.

Resume has been given at the end of each chapter. The concluding chapter presents the thesis in a nut-shell.

In this study of *Advaitasiddhi* I have tried to point out its practical relevance. As a result, I hope, the study will cater to the present-day philosophical needs. I have always been keen to be objective in my approach as well as to be brief in presentation.

More than one edition of *Advaitasiddhi* have been utilised in the present study. Unless otherwise specified page numbers of *Advaitasiddhi* referred to correspond to those of the text along with commentaries edited by Anantakṛṣṇaśāstri, N.S., of the Nirṇayasāgar edition.

The study of *Advaitasiddhi* was undertaken by me at the instance of the late Dr. S. Venkitasubramonia lyer who was the Professor and Head of the Department of Sanskrit in the University of Kerala. Dr. K. Raghavan Pillai, Director and Professor, O. R. I. and MSS. library, University of Kerala was my supervising teacher under whose guidance I could do a good deal of my work. Owing to the demise of Dr. Raghavan Pillai, I proceeded with my work under the guidance of Dr. M. Sreedharan Menon, Professor and Head of the Department of Sanskrit (Retd.), University of Calicut. Dr. Menon has always been a source of inspiration to me. I express my deep sense of gratitude to him. Dr. T. Bhaskaran, Director and Professor, O.R.I. and MSS. Library, University of Kerala, has always been a great help to me particularly in his capacity as Head of the Institute where I did research. My thanks are due to him as well. In shapping the thesis in its final form and oberving the methodological aspect I am indebted to Dr. K. Vijayan, Reader in Sanskrit, University of Kerala. It will be a dereliction of duty on my part if I do not thank Dr. K.V. Sarma of the Adyar Library and Research Institute, who has taken personal interest in my work. I am grateful to Dr. N.P. Unni, Professor and Head of the Department of Sanskrit, University of Kerala and to Prof. M.K. Gangadharan, Professor of

English, V.T.M. N.S.S. College, Dhanuvachapuram for the valuable suggestions I received from them.

I express my sincere thanks to the authorities of the University of Kerala for granting me permission to publish the thesis. The name of the original thesis was 'Advaitasiddhi—A study'. The present book form is named 'Advaitasiddhi-A critical Study. This change has been effected taking the critical nature of the study into consideration.

I am indebted to Dr. Asoke Chatterjee Sastri, Professor and Head of the Department of Sanskrit, University of Calcutta for the valuable suggestions I received form him. I am extremely thankful to him for favouring me with a brief but illuminating Foreword for the book.

Thanks are due to Dr. L. Sulochana Devi and S. Geethamony Amma, Research Associate and Research Scholar respectively of my Department, for the help they did in preparing the Index.

My obligation to Sri Satguru Publications, a division of Indian Books Centre, Delhi cannot be expressed by mere words. They have neatly executed the printing of the book in a record time.

K. MAHESWARAN NAIR

English, V. T. M. N.S.S. College, Dhanuvachapuram for the valuable suggestions I received from them.

I express my sincere thanks to the authorities of the University of Kerala for granting me permission to publish the thesis. The name of the original thesis was 'Advaitasiddhi—A study'. The present book form is named 'Advaitasiddhi-A critical Study'. This change has been effected taking the critical nature of the study into consideration.

I am indebted to Dr. Asoke Chatterjee Sastri, Professor and Head of the Department of Sanskrit, University of Calcutta for the valuable suggestions I received form him. I am extremely thankful to him for favouring me with a brief but illuminating Foreword for the book.

Thanks are due to Dr. L. Sulochana Devi and S. Geethamony Amma, Research Associate and Research Scholar respectively of my Department, for the help they did in preparing the index.

My obligation to Sri Satguru Publications, a division of Indian Books Centre, Delhi, cannot be expressed by mere words. They have neatly executed the printing of the book in a record time.

K. MAHESWARAN NAIR

PART ONE

Introduction

The world today is in an unprecedented crisis. One principal view is that the advancement of science and technology, without any regard for human values, has brought about the present crisis. The solution put forward is the convergence of science and philosophy. *Vedāntic* thought has assumed a new importance in this connection. During the last few years several important books dealing with the synthesis of science and *Vedānta* have appeared in India and abroad.

It is not within the scope of the present thesis to compare *Vedānta* and modern science. However, one thing has to be specified here. There is no rule that science and philosophy should always stand at variance. Philosophy can well become a genuine science. But the so-called modern synthetic approach to *Vedānta* and science is often at the risk of objectivity. *Vedānta* is not completely out of the reach of the scientist. However, any scientist who wants to pass judgements on *Vedānta* has to acquire a good knowledge of it. It is not an easy job too. The *Vedānta*, although frequently quoted, is little known to the people at large. Therefore, they are often made to believe anything and everything in the name of *Vedānta*. Many people take Śaṅkara's *Vedānta* as representative of the whole of Indian thought. By doing so not only objectivity but historicity is also neglected. Even the basic difference of idealism and materialism is ignored; not to speak of other differences in details. It has become a widespread tendency to depict Indian philosophy, in total, as essentially spiritual. This will not serve the larger interests of our country. Only a realistic approach, to Indian philosophy as a whole and to *Vedānta* in particular, will be in consonance with the present-day philosophical needs of our people.

The study of Indian philosophy should reveal the rich and varied philosophical heritage of India. From the very beginning, there have been a large number of philosophical views in our country. Indian philosophy represents an abundance of contradictory stand-points. Contradiction has always been the motive force in Indian philosophy.

There is difference of opinion regarding the number of Indian philosophical systems. Kauṭilya mentions in his *Arthaśāstra* only three systems: *Sāṅkhya*, *Yoga* and *Lokāyata*. Mādhava in his *Sarva-darśanasaṅgraha*, deals with sixteen systems. The traditional way is to treat Indian philosophy as nine distinct systems of basic importance. These are the *Cārvāka*, the *Jaina*, the *Bauddha*, the *Sāṅkhya*, the *Yoga*, the *Nyāya*, the *Vaiśeṣika*, the *Mīmāṁsa* and the *Vedānta*. The nine systems are grouped under two broad heads: *āstika* and *nāstika*. Among the nine systems mentioned, the first three form the *nāstika* group and the remaining six the *āstika*. Each of the nine systems, in due course, split into many schools and sub-schools on the basis of doctrinal differences.

The *Vedānta*, which is only one of the *āstika* systems, has many varieties. Three of them, namely, *Advaita*, *Viśiṣṭādvaita* and *Dvaita* are more important. All these rely mainly on the *Prasthānatraya*, namely, the *Upaniṣads*, *Brahmasūtras* and *Bhagavadgītā*, as their authoritative texts.

The Upaniṣads contain elements of a number of philosophical systems. The first comprehensive attempt to evolve a consistent philosophy out of the Upaniṣads was made by *Badarāyana* (second century B.C.) in his *Brahmasūtras*. On account of their being aphoristic *Brahmasūtras* are not easily intelligible. As a result, there originated a number of commentaries on *Brahmasūtras*. *Advaitins*, *viśiṣṭādvaitins* and *dvaitins* interpret the *sūtras* differently. The same is the case with the *Upaniṣads* as well as *Bhagavadgītā*.

It was Gauḍapāda (eighth century A.D.) who first systematised *Advaita*. He composed a verse-treatise on *Māṇḍūkyopaniṣad* known as *Maṇḍūkyakārikas*. In them he set forth the basic tenets of *Advaitavedānta*. However, *Advaitavedānta* found its full blossom in the works of Śaṅkara (788-820 A.D.). He commented on the principal Upaniṣads including *Māṇḍūkya* along with its *kārikās* by Gauḍapāda, *Brahmasūtras* and *Bhagavadgītā* virtually making them to be the *Prasthānatraya*. Śaṅkara wrote also a number of books of his own. Through all of them he revealed the leading tenets of *Advaita*.

According to Śaṅkara *Brahman* is the only eternal, infinite and amorphous reality. Everything other than *Brahman* is false and is superimposed on it. *Avidyā* is at the root of all superimpositions. Only by the realisation of *Brahman avidyā* can be eradicated and emancipation attained. And it is the goal of human life.

Śaṅkara placed the system of *Advaita* on a firm footing. For about three centuries his philosophy ruled over the realms of Indian intelligentia without any considerable opposition. Śaṅkara's name came to be first remembered in connection with *Advaita*. However, there emerged a general feeling that Śaṅkara's *jnānāmārga* ignored the theistic sentiment proper and it caused reaction.

The first theistic reaction to *Advaita* came from Rāmānuja (twelfth-thirteenth centuries A.D.). Rāmānuja accepted the basic propositions of *Advaita*; but he criticised the theory of falsity of the world. *Brahman*, according to Rāmānuja also, is the sole reality, but only including itself the entire diversity of the material world. *Brahman* is the substance and the world is its attribute. That is why the system of Rāmānuja is known as *Viśiṣṭādvaita*. Rāmānuja elevated *bhakti* as the means of emancipation. Emancipation, being dependent on the grace of *Nārāyaṇa* can be attained only through uninterrupted devotion to him.

It was Madhva (thirteenth century A.D.) who posed a robust and uncompromising resistance to the *Advaita* of Śaṅkara. Madhva's *Dvaitavedānta* holds that *Brahman* is the complete and independent basis of all that is other than *Brahman*. *Jīva* is entirely distinct from *Brahman*. Madhva discarded the theory of falsity of the world and tried to establish the reality of it. He described the *Advaita* of Śaṅkara as Buddhism in disguise. *Dvaita* may sound dualism of matter and spirit, but it is not so. It is dualism of *Brahman* and *jīva*, both being spirits. Madhva also gave importance to *bhakti*. Emancipation, according to him, is never *abheda* of *jīva* and *Brahman*. It can be attained only through the grace of *Keśava*.

In addition to the schools of Śaṅkara, Rāmānuja and Madhva there arose a number of schools of *vedāntic* thought such as those of Śrīkaṇṭha, Nimbārka, Vallabha, Bhāskara, Yādava, Baladeva and others. All these schools have inherited the regular feature of Indian philosophy that each school tries to establish its own stand by criticising other schools. The position of each system or school was strengthened by the opposition of other systems or schools. In short, diversity and contradictions have always constituted the dynamic force of development in Indian philosophy as well as in *Vedānta*. However, this fact has been persistently denied by several scholars. What has been propagated, instead, is the interpretation of synthesis whereby contradictions are simply overlooked. Even recently at the sixteenth World Congress of Philosophy (Düsseldorf, 1978), some Indian philosophers vehemently argued that Indian philosophy is an integrated whole. Of course, there is some element of truth in it; but the diametrical oppositions should not be ignored. This context makes the study of *Advaitasiddhi* relevant for the day.

Advaitasiddhi of Madhusūdanasarasvati is one of the best products of the terse theoretical fight that ensued between *dvaitins* and *advaitins*. The fight lasted for more than seven hundred years. It still continues, though not with the same vigour as in the past. The history of this fight, in which *Advaitasiddhi* of Madhūṣudana played an important role, is an eye-opener to those who still preach the simple dictum of synthesis.

CHAPTER I

The Author, His Date, Life and Works

Author

Madhusūdanasarasvati is the author of *Advaitasiddhi*. There is ample internal evidence for the same. One of the opening verses of *Advaitasiddhi* clearly mentions its author. The verse is as follows:

Śraddhādhanena muninā madhusūdanena
saṅgṛhya śāstranicayam racitātiyatnāt
bodhāya vādivijayāya ca satvarāṇa-
madvāitasiddhiriyamastu mude budhānām.[1]

The word *muninā* indicates that Madhusūdana, the author of *Advaitasiddhi*, was a *sannyāsin*. He is, therefore, to be called Madhusūdanamuni. However, tradition adds to his name the suffix *Sarasvati*. In the colophons at the end of each of the four *paricchedas* of *Advaitasiddhi*, Madhusūdana himself uses the suffix *Sarasvati* along with his name.[2]

The name *Madhusūdana* is not rare in the history of Indian philosophy. Abhyaṅkar, K.V., has pointed out that there are, in all, about twenty-five Sanskrit authors who bore the name.[3] He has further stated that five of them have the suffix *Sarasvati* along with their names.[4] Aufrecht makes mention of sixteen *Madhusūdanas* in all.[5] Of them, only one has the suffix *Sarasvati*. It is with him that Aufrecht credits the authorship of *Advaitasiddhi*.[6] The internal evidence available in *Advaitasiddhi* is enough to conclude for certain that Madhusūdanasarasvati is the author of *Advaitasiddhi*.

Date

The date of Madhusūdanasarasvati has been a subject of controversy. Madhusūdana, on his own, presents us with little information about his date. Therefore, we have to depend on other sources. Śivarāmaśāstri has stated that Madhusūdana might have flourished sometime after 1433 A.D., the date of Vallabha whose son Viṭṭhaleśa was a disciple of Madhusūdana.[7] But the date of Vallabha itself is a matter of conjecture. Some scholars hold that he flourished in 1525 A.D.[8] Telang, K.T.,[9] Rajendraghose,[10] Rāmājñasarmapāṇḍeya,[11] Karmarkar, R.D.,[12] Gopinathakaviraj,[13] Hiriyanna, M.,[14] Sūryanārāyaṇaśukla,[15] Dasgupta, S.N.,[16] Sanjuktagupta,[17] Rajagopalan, V.,[18] and others hold the date of Madhusūdana to be the sixteenth century A.D. Modi, P.M., has put forward two tentative dates: 1495-1585 or 1490-1602 A.D.[19] Divanji, P.C., after going through the different views, has fixed the date of Madhusūdana to be the sixteenth-century itself.[20]

Madhusūdana quotes from the commentary of Sāyaṇa on the *Ṛg-veda.*[21] Sāyaṇa's date is the fourteenth century. Therefore, it can be taken to be the upper limit of the date that one can assign to Madhusūdana. Nahane, A. Sulochana judges the date of composition of the *Vedāntakalpalatikā* of Madhusūdana to be 1717 A.D.[22] This can be taken as the lowest limit of the date of Madhusūdana, any scholar has assigned so far.

Ain-I-Akbari was written by Abul Fazl in 1597. It mentions the names of learned men at the court of Akbar.[23] Among the names of 'First Class' learned men of the time, we find the following:

1. Madhusarasvati	2. Madhusūdan	3. Nārāyaṇmiśra
4. Nārāyaṇharijisur	5. Dāmodarbhatta	6. Rāmtīrtha

Prof. Dineshbhattacarya has pointed out that the name Madhusarasvati, as spelt in the original Persian text of *Ain-I-Akbari*, is Mādhavasarasvati and that Madhusūdan, the name which immediately follows, is that of Madhusūdanasarasvati.[24] Roychowdhury, Makhanlal also quotes from *Ain-I-Akbari* in accordance with the same sense.[25] It is well known that Akbar promulgated his new religion after considering the fundamental principles of the philosophies and religions of the day. And for the same purpose he patronised scholars of philosophy and religion. It is quite possible that Madhusūdana was a scholar patronised by Akbar. Mādhavasarasvati, the teacher of Madhusūdana, also might have been there in the court of Akbar. Madhusūdana pays tributes to him in one of the opening verses of *Advaitasiddhi.*[26] Rāmtīrtha might be the great *dvaitin* who wrote the commentary *Taranginī* on the *Nyāyāmṛta* of Vyāsatīrtha, in refutation of *Advaitasiddhi.* Thus the historical source, *Ain-I-Akbari*, confirms sixteenth century as the date of *Madhusūdana.* Tradition also vouchsafes the same. There is no harm in reaching the conclusion that Madhusūdana lived during the second half of the sixteenth and the first half of the seventeenth centuries A.D.

Life

As in the case of many other Sanskrit authors, in the case of

Madhusūdana also biographical details are lacking. None of his works gives us information regarding his life. What we have, at present, is a lot of guess-work done by different scholars.

Rāmājñaśarmapāṇḍeya holds that Madhusūdana was a Bengali by birth.[27] It is said that in a family genealogy obtained from Kotalipara of Faridpur district in Bengal, Madhusūdana's name is found mentioned.[28] Divanji, P.C., has done a lot of work in verifying the genealogy of Madhusūdana and bringing to light the details of it.[29] One tradition holds that Madhusūdana was a South-Indian Brahmin by birth.[30] Divanji discards this view and establishes the authority of the Bengal tradition.[31] He could locate the then last extent sprout of the family of Madhusūdana. It was the Bengali scholar Cintāharaṇa-cakravarti. With his help Divanji could reconstruct the family genealogy of Madhusūdana in detail.[32] It is as follows:

- Śrīrāmamiśra
  - Mādhava
    - Gopāla
      - Gaṇapati
        - Sanātana
          - Kṛṣṇaguṇārṇava
            - Jitāmṛta
            - Ācāryaśekhara
            - Purandara
              - Śrīnāthacūdamaṇi
              - Yādavānanda
                - Gaurīdāsa
                - Viśvanātha
                - Raghunātha
                - Mādhavāvilamba-sarasvati
                  - Vāṇinātha
                    - Rudrarāma
                      - Ghanaśyāma
                        - Ramāpati
                          - Gaurīprasāda
                            - Madanamohana
                              - Jñānadakaṇṭha
                                - Cintāharaṇa[33]
              - Kamalanayana
              - Name unknown

As evident from the genealogy, Purandara had five sons, of whom Kamalanayana was one. Kamalanayana[34] later became Madhusūdanasarasvati. Purandara gave good education to his children. Kamalanayana spent his youthful days studying at Benares. It is believed that he specialised *Nyāya* and began his career as a *naiyāyika*. Slowly he concentrated on the *Advaita* of Śaṅkara. It was a time when Caitanya's cult of love and devotion opened a new era in the history of Indian culture. Madhusūdana came under the influence of the *Bhakti* movement of the day.

Madhusūdana did not enter into the *gārhasthya* stage of life. He decided to lead an ascetic life throughout. He was initiated into the ascetic life by his *guru* Śrīrāmasarasvati.[35] Madhusūdana became a *sannyāsin*.

Madhusūdana's endeavour was to integrate the paths of *jñāna* and *bhakti*. He could achieve a lot in this regard. His erudition was so profound that there originated a saying as follows:

vettipāraṁ sarasvatyā madhusūdanasarasvatī
madhusūdanasarasvatyāḥ pāraṁ vetti sarasvatī.[36]

The veracity of this saying is evidenced by the works of Madhusūdana. More than this, we have no information about the details of his life.

Madhusūdana produced a school of disciples. Balabhadra was one of his favourite pupils. This is attested by Madhusūdana in the concluding verse of his *Siddhāntabindu.*[37] Another disciple of Madhusūdana was Purusottamasarasvati. Śeṣagovinda also was his pupil. Madhusūdana dedicated his life to the propagation of *Advaita.* Some hold that he attained *Siddhi* at the age of 105 at Haridvār.[38] It is also believed that he attained *samādhi* at the age of 107 at Haridvar itself.[39]

Works

Aufrecht has listed twenty-two works of Madhusūdanasarasvati.[40] These are the following:

1. Advaitabrahmasiddhi
2. Advaitaratnarakṣaṇa
3. Ātmabodhaṭīkā
4. Ānandamandākinī
5. Ṛgvedajaṭādyaṣṭāvikṛtivivaraṇa

6. Kṛṣṇakutūhalanāṭaka
7. Prasthānabheda
8. Bhaktisāmānyanirūpaṇa
9. Bhagavadgītāgūḍhārthadīpikā
10. Bhagavadbhaktirasāyana
11. Bhāgavatapurāṇaprathamaślokavyākhyā
12. Mahimnastotraṭikā
13. Rājñaṁpratibodhaḥ
14. Vedastutiṭīkā
15. Vedāntakalpalatikā
16. Śāṇḍilyasūtraṭīkā
17. Śastrasiddhāntaleśaṭīkā
18. Saṁkṣepaśārīrakasārasaṅgraha
19. Sarvasiddhāntavarṇana
20. Siddhāntatattvabindu
21. Harilīlāvyākhyā
22. Bhāgavatapurāṇādyaślokatrayavyākhyā

Of these, *Advaitabrahmasiddhi* is not to be confused with the book of the same name written by Sadānandayati.[41] The name of Madhusūdana's work is Advaitasiddhi.[42] Aufrecht explains at another place that *Advaitasiddhi* is the shorter form of *Advaitabrahmasiddhi.*[43] In fact there is no evidence for assuming so. It is also difficult to ascribe the authorship of all the above mentioned works to Madhusūdana.

Advaitagranthakośa enlists nineteen of the above mentioned works as those written by Madhusūdana.[44] Dasgupta, S.N., mentions eighteen works of Madhusūdana.[45] Divanji, P.C. has made an elaborate study so as to finalise the number of works written by Madhusūdana.[46] After scrutinising twenty works ascribed to Madhusūdana, Divanji reaches the conclusion that ten of them can safely be believed to have been composed by Madhusūdana. These are the following:

1. Advaitasiddhi
2. Siddhāntabindu
3. Advaitaratnarakṣaṇa
4. Vedāntakalpalatikā
5. Saṁkṣepaśārīrakasārasaṅgraha
6. Gitāgūḍhārthadīpikā
7. Bhaktirasāyana

8. Bhāgavatapurāṇaprathamaślokavyākhyā
9. Mahimnastotraṭīkā
10. Īśvarapratipattiprakāśa

Divanji has bracketed '*Prasthānabheda*' along with *Mahimnastotraṭīkā*.[47] The logic behind this is unknown; for, he has not endeavoured to explain it. According to Divanji three works are of a *sannyāsin* of the same name, but cannot be confidently held to be those of the author of the above mentioned ten works.[48] These are the following:

1. Harilīlavyākhyā
2. Ānandamandākinī
3. Ātmabodhaṭīkā

The following three works are not those composed by the same author:[49]

1. Rājñāṁpratibodhaḥ
2. Kṛṣṇakutūhadanāṭaka
3. Aṣṭāvikrtivivṛti

About the authorship of the other works, according to Divanji, nothing can be confidently said.[50]

Scholars have generally accepted the authorship of Madhusūdana in case of ten works. When they come to the question of which works they are, there arises difference of opinion. From the sure-list presented by Divanji, Karl Potter drops the following three works:[51]

1. Bhaktirasāyana
2. Bhāgavatapurāṇaprathamaślokavyākhyā
3. Mahimnastotraṭīkā

Instead, Potter adds the following three works:[52]

1. Ātmabodhaṭīkā
2. Padyatrayīvyākhya[53]
3. Siddhāntaleśasaṅgrahaṭīkā.

He considers also *Prasthānabheda* as a separate work of Madhusūdana.[54]

Thankasvami, R., does not present a definite conclusion regarding the number of works of Madhusudana.[55] He numbers the same works mentioned by Potter, with the exception of *Padyatrayīvyākhyā* and states that there are a number of other works like *Ānandamandākinī*, *Bhaktirasāyana*, *Harilīlāvivekavyākhyā* etc., written by Madhusūdana.[56] Thankasvami further states that *Jaṭādyaṣṭāvikṛtivivṛti* is not written by Madhusūdana.[57]

In fact, it is very difficult to confirm the works of Madhusūdana. Only after a thorough study of all the works that go in the name of Madhusūdana, one can reach any definite conclusion. It is not within the scope of the present thesis to make a comprehensive study of all the works of Madhusūdana. One thing can be ascertained: *Advitasiddhi* is a work of Madhusūdana.

The works of Madhusūdana reveal that *Advaita* is of the supreme concern for him. His regard for *bhakti* also ranks much the same. Some of his works deal predominently with *Advaita* while some others deal similarly with *bhakti*. However, it cannot be said that he considers *Advaita* and *bhakti* as if they are in separate compartments. Infact, the works of Madhusūdana combine *Advaita* with *bhakti*. *Jñāna* and *bhakti* form two sides of one and the same coin in the works of Madhusūdana.

REFERENCES

[1]Madhusūdanasarasvati, AS, ed., Anantakṛṣṇaśāstri, N.S., (Delhi, 1982), p. 8.

[2]The colophon runs as follows:

iti srīmatparamahaṁsaparivrājakācārya srīviśveśvara Sarasvatīśricaraṇaśiṣya-śrīmadhusūdanasarasvatīviracitāyām advaitasiddhau . . .

Ibid., pp. 660; 854; 877; 900.

[3]Vide, Madhusūdanasarasvati, SB, ed., Abhyaṅkar, V.S., (Pune, 1962), Intro., p. 27.

[4]Ibid.

[5]Vide, CC, (Wiesbaden, 1962).

[6]Ibid., Pt. I, p. 427.

[7]Vide, AS, ed., Śivarāmaśāstri, (Bombay, 1937), Preface, p. 19.

[8]Vide, Potter, Karl H., EIP, Comp., (Delhi, 1983), Vol. I, p. 345.

[9]Vide, JRAS Bengal, Vol. XXVIII, pp. 368-67.

[10]Vide, AS, comm., Bagchi, Yogendranatha, (Benares, 1971), Preface.

[11]Vide, Madhusūdanasarasvati, VKL, POWSBT, No. 3, Intro.

[12]Vide, op. cit., BORIGOS, Class A, No. 3, Intro.

[13]Vide, *The date of Madhusūdanasarasvati*, POWSBSt., Vol. VII, pp. 177-82.

[14]Vide, Vimuktātman, IS, GOS, No. LXV, Intro.

[15]Vide, Sarvajnātman, SS, POWSBT, No. 69, Intro.

[16]Vide, HIP, Vol. II, (Delhi, 1975), p. 225.

[17]Vide, SPMS, (Calcutta; 1966), pp. I-V.

[18]Vide, PA, ed. Mahadevan, T.M.P., (Secunderabad, 1968), pp. 254-61.

[19]Vide, SB, Eng. Tr., (Bhavanagar, 1929), Intro.

[20]Vide, SB, ed. with Eng. Tr., (Baroda, 1933), Intro.

[21]Vide, AS, *Pariccheda*, I, *Āgamabādhoddhāra*.

[22]Vide, *Date of Madhusūdanasarasvati*, ABORI, Vol. XXX, (Pune, 1949), pp. 326-31.

[23]Vide, *Ain-I-Akbari*, Eng. Tr., Blochmann, H., ed., Phillott, D.C., Vol. I, (Delhi, 1977), pp. 607-8.

[24]Vide, IHQ, Vol. XIII, (1937), p. 31.

[25]Vide, *The Din Ilahi*. (Calcutta, 1941), pp. 236-38.

[26]Vide, op. cit., p. 8.

[27]Vide, VKL, loc. cit.

[28]Vide, SB, loc. cit.

[29]Vide, ABORI, Vol. VIII, pp. 149-58 and Vol. IX, pp. 313-23.

[30]Vide, SB, ed., Triambakaṁśāstri, CSS, No. LXV, p. 8.

[31]Vide, SB, loc. cit.

[32]Ibid. [33]Ibid.

[34]Some scholars mention the name as Kamalajanayana.

[35]This Śrīrāmasarasvati is not to be confused with Śrīrāmamisra, the great grandfather of Madhusūdana; for, as is clear from the genealogy, Śrīrāmamisra might have passed away long before the birth of Madhusūdana.

[36]Vide, AS, ed., Yogīndrānanda, Svāmi, (Benares, 1977), Vol. II

Anantakṛṣṇaśāstri, N.S. quotes the verse slightly differently and in another sense, Vide, NAAS, Pt. I, (Calcutta, 1934), Intro., p. 90.

[37]It is as follows:

bahuyācanayāmayāyamalpo

balabhadrasya kṛte kṛto nibandhaḥ.

Vide, SB, ed., Abhyaṅkar, V.S., p. 154.

[38]Vide, AGK, p. XXXXV.

[39]Vide, Yogīndrānanda, Svāmi, op. cit., Intro., p. 18.

[40]Vide, CC, loc. cit.

[41]For details about this work see infra, chapter II.

[42]Vide, AS, p. 8.

[43]Vide, CC, p. 9.

[44]Vide, AGK, loc. cit.

[45]Vide, HIP, loc. cit.

[46]Vide, SB, loc. cit.

[47]Ibid. [48]Ibid. [49]Ibid. [50]Ibid.

[51]Vide, EIP, Vol. I, (Delhi, 1983), pp. 368-70.

[52]Ibid.

[53]Aufrecht mentions this as *Bhāgavatapurāṇādyaśloka trayavyākhyā*, Vide, CC, loc. cit.

[54]Vide, EIP, loc. cit.

[55]Vide, BSAVL, (Madras, 1980), pp. 286-88.

[56]Ibid.

[57]Name of this book is differently spelt by scholars. Yogīndrānanda, Svāmi spells it *Aṣṭavikṛtivivaraṇa*, Vide, AS, loc. cit.

CHAPTER II

Siddhi-Literature of the Advaitavedānta School

Siddhi-Literature

The usage *siddhi-literature* has become common in *vedāntic* parlance. The works, the names of which are compound words ending in *siddhi*, are commonly called *siddhi-literature*.[1] The word *siddhi* stands for conclusive ascertainment as a result of careful investigation. Generally it involves discussion of a polemical nature.

Siddhi-literature of Sanskrit as a whole is vast. *Siddhi*-literature of the system of *Vedānta* also is fairly extensive. The *Vijñānāmṛtasiddhi* or *Vijñaptimātratāsiddhi* of Vasubandhu, *Sphoṭasiddhi* of Maṇḍana, *Sphoṭasiddhi* of Bhāratamiśra, *Apohasiddhi* and *Kṣaṇabhaṅgasiddhi* of *Ratnakīrti*, *Prabodhasiddhi* of Udayana, *Ātmasiddhi*, *Saṁvitsiddhi* and *Īśvarasiddhi* of Yāmuna, *Satyārthasiddhi* of Vedāntadeśika and *Bhedasiddhi* of Visvanāthapāncānana are among the principal works of the *siddhi*-literature in Sanskrit apart from those of the *Advaita* school.

The works of the *siddhi*-literature of the *Advaita* school themselves come to more than a dozen and a quarter. Thankasvami, R., has dealt with sixteen works belonging to the *siddhi*-literature of *Advaitavedānta*.[2] These, in the Sanskrit alphabetic order, are the following:

1. Advayasiddhi
2. Advaitabrahmasiddhi
3. Advaitasiddhi
4. Anirvacanīyakhyātisiddhi
5. Iṣṭasiddhi
6. Cidacicchārīrakabrahmasiddhi
7. Jñānasiddhi
8. Nairguṇyasiddhi
9. Naiṣkarmyasiddhi
10. Bodhaikyasiddhi
11. Brahmasiddhi
12. Brahmasūtrānuguṇyasiddhi
13. Mokṣasiddhi
14. Vivekasiddhi

15. Śrautākhaṇḍārthasiddhi
16. Svārājyasiddhi

A brief descriptive account of each of these works is given here. From this, *Advaitasiddhi* is excluded, since, the present thesis is a study of the same.

Brahmasiddhi

Brahmasiddhi of Maṇḍana (c. 750-850 A.D.) seems to be chronologically the first among the *siddhis* of *Advaita* about which particulars are available. It is in four chapters: *Brahmakāṇḍa*, *Tarkakāṇḍa*, *Niyogakāṇḍa* and *Siddhikāṇḍa*. *Brahmasiddhi* declares in utmost confidence the sole supreme reality of *Brahman*. Prof. Kuppusvāmiśāstri has brought out a critical edition of this important work.[3]

There is an allegation that Maṇḍana ignored the fundamental teachings of the *Upaniṣads*.[4] This has originated from one's preoccupation with Śaṅkara. Śaṅkara's contribution to the interpretation of *Upaniṣadic* teachings is very great. However, it cannot be said that Śaṅkara's interpretation is the only authoritative one. In fact, Maṇḍana has not deviated much from Śaṅkara. As does Śaṅkara, Maṇḍana establishes the unique reality of *Brahman*. The concept of *mukti* presented by Maṇḍana is the same as that of Śaṅkara. Even after obtaining realisation of *Brahman* one may remain in his mortal body. The final release is perfected at the time of severing the body.[5]

Naiṣkarmyasiddhi

Naiṣkarmyasiddhi of Sureśvara (c. 800-900 A.D.) is an elucidatory text of *Advaitavedānta*. The book is divided into four chapters. The cardinal problem dealt with in the *Naiṣkarmyasiddhi* is the interpretation of the *śruti* 'that thou art'. Sureśvara epitomises in the *śruti*, all the central teachings of the *Upaniṣads*.

Iṣṭasiddhi

Iṣṭasiddhi of Vimuktātman (c. 959-1050 A.D.) deals with all the essentials of *Advaitavedānta*. However, the stress is on the doctrine of *māyā*. The exposition of the doctrine of *māyā* in *Iṣṭasiddhi* is so complete that it can be called an *anirvacanīyasarvasva* like the *Khaṇḍanakhaṇḍakhādya* of Śrīharṣa[6]. The mastery of Vimuktātman over the dialectics of *Advaita* is evident in *Iṣṭasiddhi*. The most distinctive feature of Vimuktātman's view is that regarding the cessation of *avidyā*[7]. *Avidyā* is neither identical with nor different from *Brahman.*[8] Removal of *avidyā* is possible by knowledge gradually. Even after the complete destruction of *avidyā* some vestige of it is left over as long as a man bears his body. This is the stage of *jīvanmukti.* The final release attained as a result of the cessation of *avidyā* as well as the body is *videhamukti.*[9]

Advayasiddhi

Advayasiddhi is said to be written by *Śrīdhara* (c. 1000 A,D.). Śrīdhara is the author of *Nyayākandali*, a commentary on Praśastapāda's *Padārthadharmasañgraha.* In the *Nyayāyakandali* he makes mention of his own *Advayasiddhi.*[10] More than this we have no information about the work. The work has not come down to us.

Jñānasiddhi

Jñānasiddhi of Jñānottama (c. 1100-1200 A.D.) also has not come down to us. Pratyaksvarūpa mentions Jñānottama[11] as the author of *Jnānasiddhi.*[11]

Advaitabrahmasiddhi

Advaitabrahmasiddhi of Sadānandayati (c. 1650-1750 A.D.) is a polemical text. All shades of thought contrary to *Advaitavedānta* are subjected to discussion and discarded in this book. It reiterates the *advaitic* stand that *Brahman* which is eternal consciousness and bliss is the sole reality. It is said that *Advaitabrahmasiddhi* draws a distinction between the subjective idealism of *Yogācāra* and the absolute idealism of Śaṅkara.[12]

Bodhaikyasiddhi

Bodhaikyasiddhi of Acyutarāya (1775-1839 A.D.) has come down to us.[13] Aufrecht brackets *Bodhaikyasiddhi* with *Advaitaratnabodha.*[14] *Advaitātmabodha* is a commentary by the author himself, on the *Bodhaikyasiddhi.*[15]

Svārājyasiddhi

Svārājyasiddhi of *Gaṅgādharendrasarasvati* (c. 1780-1880 A.D.) is in verse form. The book has three chapters, namely, *adhyāropa*, *apavāda* and *kaivalya.* The intention of the author is to discard the view of *dvaitins* and establish that of *advaitins.*

Śrautākhaṇḍārthasiddhi

Śrautākhaṇḍārthasiddhi of Rāmānandasarasvati (18th century A.D.) also is in verse form. In 1119 verses Rāmānanda deals fully with the *akhaṇḍārthavāda* of *Advaitavedānta.*

Mokṣasiddhi

Mokśasiddhi of Kṛṣṇagiri (c. 1800-1900 A.D.) deals with the orderly usefulness of *karma, upāsana* and *jñāna* for attaining release. The author tries his best to show evidence for his views, from the works of Śaṇkara.

Nairguṇyasiddhi

Nairguṇyasiddhi of Gaṇapatiśāstri (c. 1850-1920 A.D.) of Mannārgudi is mentioned by Thankasvami, R. It is not known whether this book has come in print or not. Thankasvami presents a list of works of Gaṇapatiśāstri and simply states that some of them are not printed.[16]

Brahmasūtrānuguṇyasiddhi

Brahmasūtrānuguṇyasiddhi of Kṛṣṇaśāstri (c. 1870-1939 A.D.) presents in a nut-shell the quintessence of Śaṅkara's commentary on the *Brahmasūtras* of Bādarāyaṇa. Kṛṣṇaśāstri's main intention seems to be the exposition of the consonance of Śaṅkara with Bādarāyaṇa.[17]

Cidacicchārīrakabrahmasiddhi

Cidacicchārīrakabrahmasiddhi of Jagadīsvaraśāstri (20th century A.D.) is a text of the *prakaraṇa* type. It deals with *Brahman* of *Advaitavedānta.* As the name indicates the book reveals the unique nature of *Brahman.*

Other Siddhis

Anirvacanīyakhyātisiddhi and *Vivekasiddhi* are of anonymous origin. The first is incomplete. The second is in verse form. It contains only below hundred verses which deals with the fact that knowledge of *Brahman* is to be attained by the purity of mind.

Advaitasiddhi of Madhusūdana stands chronologically fourth in the *siddhi*-literature of the *Advaitavedānta* school. Madhusūdana himself has stated this in an epilogic verse of *Advaitasiddhi.* It is as follows:

> siddhīnamiṣṭanaiṣkarmyabrahmagānamiyaṁcirā-
> dadvaitasiddhiradhunā caturthī samajāyata.[18]

It is clear from this that *Advayasiddhi* and *Jñānasiddhi* which are anterior to *Advaitasiddi* were not known to Madhusūdana.

In importance *Advaitasiddhi* stands first in the *siddhi*-literature, for, as Madhusūdana states, it is the *śāstranicayasaṅgraha* originated as a result of the laborious task of a *muni* whose sole possession consists in true devotion.[19] Though the author, out of modesty, says that his effort is verily for doing good to himself,[20] it did not result so. The work is an ever lasting contribution to the polemical literature of Indian Philosophy.

REFERENCES

[1]Vide, Maṇḍanamiśra, BS, ed., Kuppusvāmiśāstri, S., (Delhi, 1984), Intro., p. XXI.

[2]Vide, op. cit.

[3]Vide, op. cit.

[4]Vide, Saccidānandendrasarasvati, VPP, (Holenarsipur, 1964), p. 94.

[5]Vide, op. cit., pp. 131-32.

[6]Vide, Hiriyanna, M., IS, Intro., p. XV.

[7]Vide, Bhattacarya, D.C., CHI, Vol. III, (Calcutta, 1975), p. 269.

[8]Vide, IS, p. 36

[9]Ibid., p. 77.

[10]Vide, Praśastapāda, *Padārthadharmasaṅgraha*, Comm., Śrīdhara, (Vizianagaram, 1895), p. 57.

[11]Vide, Citsukha, TP, comm., Pratyaksvarūpa, (Benares, 1884), p. 392.

[12]Vide, Jadunathsinha, *Indian Realism*, (Delhi, 1972), p. 225.

[13]Vide, BSAVL, p. 310.

[14]Vide, CC, Vol. I, p. 76.

[15]Ibid.

[16]Vide, Thankasvami, R., op. cit., p. 334,

[17]Vide. Kṛṣṇaśāstri, *Brahmasūtrānuguṇyasiddhi*, ed., Hariharaśāstri, (Kumbakonam, 1926).

[18]Vide, AS, p. 900.

[19]Ibid., p. 8.

bid.

CHAPTER III

Controversy between Dvaitins and Advaitins

Origin

The history of philosophy is the history of the struggle between the two trends of idealism and materialism. In India the struggle took the form of that between *ātmavāda* and *anātmavāda* or *āstikavāda* and *nāstikavāda*. Within the two streams themselves, there developed a number of substreams. However, throughout the course of their development they have remained true to their original inspirations.[1]

Philosophical controversies in which hard hits were given and taken have been a continuous affair in India. As a result, philosophical literature grew enormously too. In the history of philosophical controversies in India, controversy between *dvaitins* and *advaitins* occupies an important position.

Controversy between the *Dvaita* school of thought and that of *Advaita* is quite natural, for, though both form substreams of one and the same system, their opposition is diametrical. *Advaita* represents illusionism while *Dvaita* represents realism.

Extent

Controversy between *dvaitins* and *advaitins* cannot be confined to that between *Śaṅkarites* and *Mādhvites* alone. Controversy between *dvaitins* and *advaitins* was there even before the origin of *Mādhva-vedānta*. Bādarāyana, the author of the *Vedāntasūtras*, refutes many of the arguments of the *saṅkhyas* and *naiyāyikas* who were all *dvaitins* in the sense that they advocated the theory of many souls.[2] Gauḍapāda and Śaṅkara also refuted the arguments of the *dvaitins* so as to establish *Advaita*. The great *acāryas* who followed them also maintained the tradition. Padmapāda, Maṇḍana, Sureśvara and Vācaspatimiśra (all belonging to the ninth century A.D.) deserve special mention here. Vimuktātman (tenth century A.D.) for the first time, adopted the method of establishing *Advaita* predominantly by refuting *dvaitavādas*. His *Iṣṭasiddhi* bears testimony to this.[3] Sarvajñātman (tenth century A.D.), in his *Saṁkṣepaśārīraka*, Prakāśātman (tenth century A.D.), in his *Vivaraṇa* on the *Pañcapādikā* of Padmapāda and Ānandabodha (eleventh century A.D.), in his works such as *Nyāyamakaranda*,

Nyāyadipāvali and *Pramāṇamālā* also paid attention to refuting the *dvaitavādas*.

Śrīharṣa's *Khaṇḍanakhaṇḍakhādya* opened a new era in the history of polemical writing of the *Advaitavedānta* school. It was Śrīharṣa (twelfth century A.D.) who first adopted the method of *naiyāyikas* in refuting the *dvaitavādas*. Citsukha (twelfth-thirteenth centuries A.D.) followed suit. His *Tattvapradipikā*, popularly known as *Citsukhī*, not only refutes the arguments of *Nyāya* and *Vaiśeṣika* but also establishes the fundamental concepts of *Advaita*.

The prominence of *Advaitavedānta* began to fade as a result of the origin of the *Dvaita* proper of the *vedāntin* Madhva (thirteenth century A.D.). The very origin of *Dvaita* was a reaction, in the main, against *Advaita*. For the same reason controversy between the two schools was inevitable. *Dvaitins* vehemently criticised and retorted the arguments of the rival school. For over the last seven hundred years *dvaitins* and *advaitins* have been actively engaged in a wordy warfare. It is interesting to know how the word-war progressed through the centuries.

Madhva's works form the nucleus of *Dvaitavedānta*. Madhva maintains the *dvaita* interpretation of the *Prasthānatraya*. He holds that Śaṅkara's excessive emphasis on the *nirguṇa Brahman* was quite unwarranted and a matter of his personal idiosyncrasy.[4] Madhva defends difference: Five differences, namely, difference between God and soul, between God and matter, between matter and soul, between one soul and another soul and between one matter and another matter are real. The school of Madhva being essentially dualistic in character and realistic in approach maintains absolute reality of the manifold world on a par with that of Īśa.

Jayatīrtha (fourteenth century A.D.) wrote a voluminous commentary on the *Anuvyākhyāna* of Madhva on *Brahmasūtras* called *Nyāyasudhā*. While Madhva criticised the views of Śaṅkara, Jayatīrtha quoted and refuted Vācaspatimiśra also. In his own work, *Vādāvali*, Jayatīrtha refuted the *māyāvāda* of Śaṅkara and his followers. He quoted and refuted the *advaita* views contained in *Citsukhī* and *Vivaraṇa*.

The example of dialectical criticism of *Advaita* set by Jayatīrtha was soon followed by his successors. Viṣṇudāsa (fifteenth century A.D.) was the most notable among them. His *Vādaratnāvalī* examines, in detail, the *Advaita* principles dealt with in *Pañcapādikā*, *Citsukhī*, *Iṣṭasiddhi* etc., and refutes all of them. He establishes the validity of Madhva's interpretation of *Śrutis*.

Text-for-text controversy

It was Vyāsatīrtha (fifteenth century A.D.) who vindicated the prominence of *Dvaita*[5] and gave *Advaita* an almost fatal blow. In his work *Bhedojjīvana* he resuscitated the principle of *bheda* stifled by *advaitins*. In another work, *Tātparyacandrikā*, Vyāsatīrtha criticised the interpretations of the *Vedāntasūtras* of Bādarāyaṇa by Śaṅkara and Rāmānuja. He refuted the justifications of Vācaspati also, at times, and harmonised the utterances of Madhva and his commentators.

The masterpiece of Vyāsatīrtha is *Nyāyāmṛta*. In it he elaborately deals with the discrepancies in *Adavita*. By the composition of *Nyāyāmṛta* Vyāsatīrtha virtually pushed *advaitins* to a miserable position. *Nyāyāmṛta* contains four *paricchedas*. The first *pariccheda* repudiates *māyāvāda* and establishes the reality of the universe. The theory of degrees of rality of *Advaita* is critically analysed and rejected. The second *pariccheda* examines the *advaitin's* doctrine of *akhaṇḍārtha* and refutes the same. Difference is established to be the basis of reality. The advaita doctrine of *nirguṇa Brahman* is repudiated and the *dvaita* theory of infinite attributes of *Brahman* is established. The third *pariccheda* enquires into the means of realising Brahman or Nārayaṇa. In the fourth *pariccheda* the dvaita doctrine of *mukti* is dealt with. The *advaita* concept of *mukti* as oneness with *Brahman* is ably refuted.

Throughout *Nyāyāmṛta* Vyāsatīrtha has used a highly scholastic style employing the methodology of *Navya-Nyāya*. Advaita doctrines contained in works such as *Pañcapādikā*, *Vivaraṇa*, *Tattvapradipikā* etc., are frequently quoted and refuted by Vyāsatīrtha. The attack made by Vyāsatīrtha on *Advaita* was so fatal that it invited counters from eminent *advaitins*. It can be said that Vyāsatīrtha initiated a text-for-text controversy between *dvaitins* and *advaitins*.

It should not be taken that ever since the origin of Madhva's *Dvaita* the camp of *advaitins* had been keeping silent. Such great stalwarts like Ānandagiri (fourteenth century A.D.), Vidyāraṇya (fifteenth century A.D.), Nṛsiṁhāśrama (sixteenth century A.D.) and others were actively engaged in defending *Advaita*. Ānandagiri, also known as Ānandajñāna, through his *Tattvāloka* and a number of commentaries on the works of older *ācāryas*, waxed eloquent on the veracity of *Advaita*. Vidyāraṇya's *Pañcadaśi* is an authoritative text-book of *Advaita*. Nrsiṁhāśrama dared to make an actual counter-attack on *Dvaita*. His *Bhedadhikkāra* is an able refutation, as the name indicates, of the theory of difference advocated by *dvaitins* and an ardent defence of the theory of non-difference held by *advaitins*. There are also *Advaitadīpikā* and a number of works written by Nṛsiṁhāśrama in defence of the position of *advaitins*.

It was Appayyadīkṣita (sixteenth century A.D.) who, followed Nṛsiṁhāśrama and could make a wholesome frontal attack on the *Dvaita* of Madhva. There are more than hundred works to his credit. As far as the controversy between *dvaitins* and *advaitins* is concerned, Appayyadīkṣita's *Mādhvatantramukhamardana* is the most important among his works. The criticisms of Appayyadīkṣita were obviously *advaitins'* reactions to the challenges thrown by Vyāsatīrtha in his works.[6] However, a *verbatim* retort to the *Nyāyāmṛta* of Vyāsatīrtha was still in want, for, it tore into pieces the well-built doctrines of *Advaitavedānta*.

Beginning of encounter

The challenge thrown by Vyāsatīrtha was taken up by Madhusūdanasarasvati. Madhusūdana, in his masterpiece *Advaitasiddhi*, retorted *verbatim-et-litleratim*, to the arguments contained in Nyāyāmṛta.[7] It can be said that *Nyāyāmṛta* caused the origin of *Advaitasiddhi*. As the name *Advaitasiddhi* indicates, it re-established *Advaita* which was about to be *asiddha*. Without the origin of *Advaitasiddhi* the position of *Advaita* would have been pathetic in many ways.

The origin of *Advaitasiddhi* was important in the history of Indian philosophy due to many reasons. The most important reason was that it inaugurated the birth of a series of controversial literature. It was amazing that an advanced philosophical text came to be written exclusively for the purpose of demolishing the philosophical tenets of one school, in favour of another, of the same system.[8]

Controversy through the centuries

The origin of *Advaitasiddhi* as a retort to *Nyāyāmṛta* conduced the *ācāryas* of the rival schools to rally behind their preceptors. As sequel to both *Nyāyamṛta* and *Advaitasiddhi* there appeared a series of commentaries as well as independent works. One important feature of all these works is the employment of the Navya-Nyāya method of dialectical argument. As such *Navya-Nyāya* dialectics came to be widely applied in *Vedānta*.

Ramatīrtha (c. 1550-1620 A.D.) wrote a commentary on *Nrāyāmṛta* in complete refutation of *Advaitasiddhi*. It is called *Taraṅginī*. Rāmatīrtha writes in a clear and forcible style.[9] He reviews the criticisms and defences of *Advaitasiddhi* in close details and brings out the invulnerability of the positions taken up by Vyāsatīrtha.[10]

Taraṅginī of Rāmatīrtha was refuted by more than one scholar of *Advaita*. The first attempt came from Balabhadra (c. 1600-1700 A.D.), a disciple of Madhusūdana.[11] He wrote *Sidhhivyākhyā* on *Advaitasiddhi*, as a *verbatim* reply to *Taraṅgiṇī*. Balabhadra often quotes whole sentences from *Taraṅgiṇī* so as to refute them.

Refuting *Siddhivyākhyā* there originated another commentary on *Nyāyāmṛta*. It is *Nyāyāmṛtakaṇṭakoddhāra*. Anantakṛṣṇaśāstri attributes the authorship of this commentary to Vijayīndratirtha.[12] However, Sarma, B.N.K. refutes this view. He attributes the authorship of *Kaṇṭakoddhara* to Ānandabhaṭṭāraka (1535-1605 A.D).[13] Scholars have widely accepted the view of Śarma. The only thing is that, then, the date of Balabhadra has to be judged to be a bit more early.

Brahmānandasarasvati (c. 1600-1700 A.D.) wrote the commentary *Gurucandrikā* and its condensed form *Laghucandrikā* on *Advaitasiddhi*, in refutation, mainly, of the *Taraṅgiṇī* of Rāmatīrtha. Brahmānanda's commentary is known as *Gauḍabrahmānandīyam*. It is a successful refutation of all the objections raised against *Advaita* by Madhva's followers beginning from the time of *Nyāyāmṛta* down to the time of Kaṇṭakoddhāra.[14]

Vanamālimiśra (c. 1650-1720 A.D.) wrote two commentaries namely *Taraṅgiṇīsaurabha* and Nyāyāmṛtasaugandhya. The former, as the name indicates, is a commentary on *Taraṅgiṇī* in refutation of *Gurucandrikā* of Brahmānanda. The latter similarly, is a commentary on *Nyāyāmṛta* in refutation of *Laghucandrikā*. There are a few more works to the credit of Vanamalī. Of them *Mādhvamukhālaṅkāra*, known also as *Mārutamaṇḍana*, deserves special mention here. He wrote this in refutation of the *Mādhvamatavidhvaṁsana* of Appayyadīkṣita.

Viṭṭhaleśopādhyāya (c. 1700-1800 A.D.) wrote a commentary on *Laghucandrikā*. It is known as *Viṭṭhaleśopāḍhyāyī*. It attempts for a defence of the *advaita* position by refuting *dvaita* works especially those of Vanamālimiśra. No wholesome attept to retort Viṭṭhaleśopādhyāyī from the side of *dvaitins* seems to have taken place. However, controversy between *dvaitins* and *advaitins* did not end.

Controversy between *dvaitins* and *advaitins* was not confined to that appeared in the form of composition of *Nyāyāmṛta* and *Advaitasiddhi* and their commentaries. *Vyāsatīrtha* himself wrote works other than

Nyāyāmṛta. His *Tātparyacandrikā* is a polemical review of the interpretations of Śaṅkara, Rāmānuja and Madhva on *Brahmasūtras.* It belongs to the *adhikaraṇaprasthāna.* Thus, the controversy between *dvaitins* and *advaitins* stretched beyond the limits of the *vādaprasṭhāna. Tātparyacandrikā* is a commentary on the *Tattvaprakāśikā* of Jayatīrtha on the *Aṇubhāṣya* of Madhva.

After Vyāsatīrtha the mantle of defence of *Dvaita* fell up on his disciple Vijayīndratīrtha (1514-1595 A.D.).[15] He is credited with the authorship of one hundred and four works. He was the dualistic polymath of the sixteenth century.[16] In his commentary on the *Nyāyāmṛta,* named *Nyāyāmṛtāmoda* he attempted for an exhaustive refutation of the principal tenets of *Advaita.* Vijayīndra wrote another commentary on *Tātparyacandrikā* of Vyāsatīrtha. It is *Nyāyamauktikamāla.* In it he maintains that Madhva's interpretation of the *Vedāntasūtras* alone is in tune with the spirit of the *sūtras.* He discards all other interpretations of the *sūtras,* alleging them to be either violative or distructive of the purport of the *sūtras.* Appayyadīkṣita's *Śivārkamaṇidīpikā* and *Nyāyarakṣāmaṇī* have been subjected to severe criticism in *Nyāyamauktikamālā.*

Vādirājatīrtha (c. 1480-1600 A.D.), another disciple of *Vyāsatīrtha,* also wrote a number of works criticising the doctrines of *Advaita* and defending those of *Dvaita. Yuktimallikā* is his *maguum-opus.* It is in verse form. The views expressed by Śaṅkara, Ānandabodha and Śrīharṣa are frequently quoted and refuted in *Yuktimallikā.*

It is not within the scope of the present thesis to study the history of the controversy between *dvaitins* and *advaitins.* It is an elaborate subject fit for another research thesis. What is intended here is to present a general impression of the controversy between the rival schools of *Advaita* and *Dvaita* which has a link with *Advaitasiddhi.* Even controversy between *advaitins* and *viśiṣtādvaitins* which has direct connection with the polemical tradition, has not been considered here. It also is a subject of another elaborote study.

Though not with the same heat and light as in the past, controversy between *dvaitins* and *advaitins* continued through the ninteenth century. *Śaṅkarapādabhūṣaṇam* of Raghunāthasūri (1821-1859 A.D.)[17] bears evidence for the same. He refuted the arguments of the *Tātparyacandrika* of Vyāsatīrtha.

Raṅgappācārya (1820-1891 A.D.) who was the *āsthānapaṇḍita* at the court of the Maharaja of Cochin wrote *Candrikābhūṣaṇam* in refutation of *Śaṅkarapādabhūṣaṇam.* He wrote a number of other books also establishing the correctness of the position held by *Dvaitavedānta*.

Controversy between Rāmasubrahmaṇyaśāstri (1850-1920 A.D.) and Satyadhyānatīrtha (1913-1942 A.D.) brought the tradition of the disputation between *dvaitins* and *advaitins* to the twentieth century. The former wrote *Candrikākhaṇḍanam* in refutation of the *Tātparyacandrikā* of Vyāsatīrtha. The latter wrote *Candrikāmaṇḍanam* in refutation of *Candrikākhaṇḍanam*. Both Rāmasubrahmaṇyaśāstri and Satyadhyānatīrtha wrote a number of other works too.

Gauḍagiri Veṅkaṭaramaṇācārya (fl. 1924 A.D.)[18] also has criticised the arguments put forward by Rāmasubrahmaṇyaśāstri in his *Candrikākhaṇḍanam*. The name of Veṅkaṭaramaṇācārya's work is *Candrikāprakāśaprasara*.

Satyadhyānatīrtha was criticised by Naṭeśārya (fl. 1927).[19] Naṭeśārya was a pupil of Rāmasubrahmaṇyaśāstri. In his *Advaitataraṇi* he refuted the arguments of Satyadhyānatīrtha presented in his *Candrikāmaṇḍanam*.[20]

Anantakṛṣṇaśāstri, N.S., seems to be the last great scholar of the present century who has contributed much to *dvaita-advaita* controversial series. He criticised both Veṅkaṭaramaṇācārya and Satyadhyānatīrtha in his *Advaitadīpikā*. Anantakṛṣṇaśāstri has a number of other works also to his credit. In his *Saugandhyavimarśa* he defends the *advaita* position by refuting the charges brought home by Vanamālimiṣra against *advaitins*. As he himself has stated, in doing so, he strictly follows the foot-steps of the great scholars who preceded him.[21] In his *Advaitatattvasudhā* he rejects the objections raised against *Advaita* by Jayatīrtha in his *Nyāyasudhā*. The work done by Anantakṛṣṇaśāstri in bringing out scholarly editions of *Advaitasiddhi* also has to be applauded.

Retrospect and Prospect

It cannot be said that the controversy between *dvaitins* and *advaitins* has exhausted. It still continues in one way or other. However, the polemical rigidity of the great old *ācārayas* has become extinct. The record of dialectical and exegetical perfection set by Vyāsatīrtha and Madhusūdana stands still unaltered in the history of Indian philosophy. No historian of Indian philosophy can take the risk of ignoring it. The greatest historian of Indian philosophy, Dasgupta, S.N., has dedicated two complete chapters for dealing with the controversy between *dvaitins* and *advaitins*.[22] His stress is on the controversy between Vyāsatīrtha and Madhusūdana as evidenced by *Nyāyāmṛta* and

Advaitasiddhi.

All the controversies between *advaitins* and *dvaitins* contred round two slogans which form the keynotes of the two rival schools. These are the following:

brahmaivedaṁ jagatsarvaṁ brahmaṇonyannavidyate
brahmānyadbhaticenmithyā yathāmarumarīcikā.[23]
(advaitins)

and

yādṛśaṁ brahmaṇaḥsattvam
tādṛśaṁ syājjagatyapi.[24]
(dvaitins)

All other disputes proceeded from these two central arguments. A huge volume of controversial literature was produced. However, centuries-long arguments and counter-arguments could not effect any change in the basic positions of *advaitins* and *dvaitins*. In fact, both *advaitins* and *dvaitins* could further strengthen their positions. The most welcome outcome of the whole word war was the effective use of the dialectical method of presentation. It cannot be said that the dialectical method was quite unknown in Indian philosophy before. However, controversy between *dvaitins* and *advaitins* which employed the *Navya-Nyāya* dialectics gave a new dimension to the polemical literature. The wealth and depth of dialectics in Indian philosophy grew considerably. The creative urge and interest in exposition of both *advaitins* and *advatins* were combined with a burning zeal for dialectical conquest and doctrinal expansion.

Advaita and *Dvaita* are not mere philosophical schools. Both schools owe allegiance to theological and ritualistic interests. Both Śaṅkara[25] and Madhva[26] have established *maṭhas* in different parts of the country in view of the propagation of their *matas*. The learned pontiffs of *Śāṅkara* and *Mādhva maṭhas* continue to enrich the controversial literature of their respective schools.

Social conditions have changed. The ideological realm has considerably grown. There is no relevance today for the continuance of the controversy between *dvaitins* and *advaintins* in the very same old manner. Prospects of the controversy lie in its history being critically analysed. One who endeavours to take up that mission should have an objective approach. It is because of the lack of such an approach that one scholar depicts Madhva, the greatest theoretical rival of Śaṅkara, as a 'great harmoniser'.[27]

REFERENCES

[1]Vide, Murti, T.R.V., CHI, Vol. III, (Calcutta, 1975), p. 28.

[2]Bādarāyana dedicated the whole of the second quarter of the second chapter of Brahmasūtras for the refutation of rival views.

[3]For more about this work see, supra, Chapter II.

[4]Vide, Narain, K., OMP, (Allahabad, 1962), p. 5.

[5]Vide, Sarma, B.N.K., HDSVL, Vol. II, (Bombay, 1961), p. 38.

[6]Ibid., p. 170.

[7]See for a short comparison of NA and AS, infra, chapter IX.

[8]Vide, Chattopadhyaya, D.P., IPPI, (Delhi, May 1982), p. 24.

[9]Vide, Sarma, B.N.K., op. cit., p. 146.

[10]Ibid.

[11]Vide, SB, ed., Abhyaṅkar, V.S., p. 154.

[12]Vide, NAAS, Pt I, Intro. pp. 83-85.

[13]Vide, HDSVL, Pt. II, p. 150.

[14]Vide, Anantakṛṣṇaśāstri, N.S., op. cit., p. 90.

[15]Vide, Sarma, B.N.K., op. cit., p. 165.

[16]Ibid.

[17]Anantakṛṣṇaśāstri, N.S., has given the date as 1510-50 A.D., which Sarma, B.N.K., refutes. Sarma's view as presented here seems to be correct. Vide, op. cit., p. 358.

[18]Vide, Potter, Karl H., EIP, Vol. I, p. 516.

[19]Ibid., p. 518.

[20]Thankasvami, R., mentions the name of Nateśārya's work as *Advaitasaraṇi*. He gives his date as 1850-1910 A.D. Vide, op. cit., p. 354.

[21]Vide, Anantakṛṣṇaśāstri, N.S., op. cit. Intro. P. 92.

[22]Vide, Dasgupta, S.N., op. cit., Vol. IV, Chapters XXIX-XXX.

[23]Vide, Śaṅkara, *Ātmabodha*, V. 63. This verse has different readings. The reading accepted by *Śabdakalpadruma* is this. Vide, SKD, Vol. III, (Delhi, 1961), p. 443.

[24]Vide, Vyāsatīrtha, NA, ed., Yogīndrānanda, Svāmi, (Benares, 1977), Vol. I, p. 98. Though he quotes the verse it is of anonymous origin.

[25]Details regarding the living tradition of Śaṅkara are dealt with by Cenkner. Vide, Cenkner, William, *A Tradition of Teachers: Śaṅkara and the Jagadgurus Today*, (Delhi, 1984).

[26]Sarma, B.N.K. gives tables of the Mādhva school and its institutions. Vide, HDSVL, (1981), pp. 201-10.

[27]Vide, Rao, Alur Venkat, HMPP, (Dharwar, 1954), Intro., p.V.

CHAPTER IV

Advaitasiddhi: its Nature, Contents and Commentaries

Nature

Two types of works have originated in the vast philosophical literature of India. One type is called *adhikaraṇaprasthāna* and the other *vādaprasthāna*. The former can be generally described as topical and the latter polemical.

An *adhikaraṇa* is that which treats one subject complete in all respects. Its definition is as follows:

viṣayoviśayaścaiva pūrvapakṣastathottaram
nirnayaśceti pancāngam śāstredhikaraṇamsmṛtam.[1]

Besides these five limbs, namely, subject, doubt, view of the opponent, conclusion and relevancy, some scholars add a sixth limb too, namely, *prayojana* whereby explanation on the necessity of the view of the opponent and also of the conclusion is sought. In Śaṅkara's commentary on *Brahmasūtras* we can see *adhikaraṇa-wise* treatment of the subjects concerned. As a consequence, commentaries and sub-commentaries on Śaṅkara's commentary also have followed the same method. Commentaries of Śaṅkara, Vācaspati, Padmapāda, Prakāśātman, etc., go by the name of *adhikaraṇaprasthāna*.

Vāda is polemical discussion proper. It is, in fact, syllogism adopted in the philosophy concerned. It has also got limbs. Proposition, reason, example, application and conclusion are the limbs. *Naiyāyikas*[2] accept all the five limbs while *vedāntins*[3] and *mīmāṁsakas*[4] accept only three, namely, proposition, reason and example or example, application and conclusion. The logic behind this is that proposition and conclusion and reason and application are, in effect, the same.

Advaitasiddhi belongs to the *vādaprasthāna*. *Navya-Nyāya* has contributed much to the growth of *Vādaprasthāna* in Indian philosophy. As a result, the dialectical method of *Navya-Nyāya* came to be adopted by systems other than *Nyāya*. In *Vedānta*, Śrīharṣa in his *Khaṇḍanakhaṇḍakhādya* and Citsukha in his *Tattvapradīpikā* ably used the *Navya-Nyāya* dialectical method. When Vyāsatīrtha employed *Navya-Nyāya* method to criticise *Advaita*, Madhusūdana came forward and replied to him in the same coin. *Advaitasiddhi* is one of the best specimens of the highly polemical texts of Indian philosophy. In the polemical literature of *Advaita* it stands on a par with *Khaṇḍanakhaṇḍakhādya* and *Tattvapradīpikā*.

Contents

Advaitasiddhi consists of four *paricchedas*, of which the first is the longest and the fourth is the shortest. In different editions of *Advaitasiddhi* the topics are divided and named differently. In the present study the text mainly depended on is that which came out as the second Nirnayasagar edition. Anantakṛṣṇaśāstri, N.S., divides the whole of *Advaitasiddhi* into one hundred and eight topics.[5] The first *pariccheda* consists of sixty topics. The second *pariccheda* has thirty four topics, the third eight and the fourth six. The total number of topics will be still greater if we separate more specifically the subjects dealt with by Madhusūdana. In the present study the text of *Advaitasiddhi* will be examined under one hundred and twelve headings in the second part of the thesis.

A brief *pariccheda*-wise review of the contents of *Advaitasiddhi* is given below:

After salutation and introductory remarks, Madhusūdana opens discussion in the first *pariccheda*, on the *Advaita* doctrine of falsity. All duality has to be explained as being false in order to establish the ultimate reality of non-duality. Falsity of all duality will be proved by establishing the sole ultimate reality of *Brahman*. What is discussed in the first *pariccheda*, in the main, is the falsity of the world. Various means of proof for establishing the falsity of the world are discussed in detail. The different definitions of falsity, the different reasons that determine the character of falsity, the question whether *Brahman* also can be established to be false based on the analogy of the falsity of the world and the argument that actual worldly experience is contradictory to the world being false are fully dealt with in the first *pariccheda*. The *pariccheda* is aptly named by Madhusūdana as *saparikaraprapañcamithyātvanirūpaṇa*.[6]

In the second *pariccheda* the stress is on *Brahman*. It is on the substratum, *Brahman*, that the illusory world is superimposed. Establishment of the sole reality of *Brahman* results in proving the falsity of the world. *Brahman* is impartite, propertyless, changeless and unique. *Brahman* is existence--consciousness-bliss. *Brahman* and *jīva* are one and the same. Knowledge of *Brahman* also is not different from it. All the *śrutis* are evidences to this effect. If any *sruti*, *smṛti* or *purāṇa* goes against this the same should be explained in accordance with the vast majority of *śrutis* which deal with nondual *Brahman*. In short, what is established in the second *pariccheda* is the all-pervasive reality, *Brahman*. This *pariccheda* is called *ātmanirūpana.*[7]

The third *pariccheda* deals mainly with the means for the realisation of *Brahman*. Hearing, along with its subsidiaries thinking and meditation, is the sole means for the realisation of *Brahman*. Discussion in the third *pariccheda* proceeds from that regarding the injunction on hearing and its subsidiaries. The theory of *advaitin* that verbal testimony can create perceptual knowledge is upheld in this *pariccheda*. The *pariccheda* is called *Śravaṇādinirūpaṇa.*[8]

The fourth *pariccheda* deals with the goal of all discussions namely liberation. Liberation can be attained only through the eradication of ignorance. Eradication of ignorance can be achieved by the realisation of *Brahman*. Realisation of *Brahmon* and liberation are not different from *Brahman*. One can attain liberation while one is alive. On the extinction of *prārabdha* final release is achieved. There are no grades in liberation as conceived by *Dvaitavedānta*. Liberation is unique, single and unsurpassed since it is not different from *Brahman* which is of the same nature. The fourth *pariccheda* is called *muktinirūpana.*[9]

Commentaries

The role of commentaries in the history of Sanskrit literature is an interesting topic for study. The general nature of Sanskrit commentaries has caused the saying *ṭikāṭūkāmapekṣate* whereby it is meant that one commentary needs another commentary and it still another so as to be understood. As far as polemical and technical literature are concerned, commentaries are inevitable. Being a highly polemical text of Indian philosophy *Advaitasiddhi has necessitated commentaries.*

Commentaries on *Advaitasiddhi* belong mainly to two types: defensive and elucidative. It was when *Vyāsatirtha* created chaos among *advaitins* through the composition of his *Nyāyāmṛta* that Madhusūdana wrote his *Advaitasiddhi*. It had its repercussions from *dvaitins.*[10] This warranted commentaries of the defensive type on *Advaitasiddhi*. Since *Advaitasiddhi* is highly scholastic and involves the *Navya-Nyāya* method of argument it necessitated commentaries of the elucidative type. However, defence and elucidation of *Advaita-*

siddhi were not carried out in air-tight compartments. In fact defence involves elucidation and vice-versa to some extent.

The principal commentaries on *Advaitasiddhi* shall be enumerated here.

Siddhivyākhyā

This seems to be the first extant commentary on *Advaitasiddhi.* Balabhadra who was a direct disciple of Madhusūdana, wrote the same. He did it in defence of *Advaitasiddhi* from the attack of *Taraṅgiṇi.*[11] Some points, though not of considerable importance, raised by Vyāsatīrtha in his *Nyāyāmṛta* and ignored by Madhusūdana have been taken up for discussion and refuted by Balabhadra in *Siddhivyākhyā.* It is a pity that *Siddhivyākhyā* has not come down to us fully in print.

Gauḍabrahmānandīyam

Gurucandrikā and *Laghucandrika* are commentaries on *Advaitasiddhi* known in learned circles as *Gauḍabrahmānandīyam.* Brahmānandasarasvati wrote *Gurucandtikā* refuting Rāmatirtha's *Taraṅgiṅi. Laghncandrikā* is a condensed form of *Gurucanrikā.*[12] There is difference of opinion among scholars regarding Brahmānanda's authorship of both at the same time. One of the introductory verses of *Laghucandrikā* clearly says that Brahmānandabhikṣu is the author of it. It is as follows:

advaitasiddhivyākhyānam brahmānandenabhikṣuṇā
saṁkṣiptacandrikārthena kriyate laghucandrikā.[13]

However, some scholars raise objections. One of the concluding verses of *Laghucandrikā* is as follows:

mahanubhāvadhaureyaśivarāmākhyavarṇinaḫ
etadgranthasya kartāro lekhakaḥ kevalaṁ vayam.[14]

Based on this, scholars have said a lot. Since Brahmānanda himself says that he is only a *lekhaka* some scholars do not consider him as its author. We have to consider both the verses together. There can be three cases of conclusion. The first is that Śivarāmavarṇi is the author of *Gurucandrikā* and Brahmānanda that of *Laghucandrikā.* If this is accepted, meanings of both the verses will go against it, for, the first verse states Brahmānanda's authorship of *Laghucandrikā* and the second Sivarāmavarṇi's authorship of the same. Therefore, this case of conclusion cannot be accepted. The second is that Śivarāmavarṇi is the author of *Laghucandrikā* and Brahmānanda that of *Gurucandrikā*. If this is taken to be correct, meaning of the first verse will go against it, for, there it is clearly said that Brahmānanda writes *Laghucandrikā*. Therefore, this case also cannot be accepted. The third is that Brahmānanda is the author of both *Gurucandrikā* and *Laghucandrikā*. In this case the only adversity is that the *Kartṛtva* ascribed to Śivarāmavarni in the second verse will go against it. But this can be explained otherwise. Apart from the independent source of action, that which is the mover thereof can be called *hetu* and *karta*. Pāṇini has made provision for the same.[15] It is called *hetukartṛtva*.[16] Śivarāmavarni's *kartṛtva* in the case of *Laghucandrikā* is *hetukartṛtva*. Therefore, it can be concluded that *Brahmānanda* is the author of both *Gurucandrikā* and *Laghucandrikā*. Brahmānanda mentions *Gurucandrikā* as *Advaitacandrikā* also.[17]

Gauḍabrahmānandīyam is the best and the most complete commentary on *Advaitasiddhi* originated so far. In addition to the criticisms of *Taraṅgini* those of *Nyāyāmṛtakaṇṭakoddhāra* also are refuted by Brahmānanda in his *Gauḍabrahmānandīyam*.

Saralavyākhyā

Rāmeśvaradatta is the author of this commentary.[18] As the name indicates it is a lucid explanatory companion to *Advaitasiddhi*. The polemical rigidity of *Advaitasiddhi* needs such companions.

Bālabodhinī

Bālabodhinī also is an elucidative commentary on *Advaitasiddhi*. Bagchi, Yogendranath has intended this commentary for the benefit of students, as the name discloses. The author compares, at times, the views of *Nyāyāmṛta* and *Advaitasiddhi*. *Bālabodhinī* is not complete. It seems to be the latest commentary in Sanskrit any scholor has attempted so far on *Advaitasiddhi*. It came out in 1971.

Miscellaneous

Besides commentaries in Sanskrit, translations involving benefits of commentary have appeared in various languages. Of these *Advaitasiddhivyākhyā* in Hindi by Yogīndrānanda, Swāmi is highly useful. Commentaries on the commentaries of *Advaitasiddhi* also deserve mention here. *Viṭṭhaleśopādhyāyī* is the first to be mentioned. It is a commentary on the *Gauḍabrahmānanyīyam*.[19] Apart from this, commentaries on the commentaries on *Advaitasiddhi* also have appeared. For example, Subrahmaṇyaśāstri, V., has composed a *ṭippaṇa* on *Brahmānandīyabhāvaprakāśa* of Pancāpageśaśāstri on *Gauḍabrahmāndīyam* of Brahmānandasarasvati on *Advaitasiddhi*.

There is also other dependent works on *Advaitasiddhi*. *Advaitasiddhisiddhāntasāra* written by Sadānandavyāsa is an abstract in simple Sanskrit verse. The author himself has composed a prose commentary on his own verses. A critical summary of *Nyāyāmṛta*, *Advaitasiddhi*, *Taraṅgiṇī* and *Laghucandrikā* prepared by Anantakṛṣṇaśāstri, N.S., also has to be mentioned here.

REFERENCES

[1]Vide, SKD, Vol. I, p. 37.

[2]Vide, Annaṁbhaṭṭa, TS, ed., Eng. Tr., Virūpakṣānanda, Svāmi, (Madras, 1980), p. 98.

[3]Vide. Dharmarājādhvarindra, VP, ed., Tryaṁbakarāmaśāstri, (Benares, 1954), pp. 92-93.

[4]Vide, Nārāyaṇa, *Mānameyodaya*, ed., Eng. Tr., Kunhanrājā, C., and Sūryanārāyaṇaśāstri, S.S., (Adyar, 1975), pp. 65-66.

[5]Vide, Anantakṛṣṇaśāstri, N.S., op. cit.

[6]Vide, AS, p. 660.

[7]Vide, AS. p. 854.

[8]Vide, AS, p. 877.

[9]Ibid, p. 900.

[10]Vide, supra, chapter III.

[11]Ibid.

[12]Ibid.

[13]Vide, AS, p. 2.

[14]Ibid., p. 900.

[15]Vide, PS, I-4-54, 55.

[16]Pāṇini's actual use of the expression is *prayojakahetukartṛtva* since the *sūtra* reads *tatprayojakohetuśca*, Ibid.

[17]Vide, colophons at the end of eaeh *pariccheda* of *Gurucandrikā*.

[18]Vide, AS, ed. Rāmeśvaradatta, 2 Vols. (Bombay, 1923-24).

[19]Vide, supra, Chapter III.

PART TWO

TEXTUAL EXAMINATION

CHAPTER V

Pariccheda—1

1. Salutation

It is customary in theistic tradition to bow to *iṣṭadevatā* before embarking upon any endeavour. Accordingly, Madhusūdanasarasvati enjoins in the beginning of his *Advaitasiddhi* a verse in obeisance to *Viṣṇu*, his *iṣṭadevaṭā*. As far as an *advaitin* is concerned there is nothing other than *Brahman*, not to speak of *iṣṭadevatā*. Therefore, Madhusūdana describes *Viṣṇu* as identical with *Brahman*.

Viṣṇu, who is truth, consciousness and bliss, who is the substratum for the illusory world of duality such as *pramātṛtva* caused by *māyā*, who is to be realised by the impartite knowledge derived from the *mahāvākyas*, excels on his own as if having attained sole supreme blissful emancipation as a result of severing the false bondage and the *vikalpas* thereof.[1]

The word *viṣṇu* is used in the sense of all-pervading *Brahman*.[2] This is in consonance with the practice of earlier *advaitins*.[3] The verse consists of the gist of *Advaita* philosophy. It is verily said:

brahma satyaṁ jaganmithyā
jīvobrahmaiva nāparaḥ.[4]

Gauḍapāda,[5] Saṅkara[6] and all advaitins have upheld the idea.

Right from the first salutational verse Madhusūdana begins to retort *Nyāyāmṛta*. Vyāsatīrtha depicts in the second salutational verse of *Nyāyāmṛta* the reality of the world. He exalts *Hari* as *Satyāśeṣaviśvasyakāraṇam*.[7] It is in verbatim retort to this that Madhusūdana describes *Viṣṇu* as the substratum of the illusory world.

Having worshipped the supreme self by the first verse, Madhusūdana proceeds to pay tributes to his *gurus*. In the second verse he worships his *paramaguru* Śrīrāma, his *dikṣāguru* Viśveśvara and his *vidyāguru* Mādhava. Then in the third verse the author, out of his modesty, says that his venture will be for the purpose of doing good to himself, because there are a number of excellent longer and shorter treatises on the subject written by many scholars. This statement of Madhusādana reminds us of Kālidāsa who makes a similar statement.[8] In the fourth and final of the salutational verses Madhusūdana explains the purpose of his writing the book and also its nature. The book is a collection of the truths contained in the scriptures. It is intended for the acquisition of true knowledge and the subjugation of misguided disputants by those who have shortage of time and also for the delight of the learned.

2. *Introductory*

After having performed salutation Madhusūdana begins the text. At first the author proceeds to establish the falsity of the world. It is because *Advaita* can be established only after proving the world of duality to be false. To establish means to discard the opponent's views and substantiate one's own. Both these can be done by employing any of the three *kathās* namely *Vāda*, *jalpa* and *vitaṇḍā*.

The *Nyāya* philosophy deals in detail with the threefold *kathā*.[9] *Vāda* which is the best of the *kathās*, is disputation that leads to the ascertainment of truth. Only seekers after truth hold *Vadā*. *Jalpa* is disputation with a view only to win over the opponent. *Vitaṇḍa* is simple refutation of the opponent's view without establishing one's own. The *kathā* which is meant for serious philosophical discussion is *vāda*. Standard philosophical texts have employed it. Madhusūdana also mainly employs *vādakathā* in his *Advaitasiddhi*.

3. *Doubt arising from a diversity of opinions—the forepart of discussion*

The procedure for discussion is decided upon before the opponents begin their disputation. An umpire and a president are appointed. Since the doubt arising from a diversity of opinions is the forepart of discussion the umpire should, first of all, present the diversity of opinions. The rule that the doubt arising from the diversity of opinions is the forepart of discussion is one accepted by the *naiyāyikas*.[10] It has to be adhered to in *Vedānta* also. However, Vyāsatīrtha finds no relevance for the rule in *Vedānta* though he himself presents the diversity of opinions in the beginning of his *Nyāyāmṛta*. He says that he does it only in accordance with the practice of the *naiyāyikas*.[11] According to him the diversity of opinions has no specific use in the discussion because even without the doubt arising from it the opponents can begin their disputation. Madhusūdana objects to Vyāsatīrtha. He holds that the diversity of opinions has to be presented because it is the doubt arising from it that initiates discussion. It is true that even after presenting the diversity of opinions no doubt may arise, sometimes, because of the knowledge of the real state of things by the persons concerned. However, diversity of opinions has the immanent quality to produce doubts. So it is the duty of the umpire to present the diversity of opinions before embarking upon discussion.

4. *Real character of that with regard to which falsity is predicated*

Now diversity of opinions on the falsity of the world is being presented. Whether it is, that which cannot be contradicted by any true knowledge other than that of Brahman, which is fit to be perceived as existent, which is different from consciousness and which is the counter-correlate of non-existence of all the three points of time in what is taken to be the locus of itself, or not? Whether it is the counter-correlate of non-existence in the said manner eternally or not? This is with regard to the world as a whole. Diversity of opinions can be exhibited individually also. Whether ether is false or not? Whether earth is false or not?

Madhusūdana now exhibits the inference, on the falsity of the world, coined by earlier *advaitins.* Ānandabodha says: the world under dispute is false because it is coginsable, material and finite like shell-silver.[12] Eventhough Ānandabodha uses all the five limbs of syllogism[13] Madhusūdana does not insist on the number of limbs because as far as *Vedāntins* are concerned three limbs will do.

Inference originates from the combined knowledge of pervasion and being the essential attribute of the subject; but there is a condition. It is being the subject itself. So as to specify the being of the subject beyond doubt, the essential characteristic of the subject has to be identified. In the case of the inference on the falsity of the world the diversity of opinions itself can be taken to be the essential characteristic of the subject. Vyāsatīrtha also has no objection in this matter.[14] The essential characteristic of being the subject of the diversity of opinions itself can be taken to be the essential characteristic of the subject. Ānandabodha and other earlier *ācāryas* have used the term *vimatam* in the sense of that which is qualified per proprium by the essential characteristic of being the subject of the diversity of opinions.

5. *Falsity of the world*

What is this falsity that you seek to prove? Only after defining falsity one can proceed to establish the falsity of the world. All the definitions of falsity put forward by earlier *advaitins* have been vehemently criticised and discarded by Vyāsatīrtha. Therefore, Madhusūdana examines the question in detail. Vyāsatīrtha subjects to criticism, in all, five definitions put forward by earlier *advaitins*. Madhusūdana refutes the arguments of Vyāsatīrtha and establishes the validity of all the five definitions.

6. *First definition of falsity*

The first definition of falsity under dispute is that which we find in the *Pancapādikā* of Padmapāda. Padmapāda says that falsity is indefinable.[15] This means that falsity is distinct from both reality and unreality. Therefore, the *pañcapādikā* definition of falsity can be taken to be not being the locus of either reality or unreality. Silver superimposed on sea-shell is the example.

Vyāsatīrtha contends that this is an ambigous definition. Not being the locus of either reality or unreality can have at least three senses. Firstly, it may mean eternal absence of reality qualified by unreality. Secondly, it may mean the two eternal absences of reality and unreality. Thirdly, it may mean something qualified by both the absences of reality and unreality. Of these, the first sense is not tenable because absence of reality qualified by unreality is already there in the world which is only real and for the same reason it would involve the fallacy of the establishment of what is already established. The second sense is not tenable because it would involve all the three fallacies of *vyākhāta*, *arthāntara* and *sādhyavaikalya*. The third sense also cannot be accepted because of the presence of the same three fallacies.

Madhusūdana refutes the charges. There is no harm in taking the definition in the second sense: the two eternal absences of reality and unreality. It would not involve any of the fallacies alleged by Vyāsatīrtha.

The first fallacy alleged is *vyākhāta*[16] which is the violation of the law of contradiction. It can be in three ways. First is in the form of mutual absence of reality and unreality. The second is in the form of being the pervader in the mutual absence of reality and unreality. The third is in the form of being the pervaded in the mutual absence of reality and unreality. Of these, the first form of allegation is to be summarily rejected because *advaitins* do not accept the mutually absent nature of reality and unreality. Reality is that which is not contradicted throughout the three points of time, namely, past, present and future. Unreality means not being the locus of being presented as real at any substratum. The absences of the said reality and unreality are what are intended. For the same reason the second form of allegation regarding *vyākhāta* also has no ground. Since reality and unreality are not mutual absences, being the pervader in the mutual absence of reality and unreality can never be established. The third form of allegation of *vyākhāta* is baseless because being the pervaded in the mutual absence is not conducive to *vyākhāta.* We see that the mutual absences of cow and horse, though they are pervaded, co-exist in camel.

There is also no presence of the fallacy of *sādhyavaikalya.*[17] *Sādhyavaikalya* is the absence of probandum in the example. Silver superimposed on sea-shell is the example here. Probandum is the absences of reality and unreality as defined earlier. There is that probandum in shell silver.

The fallacy of *arthāntara*[18] also is not present in the definition of falsity. *Arthāntara* is establishing something quite different from what is actually intended. Vyāsatīrtha alleges that *advaitins* establish reality of the world instead of its unreality. This is baseless. *Advaitins* hold the reality of *Brahman* alone.

Now *dvaitins* may say that, since according to them, the world is real, absence of unreality is there in the world and that for the same reason there is the fallacy of partial establishment of what is already established. However, it also is baseless. Both the absences of reality and unreality are intended as probandum and therefore, the presence of a part of it cannot be taken for granted for both.

For the reasons presented, there is no harm in taking the third sense of the definition of falsity also. In short, the *Pañcapādikā* definition of falsity that it is not being the locus of either reality or unreality is faultless.

7. *Second definition of falsity*

In his commentary *Vivaraṇa* on the *Pañcapādikā* of Padmapāda, Prakāśātman puts forward two alternative definitions of falsity. Madhusūdana now deals with the first alternative. It is as follows: falsity is being the counter-correlate of negation for all the three points of time in the very same locus where it appears to be.[19]

Vyāsatīrtha discards this definition. He asks whether being the counter-correlate of negation in the locus where it appears to be is absolute or practical or apparent. If it is absolute then *Advaita* is in danger. If it is apparent then there is the fallacy of establishing what is already established. If it is practical then it will be negated later and therefore it will not contradict the absolute *Brahman* and for the same reason the reality of the world is not questioned in any way. This in its turn will present the fallacy of *arthānara*, nullify the validity of such *śrutis* as 'there is in it no diversity'[20] and finally establish the absolute reality of the world.

Madhusūdana now replies: Even if being the counter-correlate of negation in the locus where it appears to be is taken to be absolute there is no danger for *Advaita* because the negation is not different from *Brahman*. The world is enternally negated in its locus *Brahman*. This eternal negation is absolutely non-different from *Brahman*. The negation can be considered to be practical also. Of course, then it will be sublated by the knowledge of *Brahman*. This will not go against the falsity of the world or present its reality. Therefore, there is no relevance for the fallacy of *arthāntara* also. Falsiiy of falsity does not imply reality of its substratum. When dream is negated the objects seen in dream are also negated. There is no rule that negation of negation is reaffirmation. It is only when reality and negation have the same status and identically the same scope that negation of negation means reaffirmation. Otherwise, negation of negation does not imply reaffirmation. Take for instaece the case of silver superimposed on sea-shell. Shell-silver never existed, never exists and will never exist. Therefore, attribution of falsity on it also cannot but be false. However, reality of shell-silver is not reaffirmed. Similarly, negation of the world which is practical also is negated further and it does not present reality of the world. Apparent nature of negation of the reality of the world is never accepted by *advaitins*.

As far as the validity of *śrutis* is concerned there is no harm. *Śrutis* have practical validity. Practical reality of the world is never negated. So *śrutis* do not go invalid. What is negated is the absolute reality of the world?

The opponent argues: The negation of shell-silver and of the world cannot be originally. In the case of the negation of silver the knowledge that contradicts is 'here silver did not exist'. The positive counterpart in this case is practical silver. It never contradicts the existence of apparent silver. Similarly, the positive counterpart in the case of the practical world is absolute *Brahman*. *Brahman* contradicts the absolute nature of the world and not practical. If this is accepted it will result in contradicting what *Vivaraṇa* says. *Vivaraṇa* says that, of absolute negation the positive counterpart in its own form may be the practically real silver as found in the silversmith's shop 'or' in its absolutely real form may be apparent silver itself.[21]

Madhusūdana replies: This is not so. What is meant by *vivaraṇakāra* is that the positive counterpart of the negation is nothing other than apparent silver conceived as identical with practically real silver. What is meant by 'or' is that the author is not particularly concerned whether this apparent silver be negated in its own form or absolutely. In fact, there is no harm in taking the negation originally. In the case of shell-silver the positive counterpart is apparent silver appearing identified with the practical silver. Such silver is eternally negated. Similarly, the practical world taken to be absolutely real is negated eternally.

One may ask: Is the world as non-existent as *tuccha*? The reply is that there is difference. *Tuccha* has not even a seeming appearance anywhere; the world appears as really existent until it is contradicted. It must also be noted that the negation which leads to falsity must have the same relation, extent and scope as the content which is being negated has. *Advaitins* do not accept negation as a separate category; but consider it to be identical with the locus where it appears. *Brahman* has no quality. This negation of all qualities in *Brahman* simply means *Brahman* itself and nothing else.

The opponent says: If *Brahman* is without any quality, *śrutis* like 'Brahman is truth, consciousness and infinite'[22] will go wrong. Here Madhusūdana says that these are not qualities of *Brahman*. By truth untruth is negated, by consciousness unconsciousness and by infinite finite. All negations ultimately mean *Brahman* itself. Therefore, the *Vivaraṇa* definition of falsity that it is being the counter-correlate of negation for all the three points of time in the very same locus where it appears to be is faultless.

8. *Third definition of falsity*

The third definition of falsity dealt with in *Advaitasiddhi* also is that put forward by Prakāśātman in his *Vivaraṇa*. Falsity is the state of being discarded by cognition.[23]

Vyāsatīrtha criticises this definition also. He says that this also cannot be a true definition of falsity. Cognition of past events and things, eventhough false, ceases by itself without waiting to be discarded by right cognition. It is also not felt that silver is discarded by cognition of sea-shell. Moreover, every cognition would be discarded by the cognition that follows and therefore, all cognitions have to be considered false.

Madhusūdana replies: It is not so. What is meant by the state of being discarded by cognition is that it has its existence denied by a general negation proceeding from the true knowledge of the substratum. This existence may be in its own form as effect or in the form of its cause. The effect has an existence in the cause. When a jar is smashed by the stroke of a stick, eventhough the jar ceases to exist in its own form it still exists in the form of its material cause, the particles of earth. And this two-fold existence of anything could be negated only by the true knowledge of *Brahman*. Therefore, falsity is the state of being negated by knowledge in its function as knowledge. All cognitions need not be considered false because one cognition does not negate the preceding cognition by its function as cognition, but it does so on account of its posteriority.

Vivaraṇakāra defines negation as the sublation by cognition along with the effects either latent or apparent.[24] *Vārtikakāra* also agrees with him.[25] He says that as soon as there appears the true knowledge arising from such declarations as 'that thou art' there is, was or will be no ignorance or its product.

One objection that may arise still is that memory by its function as knowledge destroys the unconscious trace of the past percept and that therefore, the definition of falsity is too wide. However, this also is not a harm, for, there is no evidence to the effect that memory destroys the unconscious trace of the past percept. Even if it is admitted that memory destroys the unconscious trace there is no difficulty. In that case the definition has to be interpreted in another way. Falsity is the state of being discarded by cognition as being cognition of the perceptual type. Memory is not a cognition of the perceptual type.

9. *Fourth definition of falsity*

The fourth definition of falsity is that given by Citsukha in his *Tattvapradīpikā*. It is being the counter-correlate of the absolute negation existing in the locus where it appears to be.[26]

Vyāsatīrtha alleges the very same defects as he did in the case of the second definition, taking this to be a replica of the second definition. Madhusūdana disagrees with him. This definition is not a replica of the second definition. Here it is to be taken to mean appearance in the very same locus where there is actually its own eternal absence.

Opponents may argue: When a jar is produced it discards its eternal absence. Then how can the jar and its eternal absence coexist?

Madhusūdana replies: Both the jar and its eternal absence can coexist at the same time, for the jar exists in its cause while its absence exists on the floor. Similarly, the jar and its absence can coexist at the same place too. Though the jar becomes absent in its *kapāla* there is no violation of the law of causality, The antecedent negation of a particular jar resting with a particular *kapāla* regulates the production of that particular jar from the particular *kapāla*. As in time, in place also the antecedent negation and the eternal absence of the same object can coexist.

Objection: As regards time, coexistence of antecedent negation and eternal absence can be accepted on the strength of such ideas as 'at present we have the absolute negation of the jar' and 'at present we have the antecedent negation of the jar'. However, as regards place we have no such grounds for admitting the coexistence of both.

Reply: For admitting the coexistence of antecedent negation and eternal absence in the same place also we have valid grounds. Inference and *śrutis* prove their coexistence.

Objection: Such *śrutis* as 'in the beginning all this was nonexistent'[27] point to the real existence of the nonexistent. The said definition of falsity will unduly include this non-existence too.

Reply: What the *śruti* speaks of is only the opposite of the idea 'this was existent in the beginning'.[28] Therefore, it does not mean to assert the existence of non-existence in the beginning. Otherwise, there will present contradiction between the *śrutis* dealing with 'existent' and 'non-existent' in the beginning.

Moreover, all the reasons set forth in connection with the substantiation of the former definitions can be applied here also. Therefore, the fourth definition of falsity also is without any fault.

10. *Fifth definition of falsity*

The fifth definition of falsity is that which Ānandabodha deals with in his *Nyāyadīpāvalī*. It is being something different from existence.[29] That an object exists means that it is recognised by the valid means of knowledge. The validity of the means exists in its being unaccompanied by deficiencies or discrepancies. Thus, falsity comes to be the character of being distinct from that which is established by valid means of knowledge. Everything other than that which is established by valid means of knowledge is false like dreams. This definition will, however, apply to absolute non-entities as well as to *Brahman* which is devoid of any character. Hence, it becomes necessary to supplement the definition further. Falsity of an object consists in its being distinct from existence and yet being cognised as existing. This will not apply to either non-entities or *Brahman* because both are never known as existing.

Objection: In the definition what is meant by existence? Is it that which is the substratum of the general essence of being or which is incapable of being denied or which is of the nature of *Brahman*? In the first case the definition of falsity will be inapplicable to jar etc., since in them also there is the general essence of nescience. In the second case the definition will be reduced to undeniability. In the third case the argument will be superfluous, for, none of the opponents objects to it.

Reply: Any of the three alternatives is not acceptable. Infact, here in the case of this fifth definition of falsity also all the reasonings put forward in the case of the first definition are relevant. Falsity is distinct from both existence and non-existence. Thus the fifth definition of falsity also is without any fault.

11. *Falsity of falsity*

Vyāsatīrtha now poses a dilemma.[30] Is this falsity itself false or not? If false, it would mean that the world the falsity of which is false is rather real. If falsity is not false then also the reality of the world is established. In both cases *Advaita* is in danger.

Madhusūdana overcomes the dilemma. Falsity is false. It will not present the reality of the world. Falsity of falsity implies reality only when both the cases of falsity have not the same metaphysical status. The silver superimposed on sea-shell and the eternal absence of that silver do not have the same metaphysical status. Therefore, the falsity of silver implies the reality of its eternal absence and vice-versa. In the case of the falsity of the world both falsities have the same metaphysical status because both are appearances liable to be contradicted by the knowledge of *Brahman*. So the falsity of the falsity of the world does not imply the reality of the world. Falsity of falsity and falsity of the world do go together.

12. *Cognisability*

One of the proofs of the inference on the falsity of the world put forward by Ānandatīrtha is the cognisability of the world.[31] Vyāsatīrtha analyses this proof. What is meant by the term cognisability? Is it being the pervaded of a mental state? Or is it being the pervaded of the resultant shape of the mental state? Or is it both? Or is it that which forms at some time and in some way the object of consciousness? Or is it dependence for its own activity upon something different from itself in the form of cognition? Or is it the absence of self-luminousness?

It can not be the first because in that case cognisability will apply to *Brahman* also. For the same reason it cannot be the third also. It cannot be the second, for, eternal substances, substances not cognisable and misconceived substances such as shell-silver are not pervaded of the resultant shape of the mental state. It cannot be the fourth or fifth because then it will apply to *Brahman* also. It cannot be the sixth because self-luminousness is nothing more than non-cognisability coupled with incapability of direct recognition. If such self-luminousness is accepted as cognisability then it will not apply to shell-silver.

Madhusūdana discards all these objections. With the exception of the second all the alternatives are correct. Pure consciousness which is self-luminous is never the content of any cognition. It only appears to be so in association with ignorance. Only modifications of ignorance can become the content of cognitions. Cognisability through simple verbal means has to be excluded. Though one may be aware of *tuccha* through verbal propositions, it cannot on that account, be called false, for, it is absolutely non-existent and cannot be called either false or real.

Madhusūdana further explains cognisability as that which has a definite formal content. By the term formal is meant any describable characteristic whereby *Brahman* is excluded. *Brahman* has no describable characteristic. Even the cognition of negation has to be described as having the character of negativity. The effect of this interpretation is that cognisability is limited to all that comes within the purview of relative and pragmatic experience.

13. *Materiality*

The second proof produced for the falsity of the world is materiality.[32] Vyāstīrtha now asks: What is this materiality? Is it the character of the non-cogniser? Or is it the character of non-cognition? Or is it the character of the non-self?

It cannot be the first, for, it will apply to pure *Ātman* also. It cannot be the second because the character of non-cognition will be applicable to the mental state also. It cannot be the third too because it cannot be ascertained what the character of the non-self is, for the character of the self itself is difficult to be understood.

Madhusūdana replies: There is no harm in the second and third explanations suggested. If we regard unconsciousness as the character of non-cognition it will never apply to *Ātman*. Even during the state of liberation *Ātman* does not lose its consciousness.

Vyāsatirtha now alleges inconstancy for the second explanation. However, Madhusūdana discards the allegation. If knowledge is defined as that which illuminates an object then even during emancipation objects would be illuminated. In fact, the relation of knowledge to objects is extraneous and therefore illusory.

Objection: If no objects are revealed during emancipation bliss also will have to be said to be not revealed whereby it will result that no one would care for emancipation.

Reply: The state of emancipation itself is bliss and there is no separate manifestation of bliss obtainable therein. The association of object is perceivable only in sense-knowledge. Knowledge of *Ātman* which is non-different from emancipation is not produced of sense contact. The character of non-self also fits in as the meaning of materiality. The opponent alleges inconstancy in this case also. Madhusūdana discards it also. Self is distinct from non-self and therefore the definition does not apply to *Ātman*. Thus the proof of falsity of the world, materiality also is quite suitable.

14. *Finiteness*

The third proof introduced in the inference on the falsity of the world is finiteness.[33] Finiteness can be of three kinds: by time, space or object.

Objection: Time and space are universals which cannot be considered to be finite either by others or by themselves. Even *Brahman* is spoken of as existing always and everywhere. Therefore, finiteness by time or space cannot be considered as proofs for falsity. Finiteness by object is nothing other than mutual negation which *advaitins* do not accept since they do not approve of reality of any difference.

Reply: Since *advaitins* do not admit universals time and space cannot be considered to be universals. It is nonsense to suppose that in all cases of existence of cow there is a cow-universal which persists throughout. The same is the case of all supposed universals. Therefore, the world is to be taken as limited by time and space. The *śrutis* such as 'from that *Ātman* sprang ether' etc.,[34] clearly state the origin of the world. That which has an origin has an end also. That is why the world is considered false. The world is limited by objects also. *Brahman* is the only reality which is unlimited. *Brahman* is devoid of all the four dimensions: shortage, length, subtlety and grossness.[35] Thus finiteness also is evidence for the falsity of the world.

15. *Citsukha's inference on falsity*

Citsukha has presented an inference on falsity. The cloth is the counter-correlate of the absolute negation in the yarns because it is a composite whole just like other composite things.[36] It can be concluded from this that a thing is false if it is capable of being absolutely denied with regard to its material components.

Objection: The effect is non-different from its material cause. Therefore, falsity of all effects is already established. In that case your argument is open to the fallacy of establishing the established. If your argument is in the sense that the effect is not contained in the cause or that it is contained in something else then it will be open to the fallacy of *arthāntara*.

Reply: The experience of cause and effect is there. It necessitates the assumption of some difference between them in spite of the fact that cause and effect are identical. It may be argued that this will go against the non-difference of cause and effect laid down by Bādarāyaṇa.[37] However, there is no such contradiction. All that is meant by the *sūtra* is that the effect has no existence apart from its material cause. Therefore, there is no presence of the fallacy of establishing the established. As regards *arthāntara*[38] it can be excluded by adding a qualifying adjunct to the subject of the argument whereby it becomes that the effect is contained in that particular cause only.

Objection: Perception shows that the whole is dependent on parts. Therefore, non-existence of whole in parts cannot be admitted.

Reply: Opposition of perception is no matter, for, perception is often illusory.

The opponent alleges that the character of not being produced out of the yarns serves as an extraneous adjunct in the inference propounded by Citsukha. However, Madhusūdana discards it. An extraneous adjunct invalidates the inference only when it is possible to prove the negation of the probandum of that inference by the negation of the extraneous adjunct in question. In the case of Citsukha's inference it is not possible. Based on the arguments presented, the inference propounded by Vidyāsāgara also can be successfully explained. The inference is as follows: The world under dispute has no existence apart from consciousness because it is never cognised apart from consciousness just like a dream. What is meant by non-existence apart from consciousness is any of the forms of falsity described above. What is meant by non-cognisable apart from consciousness is that it is cognisable only when there is an illumination of consciousness. In this manner inferences put forward by other *advaitins* can also be explained.

16. *Denial of the presence of extraneous adjuncts*

Mādhvas allege the presence of extraneous adjuncts in the proofs set forth in the inference on the falsity of the world.[39] An extraneous adjunct is that which has reciprocal pervasion with the probandum and absence of pervasion with the probans at the same time.[40] In the inference on falsity, being other than the subject is the extraneous adjunct. It has reciprocal pervasion with the probandum falsity and the absence of the same with the probans cognisability etc. Therefore, the proofs set forth in the inference on the falsity of the world have extraneous adjuncts.

Madhusūdana discards the allegation. The alleged extraneous adjunct is not present in the cognition of the unity of body and self which is false and which will be sublated only by the knowledge of *Brahman*. Moreover, the probandum can be regarded as concomitant with only that thing the negation of which will prove the negation of that probandum simply because in support of any further phase there will be no corroborative instance. Take for instance the inference 'the earth is not produced by a creator, because it is not produced by a material body'. Here, we find that all cases of being produced by a creator are not concomitant with the character of being produced by a material body because the qualification 'by a material body' is absolutely useless. The same is the case with the falsity of ether etc., also. Therefore, the proofs set forth in the inference on the falsity of the world do not present any extraneous adjunct.

17. *Denial af similarity with pseudo-inferences:*

Vyāsatīrtha now alleges similarity of the inference on the falsity of the world with pseudo-inferences. We have such inferences as the world has apparent reality because it is cognisable' and '*Brahman* is false because it is an object of empirical usage or because it is different from non-entity like the shell-silver'.

Madhusūdana objects to the argument. If the world has no practical reality it will not be possible for us to subject it to empirical usage. Similarly, if *Brahman* is false it will make everything non-existent and absolute nihilism will be the result. Moreover, apparent nature has to be defined. Is it the state of being contradicted by knowledge other than that of *Brahman*? Or is it the state of having only an apparent body? In the former case it has inconstancy in the cognition of the unity of body and self and also the fallacy of non-efficiency. In the latter case there is the fallacy of establishing the established.

As regards the second proof put forward by the opponent to prove the falsity of Brahman, it is to be pointed out that it will not apply to *Brahman*. What is meant by a thing being an absolute non-entity is that it is incapable of being cognised in connection with any state. A thing can be said to be different from absolute non-entity when it is contrary to what has been said. This latter character cannot belong to *Brahman* in its pure sense. As regards *Brahman* in association with ignorance we also admit its difference from non-entity.

Lastly, the example of shell-silver you pointed out has no connection with the probans. Therefore, the inference put forward to establish the falsity of the world is not open to the charge of similarity with pseudo-inferences.

18. *Denial of contradiction by perception*

Mādhvas urge that the inference on the falsity of the world held by *advaitins* is contradicted by perception such as 'the jar exists'. Madhusūdana retorts that it is baseless because before alleging contradiction of the inference with perception, the opponent has to establish existence which can be cognised by perception and which is contradictory to falsity.

Vyāsatīrtha attempts for a definition of existence with a view to establish it. He puts forward a number of alternative definitions. Existence is being the object of true cognition. It is the capability of true cognition. It is not being the object of erroneous cognition. A number of objections can be raised against each of these definitions. Since true cognition apprehends and presupposes existence and is not perceivable by the eye and other sense-organs existence cannot be defined in terms of true cognition. Therefore, further alternatives are suggested. However, those alternatives also meet with the same deficiences. At last the opponent says: by existence is meant reality. What is meant by the reality of the world is exactly what is meant by the reality of *Brahman*. It is said: 'the world has the same kind of reality as *Brahman* has; if the reality of *Brahman* is undefinable that of the world also is undefinable.'[41]

Madhusūdana retorts sarcastically: At the time of marriage, being questioned by the bride's father as to his *gotra* the bridegroom replies: 'my *gotra* is exactly the same as yours'. The *dvaitin* is the true brother of that bridegroom. If father-in-law and son-in-law belong to the same *gotra* the marriage cannot take place. Similarly, if the world and *Brahman* have the same being the world is absolutely false. The being of *Brahman* consists in that it is self-luminous, non-dual intelligence. This is the true nature of the world which is admittedly non-intelligent. So the world will be proved to be essentially false because its true being is that of *Brahman*.

Vyāsatītha still persists to define existence. Existence is that which cannot be denied at any time and at any place. It can also be defined as that which, being different from non-existence, is not a false imposition or as that which at some time or other is directly and rightly perceived as existing.

Madhusūdana retorts that in the definitions presented, falsity is conceived as non-existence at all times and all places and reality as the opposite. Sense-perception can never bring to us such a negation binding all times and places and therefore, it cannot bring to us the opposite of negation, namely, reality also. The fact that some things are perceived to exist somewhere at some time is irrelevant, for, even a false appearance may have such a temporary perceptual existence.

Vyāsatīrtha now contends that as admitted by *naiyāyikas*, there is a special mode of presentation of universals called *sāmānyapratyāsatti*[42] by which all the individuals that come under such universals are perceived in consciousness. It is by this means alone that inductive generalisation leading to deductive inference is possible. Thus though all negations of an entity at all times and places may not be visually perceived, they may be presented to consciousness by the said *sāmānyapratyāsatti*. This being the case, their negation reality also can be conceived.

Madhusūdana, however, discards the validity of *sāmānyapratyāsatti*. He indulges in a terse polemical fight against *naiyāyikas* and shows that deductive inferences are possible not through *sāmānya-pratyāsatti* but through the association of the special characteristics of the universals in determining the concomitance. Therefore, all negatives at all times and places cannot be presented to consciousness. For the same reason their opposite, reality, also cannot be perceived.

Vyāsatīrtha continues his arguments. It is through the perception of *sākṣin* that *advaitins* establish the falsity of the world. The reality of the world also may be similarly claimed to be perceived by *sākṣin*. If the perceptions of the *sākṣin* are susceptible to truth and error alike, the perception of oneness by *sākṣin* also will be open to the same kind of uncertainty. In that case the reality of the world of difference will be automatically established.

Madhusūdana replies that the perception by *sākṣin* is capable of revealing only already existing realities. It cannot reveal things of the future. The world is practically real. Perception by the *sākṣin* cannot in any way show whether the reality of the world will be contradicted in future or not. Perception by *sākṣin* is thus incapable for a future denial of the falsity of the world. In fact, it is the knowledge of *Brahman* that discards the reality of the world. In short, perception, whether it be sense-perception or perception born of *sāmānya-pratyāsatti* or perception by *sākṣin*, is not capable of contradicting the validity of the proofs set forth in the inference on the falsity of the world.

Vyāsatīrtha now objects to the thesis of *advaitin* that there is only one existence identical with pure consciousness on which all the so-called objects and contents of knowledge are superimposed. The mere fact that one experiences that a jar exists does not prove that the jar is imposed upon pure existence, for, pure existence can never be perceived and all the characteristics including false appearances may also be considered to have the same existential character as existence itself has.

Madhusūdana replies that it is better to admit one constant existence on which various forms of objects are imposed than to admit a number of individual entities.

Vyāsatīrtha now urges that perceptual evidence by itself is stronger than inference. Inference is slow in establishing itself on account of the various conditions it has to depend on.

Madhusūdana discards the argument. Perceptual evidence is inferior in validity to inference and verbal testimony. When perception is contradicted by inference or verbal testimony it is the latter that stands.

So perception also has to depend on its non-contradiction with other means of proof for its validity. All means of proof are relatively dependent on, and inferior in validity to, verbal testimony. *Vedic* scriptures are not man-made and they have therefore, an inalienable claim to validity. Perception through one sense, for instance the visual, has often to be woven together with perception through other senses, for arriving at valid conclusions as in the perception 'fire is hot'.

It is true that in certain cases perception may dispel an ignorance which is not removed by inference. However, this does not establish the superiority of perception. The argument that perception is quicker than inference is not valid, for, authority depends on proper examination and discovery of faultlessness and not on mere quickness. However, the validity of perception in its relative field is not hampered in any way. *Śrutis* dealing with the absolute onencss of reality are the most valid. Inference also accordingly has to prove the falsity of the world.

19. *Denial of superior validity of perception*

Vyāsatīrtha argues that since inference and verbal testimony depend on visual and auditory perception respectively, it will be wrong to think that perception is invalidated by inference and verbal testimony. If perception is not valid by itself all inferences and verbal testimonies will also be invalid because they depend on perception for their data.

Madhusūdana replies that verbal testimony does not challenge the data supplied by perception, but it challenges their utlimate validity which can never be supplied by perception. The simple fact that one knowledge springs after another is no reason for considering it less valid than the former. In that case the judgement 'this is not silver, but is sea-shell' will have to be deemed less valid than its previous perceptual error that 'this is silver'.

Vyāsatīrtha argues further that the validity of sense-evidence is determined by a critical examination depending on correspondence. Madhusūdana replies that he, as well as other advaitins, has no objection to the validity of an awareness according to correspondence. What is contended is that the ultimate validity cannot be revealed by any critical examination.

Vyāsatīrtha still holds that if perception is invalid the knowledge of concomitance arrived at through it will also be invalid and for the same reason all inferences will have to be considered invalid. Madhusūdana syas that this argument is wrong because even by a false reasoning a right inference may be possible. From a reflection which is illusory it is possible to infer the existence of the thing reflected. Moreover, falsity of the evidence does not necessarily imply the falsity of the thing known. Therefore, the contention that if perception is not regarded as superior in validity to inference and verbal testimony, then all knowledge will become invalid, is illegitimate.

20. *Contradiction of Perception by inference*

Dvaitins argue that if perception is contradicted by inference the whole of *Mīmāṁsā* will be invalidated. *Mīmāṁsā* admits in various places the puperior validity of perception and recommends at times a twisting interpretation of such scriptural passages as are not in harmony with perception.

Madhusūdana replies that it is indeed true that certain scriptural passages which deal with mundane things are brought into harmony with perceptual experience by interpreting them likewise. However, it is no reason for assuming that those texts which deal with ultimate reality and which do not refer to the accessory details of sacrifices also should be subordinate to perception.

Vyāsatīrtha argues that if perception is contradicted by inference fire can be inferred to be cold and a hare as having horns. Madhusūdana replies that all inferences cannot be regarded as superior to perception and cannot therefore contradict it. It is well known that an illegitimate inference does not lead to valid conclusion. An illegitimate inference is therefore not superior to perception. It cannot also be denied that there are many instances of illegitimate perception being rightly denounced by inference.

21. *Contradiction of perception by verbal testimony*

Mādhvas argue that if perception is contradicted by verbal testimony the whole of both *Mīmaṁsā* and *Vedānta* will be invalidated. If verbal testimony were to contradict perception *Jaimini* would not have dealt with the figurative meaning of the *arthavāda* texts of the Vedic scriptures.[43] *Arthavāda* has often observations which are against perception.[44] Take for example the figurative description 'the sacrificer is the grass-bundle'.[45] In *Vedānta* also secondary implication would not have been accepted in the case of the *śruti* 'that thou art'.[46] In fact, there it is accepted in order to patch up the contradiction with perception.

Madhusūdana now replies: The validity of perception is not always contradicted by verbal testimony. Perception has empirical validity. It is the absolute validity of perception that is contradicted. If figurative statements are taken in their expressed sense the empirical validity of perception will be contradicted. It is only to avoid such contradictions the figurative meanings of such statements are taken. As regards the secondary implication in the case of the *śruti* 'that thou art' the opponent's argument is wrong. It is only in fitness of things to say that secondary implication is adopted in the text so as to get the valid cognition of non-duality non-apprehensive of relation. The six proofs which help to decide the purport of a text, namely, commencement and conclusion, reiteration, novelty, profit, eulogy and demonstration[47] and also the general intention of the *śrutis* show that the purport of the *śruti* 'that thou art' is the impartite unity of *Brahman* and *jīva*. Infact everywhere secondary implication is adopted so as to obtain the purport of the text.

It may be argued that if secondary implication is accepted in the *śrutis*, *śrutis* in general will have to be considered secondary. This argument is wrong. The *śruti* dealing with non-duality of *Ātman* is secondary to none.

Objection: To be part of other texts and otherwise are not causative of secondary and primary meanings respectively; but to be in contradiction with other evidences and otherwise are causative of secondary and primary meanings respectively. If verbal testimony contradicts preception the very validity of perception will be questioned.

Reply: To have primary meaning means to import purport. To import the purport of something else means to have secondary meaning. Adoption of secondary implication does not necessarily mean that the meaning is secondary. In the case of *śrutis* dealing with non-duality, even if there is dependence on secondary implication in the matter of import of the purport there is no harm for their having primary meaning. And for the same reason *śrutis* dealing with non-duality are capable of contradicting perception.

22. *Denial of inequality with apacchedanyāya*

Madhusūdana explains that verbal testimony must be regarded as superior in validity in accordance with the *apacchedanyāya*. In the *apacchedādhikaraṇa* of *Mīmāṁsa* the procedure for the performance of penance has been laid down.[48] The sacrifice, at which all the belongings of the sacrificer have to be given away and which is laid down as to be performed in expiation of the anomaly incurred in the line of priests passing out being broken by the *pratihartṛ* priest, is set aside in favour of the sacrifice at which no gifts have to be given and which is to be performed in expiation of a similar breaking of the line by the *udgātṛ* priest. The reason given for this is that the passing of the *udgātṛ* comes after that of the *pratihartṛ*. In accordance with this law it is only right to assume that perception which is the fore-runner of all forms of cognition should be sublated by verbal as well as inferential cognitions.

Objection: In the case of the breaking of line done by the *pratihartṛ* alone or by both the *pratihartṛ* and the *udgātṛ* occuring either simula-taneously or one after the other, there is room for the performance of rites connected with the passing of the *pratihartṛ* even after the performance of that connected with the *udgātṛ*. Otherwise, the *Vedic* injunction that prescribes giving away of all the belongings in connec-tion with the passing of the *pratihartṛ* will be violated. That is why an option as to the performance of the expiatory rites has been pro-vided.[49] In short, *apacchedanyāya* is applicable only to those actions for the performance of which there is some room left. If we apply the same *nyāya* to the case of validity of perception and *śrutis* we will have to discard perception in total as invalid.

Reply: As in the case of the performance of the rites mentioned in the *apacchedādhikaraṇa*, in the case of perception also there is room for validity in regard to the practical state of things. Perception reveals the world to be true for all practical purposes. Certain *śrutis* reveal *Brahman* as qualified and phenomenal. *Śrutis* dealing with the unqualified and transcending *Brahman* contradict with the said percep-tion and *śrutis*. It is in this connection that the *apacchedanyāya* is relevant. Therefore, the opponent's claim that the case of sublation of perception by verbal cognition is not amenable to the *apacche-danyāya*, is as a result of sheer ignorance.

23. *Denial of equality with the inference on fire being cool*

Objection: If inference contradicting sense-perception were to be accepted as valid we must also regard the inference that 'fire is not hot' as valid. Then there can be no talk of the fallacy of *Kālātyayā-padiṣṭa*.

Reply: It is not proper to equate the inference on the coolness of fire and that on the falsity of the world. The hotness of fire can be perceived. The same perception is that which contradicts the inference on the coolness of fire. This is not the case with the inference on the falsity of the world. There is no perception that can contradict the inference on the falsity of the world. It may be said that the perception, 'the jar exists', is capable of contradicting falsity. However, it is not so. The perception, 'the jar exists', does not prove existence. Existence that is absolute cannot be perceived. The jar has only empirical existence. A perception on empirical existence can never contradict the absolute falsity proved by inference.

The opponent strives his best to establish that inference is dependent on perception and that therefore perception cannot be contradicted by inference. Madhusūdana refutes the contention. Mere dependence is not capable of standing in the way of contradiction. In fact what is misleading is independent reasoning. That is why Bādarāyaṇa enjoins the aphorism 'because reasoning has no conclusiveness'.[50] The commentators have interpreted the aphorism in the same sense too.

The falsity of the world is not a matter of mere inference. *Śrutis* hold the absolute reality of *Brahman* alone. Therefore, the falsity of the world cannot be otherwise. It is the relevance of inference also. Inference on the falsity of the world is not similar to that on the coolness of fire.

24. *Sublation of the non-contradiction of perception*

The greater validity of a cognition depends on its being tested well and not either on its being the basis for other cognitions or its being direct or immediate. We find that perception is actually amenable to rejection by inference and verbal testimony. Direct perception of shell-silver is set aside by inference. Such perception as 'I am fair', 'the moon has a disc of the size of about six inches' and 'I am in this house' are all set aside by verbal testimony and inference.

Objection: As a matter of fact, a misconception pertaining to direct perception is set aside by another more reasonable perception. If otherwise inference were capable of setting aside immediate perceptual misconceptions, the attempt of *advaitin* to prove that cognition obtained from *śruti* to be immediate and direct would be absolutely unnecessary.

Reply: What occurs in the case of an ordinary misconception is this: A man sees something lying on the ground. He sees it as a snake. Then comes a trustworthy assertion 'this is not a snake'. This verbal knowledge does not completely destroy his ignorance which caused the misconception of snake on the rope. However, the knowledge is capable of establishing the falsity of the knowledge of snake and also snake on the rope. Delusion on the validity of the knowledge of snake on rope and that of snake on rope are not in demand of immediate or direct perception so as to be sublated. Therefore, the view that direct perceptual illusions are sublated by more reasonable perceptions is wrong. Perception is contradicted by inference and verbal testimony.

It may be argued that this will go against what *vivaraṇakāra* has said. He says that in certain cases, without due consideration, a certain cognition may, in a hurry, be regarded as sensuous and such a cognition may be rejected by inference and cast out of ordinary usage; but when we come to examine the comparative authority of such sensuous and inferential cognitions as have been found to be so after due deliberation, what we find is that no inferential cognition can ever prove the reality or falsity of a sensuous cognition.[51] This declaration must be taken as referring to such verbal knowledge as has its validity not duly ascertained and to inference based on it. Once the validity is duly ascertained there is no question of enquiring into its higher or lower status.

25. *Fitness of future contradiction*

Madhusūdana holds that the validity of perception cannot be established unless there is surety to the effect that it will not be contradicted in future. In fact there is no surety to that effect, for, the present perception of the reality of the world will be ultimately contradicted. The perception, 'this jar exists', is set aside by the *śrutis* which proclaim the falsity of the world.[52]

Objection: If we are to invalidate any knowledge for fear of future contradiction the rule will be applicable to every knowledge and as a result all knowledge will have to be considered invalid. Ordinarily, experience of wake contradicts that of dream. If experience of wake also is said to be contradicted there will be nothing to contradict experience of dream. Again, one knowledge that contradicts another must have a content because a knowledge without any content will have no objectian to any other knowledge. *Advaitins* hold that the knowledge of *Brahman* is contentless. They also certify monistic experience on the basis of monistic *śrutis*. Similarly, *dvaitins* can also certify experience of *Ātman* as dualistic based on dualistic *śrutis*.[53] Finally, the monistic experience which is said to contradict the world experience, being itself an experience would be liable to contradiction. Therefore, if perceptual experience is doubted to be liable to contradiction there would be no end to such doubts.

Reply: The essential character of a knowledge that contradicts another is not to have a content. What is important is that a right knowledge should realise reality and negate false knowledge. When true knowledge of *Brahman* negates world experience and establishes reality there is no involvement of affirmation of duality. The very knowledge of *Brahman* is in the form of reality by which falsity, which has only appearance and no existence, dissolves away. Doubts regarding the validity of the knowledge of *Brahman* can arise only if defects are known in it. The knowledge of *Brahman* is supreme and therefore there can be no question of doubt. In short, inference on the falsity of the world is valid and no perception can contradict it. On the contrary, inference contradicts perception on account of its indefiniteness regarding future contradiction.

26. *Denial of inference on the reality of the world*

The opponent says: Let perception not reject the inference on the falsity of the world. There are inferences themselves that will serve to reject the inferential cognition on the falsity of the world. Everything other than *Brahman*, or the thing under discussion which is not the substratum of falsity by reason of its not being rejected by any other right notion save that of *Brahman*, or save the knowledge obtained from the right apprehension of the true import of the *Vedānta* texts or save such knowledge as that brings about liberation, is real or absolutely real because not being the substratum of merely apparent reality it is totally different in character from a false thing like *Brahman* or like the hare's horn.

Madhusūdana replies: This inference is fallacious because in accordance with the view of *dvaitins*, that which is only apparently real is false and as such the qualification in the above inference, 'not being the substratum of mere apparent reality', is superfluous. This would make the proof of the inference open to the fallacy of *vyāpyatvāsiddhi*.[54] If you put the proof in accordance with the view of distinguishing absolute and apparent reality, then it will fail to prove the conclusion because it will not apply to the identification of soul with body which is not subject to rejection by anything other than the knowledge of *Brahman*. A thing is called apparently real only if it is such as is set aside by the knowledge of *Brahman*. Then again, with the sole view of excluding from the subject of your syllogism the apparently real things like shell-silver you have introduced three alternative qualifications in the statement of your subject. The first of these is in accordance with the view that *Brahman* is pervaded over by mental state. The second is introduced in accordance with the view that there is no such pervasion and that the right knowledge of the import is a necessary condition in all right verbal cognitions. The third is added in accordance with the view that the knowledge of import cannot be regarded as necessary in verbal cognition. All these involve a vicious circle.

Arguments and counter-arguments continue between Madhusūdana and the opponent. In all, *Vyāsatīrtha* puts forward eight particular inferences to prove the reality of the world. Madhusūdana discards all of them. He establishes beyond doubt that no inference can contradict the falsity of the world or prove the reality of it.

27. Particular inferences on the falsity of the world

Having refuted all the charges of the opponents against the falsity of the world Madhusūdana proceeds to present the particular inferences on the falsity of the world.

1. Note being the substratum of the negation of things other than *Brahman*, which are not contradicted by anything other than the knowledge of *Brahman*, cannot subsist in the substratum of absolute reality because it does not subsist in *Brahman* like the character of shell-silver and like the difference from absolute reality.

2. The world under dispute is false because it is something other than *Brahman* like shell-silver.

3. Absolute reality cannot subsist in anything that is the object of a mutual negation subsisting in itself because it never subsists in anything but an absolutely real entity like the state of *Brahman*.

4. The character of absolute reality is invariably concomitant with the character of *Brahman* or with unity because these two characters are coexistent with reality like the character of being different from falsity.

5. The jar and other things having a pervasive existence are objects of only such negation as co-existent with its substratum and is other than those that are produced because they are the objects of negation like nameability.

6. Absolute negation subsists in the whole of its object because it is eternal negation like mutual negation.

7. The character of absolute negation subsists only in that which resides in the substratum of all that forms the object of that negation or it subsists in that which resides in all the objects of the negation because the negation is an eternal one like mutual negation.

8. The character of the absolute negation of the jar subsists in that which is co-existent with the negation, this negation being the antecedent negation of the object that is productive of the object of that negation because it consists in the negation of a certain jar which is coeval with a certain piece of the jar like the character of cognisability.

9. The piece of the jar is the substratum of the absolute negation of that jar because it forms its receptacle like the jar.

10. The character of *Brahman* cannot belong to any object of mutual negation subsisting in an absolutely real thing because it belongs to *Brahman* like the character of being different from falsity.

11. Any distinction from or negation of the absolutely real thing cannot subsist in any absolutely real thing because it has for its object an absolutely real thing like negation that has for its object all things having absolute reality.

12. All negations must belong either to an object other than the real or to the substratum of such an object because they are negations like the negation of shell-silver.

13. The negation residing in the absolutely real thing cannot have that thing for its object because it resides in an absolutely real thing like the negation of shell-silver.

14. Falsity is invariably concomitant with all things except *Brahman* and the absolute non-entity because it belongs to all false things or because it is not the object of that absolute negation which is co-existent with falsity like the character of perceptibility.

15. Perceptibility cannot belong to the absolutely real thing because it resides only in nameable things like the character of shell-silver.

16. Perceptibility is invariably concomitant with the character of differing from the absolutely real thing because it is a character not residing in things other than perceptible like the character of apparent reality.

17. That which according to both disputants, is not false can never form the substratum of any character that is not co-existent with falsity because it is the receptacle like shell-silver.

18. That place which is occupied by an object is the substratum of

the absolute negation of that object because it is its receptacle like time.

19. Anything endowed with the character of the self is devoid of that negation which has for its object something possessed of absolute reality because it is absolutely real like all things possessed of absolute reality.

20. Shell-silver does not in any way differ from the world in respect of falsity because it forms the object of ordinary activity like *Brahman*.

21. The world under dispute is false because while not being the object of that knowledge which leads to deliverance, it is something other than an absolute non-entity like shell-silver.

22. Being the object of that knowledge which leads to deliverance is such that absolute reality is invariably concomitant with it because it is co-existent with absolute reality like being spoken of in the *śrutis* as absolutely real.

23. The absolute negation of a certain piece of clothe is located in the yarn because it is the beginningless negation of the cloth like the mutual negation of the cloth.

24. That which is devoid of the character of having partial existence, in the sense that the subject is meant to be such as does not exist on only a part of its substratum and which has the character of the subject of the preceding inference, is the object of that absolute negation which is co-existent with itself because it is non-self in the sense that it is unconscious like conjunction.

25. Everything besides eternal substances, which is not the substratum of partial existence and has the characteristics of the aforesaid subject, is the object of such absolute negation as is not itself the subject of absolute negation because it is a thing like the eternal substance.

26. Any differentiation from the self cannot have for its object an absolutely real thing because it has not the self for its object like the differentiation of shell-silver.

In this manner any number of particular inferences can be coined by the learned. Therefore, the falsity of the world can never be questioned by the opponents.

28. *Denial of contradiction by scriptures*

Vyāsatīrtha alleges contradiction of the inference on the falsity of the world by Vedic and other scriptures as well as aphorisms. Vedic texts such as 'the world is real',[55] 'that which is regarded as real is false'[56] and 'for eternal years he created things in reality'[57] reveal the reality of the world. Similarly, *smṛti* says 'they declare the world to be false, unstable and without God, out of ignorance'.[58] There are also aphorisms: 'external objects are not non-existent because they are perceived'[59] and 'because of the difference of nature the waking state is not false like dream'.[60] All these contradict the falsity of the world.

Madhusūdana discards the allegations. The scriptures have no purport as the opponent interprets. The first of the *śrutis* cited is addressed to Indra and Brahmaṇaspati. It says that all the world that seems to be true is created by both of them. It may also mean that all the prayers offered to them both are true. Therefore, the same has no purport as to the reality of the world. In the second *śruti* cited the deity is Indra. It means that Indra the blue-coloured bird, vigorous, mighty, heroic, ancient, nestless from eternity, knows all that is truth and is not vain. Thus it also does not deal with the reality of the world. The words of the *Īśāvāsya Upaniṣad* also do not prove the reality of the world. It means only that the creator created the world as it was in the past. In fact all the *śrutis* are restatements and not injunctions.

Objection: The *śrutis* do not make any restatement. *Advaitins* cannot say so because as far as they are concerned there is no reality other than that of *Brahman*.

Reply: The reality of *Brahman* is perceived as that of the world. Up to the realisation of *Brahman* the world has its reality too. Therefore, the *śrutis* can restate that reality of the world. All this does not make any change to the fact that the reality of the world will be contradicted by the knowledge of *Brahman*.

The words from *Bhagavadgītā* also do not in any way prove the reality of the world. It is true that those words condemn the unrealistic view. However, they only mean the *advaitic* view that the world is beyond being defined as real or false.

The *sūtras* also do not vouchsafe the reality of the world. The *adhikaraṇa*[61] where occur the *sūtras*, is intended to refute the view of the *Vijñānavāda* sect of the Buddhists. According to *Vijñānavāda* all dealings concerned with the means, objects and ends of knowledge become possible as subjective occurrences superimposed on consciousness. Even though an external object may exist, there can be no activity of the means etc., of knowledge unless it is through a superimposition on consciousness. In short, according to them there is no external object. Retorting to this, the first *sūtra* cited says that the external objects are not non-existent, for, they are perceived. The *vijñānavādin* may say that he does not negate the perception of any object but does negate the perception of anything apart from that perception. The reply to this is that something other than the perception has to be admitted just because there is perception. That 'something' is the object of that perception.

Vijñānavādins further say that perception of things like pillar occurs in the waking state even in the absence of any external objects just as it happens in a dream. It is to deny this argument that the second *sūtra* cited is enjoined. The waking state and dream are actually different in nature. And for the same reason the said thing is not correct. Thus the *sūtras* are in refutation of the view of *vijñānavādin* and not to establish the reality of the world. The inference on the falsity of the world cannot be contradicted by scriptures of any kind.

29. *Fitness of non-existent to be the probans*

Vyāsatīrtha still argues that the inference on the falsity of the world is invalid whereas the same on its reality is valid. He raises a question: Whether the inference on the falsity of the world establishes the falsity of the subject and the like of the promise and the like or not? If not, the whole world cannot be considered to be false. If it establishes, then, there is conflict between the promise and the inference because the former tries to establish the reality of the world while the latter its falsity. Moreover, if the subject and the like are false there will be the fallacy of non-establishment of the base and the like in the inference.

Madhusūdana replies: There is no such conflict as interpreted by the opponent. The inference does not establish the reality of the subject and the like in the form of non-contradiction throughout the three points of time. It may be argued that the absolute reality of the subject and the like has to be presumed; but it is not so. The reality denoted by the statement 'the jar exists' is not absolute but practical. It is distinct from the apparent reality of the blue sky. The reality of the subject and the like of the inference is such. In fact the nature of the reality conceded to the world is that it is not contradicted by anything other than the knowledge of *Brahman*. There is no harm in assuming that kind of reality to the subject and the like of the inference.

Vyāsatīrtha then proceeds to criticise the practical reality itself. He holds that if the subject, promise and probans are false there can be no inference at all, for, all of them being non-existent the inference will not proceed. Madhusūdana says that the practical reality will explain everything other than *Brahman*. Practical reality of the world including every component of the inference on the falsity of the world is never rejected by *advaitins*. Therefore, even if the subject and the like of the inference are false there is no harm for the inference.

30. *Sublation in the absence of probanshood for the non-existent*

It appears to be much simpler to admit the reality of the inferential components than to regard them as something different from an absolute non-entity. When there are parsimonious qualities why should we go in for prolix ones?

Madhusūdana answers: The quality, existence, may seem to be parsimonious verbally but it is prolix in meaning. Its meaning is the absence of sublation throughout the three points of time which is more prolix than difference from an absolute non-entity. In fact absolute reality is not applied for in the probans. The case of reflection can be cited as an example. The reflection has no reality other than that in the form of its original figure. However, it is capable of establishing the presence of the figure which is real. Similarly things seen in dream, though not real, are indicators of the auspicious and unauspicious. In the same way the redness felt on the crystal is also not real though it is probans for the presence of the china-rose.

Objection: The redness in the crystal is not false. What happens actually is that redness reflects independent of its substrate.

Reply: The redness being an attribute cannot reflect on its own independent of the substrate. The colour of face cannot reflect itself independent of face. Padmapāda has explained the same.[62] He considers redness on the crystal to be false.[63] Infact the redness on the crystal is not a reflection but an imagination.

In this connection it is interesting to note what Śaṅkara has said in his commentary on *Brahmasūtras*.[64] The so-called letters 'a' etc. are not real. We call literal scribblings as letters. Though not real letters they represent real letters. From the false perception of letters in the scribblings the true letters are grasped.

Objection: Meaning is grasped from the letters and not from the scribblings. When we see the scribblings the letters are reminded of and from the letters in our memory meaning is known.

Reply: The memory and perception are of the same object. Letters in the form of scribblings convey the meaning. It is common knowledge that the scribblings and letters are not distinguished. The qualities of sounds such as lengthening and shortening are superimposed on the letters in the form of scribblings, whereby difference in meanings are grasped. Vācaspatimiśra has explained the same.[65] No one misunderstands *nāga* and *naga*, for, the lengthening differentiates the meaning.

Objection: If the lengthening and shortening are superimposed they cannot indicate the correct meaning. No one is able to infer fire from the superimposed smoke.

Reply: The probans should have the essential quality of probanshood so as to be the probans. Whether it is superimposed or otherwise is immaterial. Vācaspatimiśra has said the same thing.[66]

In short, a false probans also can give birth to a true knowledge. Therefore, probanshood for the non-existent cannot be denied in any way.

31. *Denial of cogniser-cognisable relation*

Vyāsatīrtha alleges the fallacy of non-efficiency in the inference on the falsity of the world. He argues that there can be cognisability in the world even if it is real. Therefore, the probans cognisability is non-efficient.

Madhusūdana discards the view by putting forward a favourable counter-argument: If the world is not false it cannot be cognisable too, for, the real cannot be cognisable. A cognition cannot reveal its object without any contact with it. Otherwise it would have to be accepted that one can cognise the whole world at one stretch. And there can be no contact between the subject and object too because it cannot be conjunction or inherence and there can be no superimposed contact other than the two.

It may be argued that being the subject and object itself is the relation. This cannot be admitted because relation should exist in both; but in this case subjecthood is in the subject and objecthood in the object. The exact relation cannot be defined. Madhusūdana then proposes nine possible alternatives for explaining the notion of relation between the subject and object and discards them all.

Objection: Learned people say that 'this is the object of that cognition' and therefore there should be some relation between the two.

Reply: It is true that such assertions show object as a notion in general, but not the object of any particular cognition.

Discussion on the relation between subject and object prolongs. Madhusūdana concludes that there can be no cogniser-cognisable relation in case the world is real. It is therefore necessary to admit the fact that the relation as well as the world is false.

32. *Reasonings in support of the falsity of the world*

The opponent puts forward fresh arguments regarding the reality of the world. Let the entire perceptible world be superimposed on *Brahman* and the cognition also accordingly. Yet, for the purpose of explaining the well-known phenomenon that only one particular thing appears in consciousness at a particular point of time, there should be some sort of relation between the cognition and the thing cognised through a certain mental state which takes the form of the thing. *Advaitins* admit that the mind and the thing enter into contact through the sense-organ and form a continuum by way of the mental state.

Madhusūdana answers: As a matter of fact every source of light illuminates directly the object that comes into contact with it. Consciousness cannot illuminate an object indirectly through the intervention of a relation. Hence it can be concluded that the consciousness which forms the substratum of an object illuminates that object without being intercepted by any relation. It is the removal of such interception that is done by the organic mental state postulated by *advaitins*. It is for the mental state to proceed that an imposed relation is also accepted.

Objection: An imposed relation is possible only when all real relations have been rendered impossible. Here how can we say that all real relations are impossible?

Reply: Real relation is rendered impossible by the simple fact that we do not perceive that with which it is invariably concomitant.

Objection: In accordance with the absence of relation in the case of cognition there would be no relation between destruction and the past thing, absolute negation and its counter-entity, potency and its objective, ignorance and its object, desire and the object desired, usage and the object with which it deals, verbal expression and the thing expressed and cognition in the form of emanation and the thing cognised.

Reply: It is true that in view of the parity of reasoning there can be no real relation between the members of the pairs cited. However, we do not absolutely deny the character of counter-entity, relativity and the like because they are duly recognised in our experience. What we say is that they are all false. They do not pertain to the category of real or imposed.

Argument: In this way the relation of the cogniser and cognisable also should stand on the same footing as that of counter-entity and negation.

Counter: Not so; because the said relation has to be assumed, on the ground of the impossibility of any such relation as that of mutual imposition.

Argument: *Brahman* as the object of nescience cannot be imposed upon the subject ignorance so that the general proposition that the object is always imposed upon the subject cannot be accepted as true.

Counter: As we do not hold any such proposition at all, all that we mean is that imposition is the relation that subsists between cognition and nescience with their respective objects. This is in accordance with our experience that the cognised object is imposed on cognition and that nescience is imposed on uncognised object. Therefore, nescience and cognised object cannot serve as an effective counter-instance in the denial of imposed relation.

Madhusūdana, then, examines in detail, different arguments put forward by the opponent and discards them all. He presents a number of further reasonings in support of the falsity of the world. The world is a product of ignorance of consciousness only and it is set aside also by the knowledge of the same consciousness. The things of the world are actually found to be cognised as related to the substantive consciousness which is duly apprehended. From all this it is firmly established that if things are real the relation of cognition and the cognised is not possible at all.

33. *Pratikarmavyavasthā*

Dvaitins argue that if the world is superimposed the *pratikarmavyavasthā* accepted by *advaitins* will not fit in, because it is dependent on the relation between subject and object and *advaitins* consider the relation also imposed as in the case of apparent objects. Madhusūdana discards the argument and establishes that there is no harm for the *pratikarmavyavasthā* accepted by *advaitins*.

Since the jar and the like are superimposed on consciousness even before the origin of the mental state there is difference of it from the case of apparent objects. It is thus: The mind, like the eyes, is constituted of light. It goes out through the sense-organ to the object in contact and takes the same shape after extending on it. It is just like the water of a tank going out through a hole, entering fields through channels and taking shape of the fields. This is what is called mental state. Eventhough the basic consciousness is single, it assumes the forms of content, cogniser and cognition. Therefore, there is no harm for the *vyavasthā*.

Objection: The *pratikarmavyavasthā* does not fit in because if the jar and the like are there even before the origin of knowledge through the sense-organ in contact with them, there cannot be any imposition pervasive with apparent body alone.

Reply: Imposition is not pervasive with apparent body alone because the rule will collapse in the case of the imposed world.

Objection: It is not proper to assume that the mind goes out of the body. In order to distinguish between perception and imperception it is better to assume that consciousness proceeds to the object in the case of perception.

Reply: It is not the mind's forming of the shape of the object alone that governs the procession of consciousness because in that case it will apply to imperception also. It is the mingling of the mind with the object that governs the procession of consciousness and for that mind has to go out.

Objection: Since you accept the view that the objects are imposed on the subject there arises the question: Who is the cogniser, *jiva* or *Brahman*? If it is *jīva*, imposition cannot take place. It cannot be *Brahman* too, for then also imposition cannot take place.

Reply: There is no harm in assuming *Brahman* as the cogniser. The basic igorance does not get itself rid of as a result of a mental procession in the form of a jar. However, the mental procession dissolves the ignorance extending on the jar.

Objection: It is not correct to admit ignorance or its powers on something which also is the resultant of ignorance.

Reply: We do not do so. It is on consciousness that we admit everything imposed. Sarvajñātman has made it very clear. Undifferentiated consciousness is the locus as well as the object of ignorance. Everything that comes into being as a result of ignorance is neither the locus nor the object of ignorance which exists prior to them.[67] Sarvajñātman has concluded thus: What is the use of elaborating the point? The essence of the tenets of *Advaita* may be stated as follows: The pure consciousness transcends mind and speech and comes within the range of mind and speech.[68]

The gist of the *pratikarmavyavasthā* is as follows: It is the content-consciousness that illuminates the object. Consciousness defined by the mind is its cogniser. Consciousness defined by the mental state is the cognitive one. However, it is he, whose mind goes out through the sense of sight and the like to the object forming a mental state and whose cogniser-consciousness becomes one with the content-consciousness, that knows that object and no one else and nothing else. It is he who has the direct perceptual knowledge that this is a jar. It is only in the case of perception that the mental state has direct relation. In the case of inference etc., the relation is indirect. Therefore, the *pratikarmavyavasthā* fits in well even though the objects are false.

34. *Denial of reasoning against the falsity of the world*

Vyāsatīrtha argues that the inference on the falsity of the world is invalidated by counter-reasonings. He points out eight such reasonings all of which Madhusūdana discards well.

1. If the world is imposed it should have a substratum; it has no such substratum. A substratum is that which is generally known and particularly unknown. *Advaitins* view *Brahman* as the substratum of the world. It cannot be so because *Brahman* has no general and particular forms.

This reasoning does not stand the test. Substratum is that which is generally known and particularly unknown; but this does not mean that there should be any general or particular quality in it. Therefore, there is nothing against *Brahman* being the substratum of the world.

2. If the world is imposed it is subsidiary whereby a principal is anticipated. You do not concede any principality to the world. Therefore, the world is not imposed.

This reasoning also is not correct. The principal world belonging to the same category as that of the false world is there according to our view also. Superimposition takes place only on the similar.

3. Similarity means that in form or quality. If the world is superimposed on *Brahman* both should have common form or quality. Therefore, there can be this reasoning: If the world is superimposed there should be the similarity of reality in both the world and *Brahman*.

In the case of the superimposition of *jīva*, Īśa, pure consciousness, difference between *jīva* and *Īśa*, ignorance and combination of ignorance and consciousness no particular ground is necessary. Therefore, similarity also is not necessary. And for the same reason there is no harm in the world being false and *Brahman* real.

4. If superimposition takes place without any defect it is applicable to the invalidity of the superimposition also. Therefore, this reasoning can be there: If the world is imposed it can be without any defect too.

In the case of the superimposition of the beginningless six categories mentioned above there is no need of defect also. But that is not the case with the invalidity of superimposition. Therefore, the reasoning presented is not correct.

5. If bondage is in the form of the counter-correlate of absolute negation which is called illusion, who would take the pain to get rid of it? Therefore, there proceeds the following reasoning: If the world is imposed no one would try to get rid of it.

Brahman is real by nature. Therefore, it can never be contradicted. Similarly, if the world is not false, it has to be said that it also is real and for the same reason it cannot be contradicted. Therefore, the world being false is capable of being contradicted.

6. If the world is superimposed on *Brahman* then it will not be a subject to negation as a result of the realisation of *Brahman* obtained through the meditation of it.

7. If the world is superimposed on *Brahman* then it will not be a subject to negation as a result of the knowledge of *Brahman* depending on *adṛṣṭa* produced by means of hearing etc.

Both these reasonings are wrong. Silver superimposed on sea-shell is negated by the realisation of the sea-shell. From this it is to be imagined that the realisation of *Brahman* will surely negate the false world. What is said about the dependence of realisation on *adṛṣṭa* is not correct. Realisation depends on *adṛṣṭa* but not release. That is what Bādarāyaṇa also has stated.[69]

8. If the world is superimposed the origin etc., of it dealt with in the *janmādisūtra*[70] will not suit. The *śruti* 'that from which these beings are born'[71] clearly deals with the orderly origin of the world. In the *sūtra ikṣaternāśabdam*[72] and in the *śruti* 'it thought' etc.,[73] it is said that *Īśvara* created this world after thinking clearly about it. Similarly, there are a number of *śrutis* and *sūtras* that can be pointed out in favour of the origin of the world. The reverse order of dissolution also is dealt with in the *śutra viparyayeṇa kramota upapādyate ca.*'[74] All these will go against, in case the world is false.

It is not to be presumed that only the apparent can be superimposed. In fact the practically real also can be superimposed. Everything including the origin etc., of the practically real world can be considered to be superimposed. *Śrutis* deal with the origin of things of dream. Similarly, the superimposed serpant creates fear etc. Thus the origin of the world which is superimposed also can be substantiated. In fact it is *Brahman* itself that evolves in the form and name of worldly objects.[74] It is the crux of the *vivartavāda* held by *advaitins*.[76] Śaṅkara explains the same thing.[77] It is verily said that the greatness of God makes the *Brahma*-wheel turn.[78]

There is no rule that superimposition goes against origin etc. In fact nothing originates without superimposition. That is the meaning of the *anirvacanīyavāda* held by *advaitins*. Thus since all the world is superimposed on *Brahman* which is unique there can be no reasoning against it.

35. *Fitness of śrutis on the falsity of the world*

Madhusūdana says that the inference on the falsity of the world has the support of such *śrutis* as 'one only without a second'.[79]

Objection: The *śruti* does not make known its own form, authority and qualification. For that there is dependence on perception. The form, authority and qualification of *śruti* cannot be considered false also. Therefore, everything other than *Brahman* does not necessarily come to be false. Moreover, as per the maxim 'that which is taught in a rule, the application of which is occasioned by the combination of two things, does not become the cause of the destruction of that combination'[80] the jar and the like known by perception do not come to be false. Perhaps it can be said that the *śruti* declares its own form, authority and qualification also to be false. In that case the *śruti* loses its authority because what is known by verbal testimony is of the same status of reality as that of verbal testimony, its own authority and the like.

Reply: The status of what is known by verbal testimony and that of verbal testimony, its authority and the like are not concomitant because of inconstancy. Moreover, quality of their status is non-efficient. Imperceptibility, non-eternality and the like can be pointed out as extraneous adjuncts too. Therefore, eventhough *śruti* makes known the falsity of its qualification etc., there is no harm in its meaning being true. The maxim quoted from the *Mahābhāṣya*[81] does not fit in here because the subject dealt with in it is entirely different from what is being dealt with here. It can be explained: Pāṇini says that the numerals having *ṣa* or *ṇa* as their finale are called *ṣaṭ*.[82] He further stipulates that the nominative and accusative plural endings are elided after the numerals called *ṣaṭ*. *Pañca* etc., are examples. However, this rule does not apply in the case of the numerals *śatām* and *sahasrāṇi*. The reason is the maxim cited. In both cases there is the affix *num*[83] provided by the presence of the case-suffix *śi*[84] which has got the name *sarvanāmasthāna*.[85] It is the same *num* that ought to cause the elision of *śi* in the case of *śatāni* and *sahasrāṇi*. Therefore, the maxim applies and bars the elision. Here one thing has to be specially noted. It is the *sarvanāmasthāna* which is present that provides the application of the maxim. If it were lost, on the basis of the rule that when elision of an affix has taken place the affix still exerts its influence, and the operations dependent upon it, take place as if it were present,[86] *num* would have come. In that case the maxim would not apply. Similarly, in the case of *śruti*, if it had depended on perception and the like based on their reality, the maxim would have had application. But perception and the like have application here only as being perception and the like and not being real. Therefore, the maxim also has no applicatien. Vācaspatimiśra has stated the same thing by the words: 'since there is no opposition to the originator.'[87] Infact, the qualification etc., of the *śruti* only are relevant and not their reality too. There is no need of any imposition in the case of the *śrutis*, '*Brahman* is truth, consciousness and without end',[88] 'It is true, it is the self'[89] and the like as in the case of *śrutis* dealing with the origin etc., of the world.

Vyāsatīrtha then argues further to establish contradiction with perception etc., in the *śruti* dealing with the falsity of the world. However, Madhusūdana discards the argument. He establishes that the *śruti* 'one only without a second'[90] is evidence for the falsity of the world.

36. *Denial of sublation of the śruti dealing with non-duality*

Dvaitins say: Infact the general sense cannot be taken to be that of the Vedic texts because the *śruti* 'who is that intelligent person who knows the purport of the *Vedas*'[91] and the *smṛti* '*Veda* fears him who has very little knowledge of it'[92] clearly mention the depth of the meaning of the *Vedas*. Otherwise, *Mīmāṁsā* will become futile. The meanings of the *Vedas* are to be obtained by rapprochement and it is for the same that *Mīmāṁsā* is depended on. For example, the *citrādhikaraṇa* of *Pūrvamīmāṁsā*[93] deals with meaning of the instruction *ājyaiḥ stuvate* and the *ākāśādhikraṇa* of *Uttaramīmāṁsā*[94] deals with the meaning of the *śruti* 'all these beings originate from ether'.[95] In short, based on the evidences like perception etc., and also the internal contradiction of the *śrutis*, non-duality cannot be taken to be the meaning of the *śrutis*.

Madhusūdana retorts: Perception which grasps duality is only false like that which perceives moon to be located at a spot. Therefore, it cannot contradict *śrutis* dealing with non-duality. In fact, as pointed out earlier,[96] it is the faultless *śruti* that contradicts perception which is false. Moreover, the scope of perception is very limited whereas that of *śruti* is very wide. Therefore, *śruti* deals with non-duality without any difficulty.

Objection: Are the two, between which the *śruti* dealing with non-duality establishes non-difference, present at the time of discarding difference or not? It cannot be the latter, for non-difference of two things which are not present cannot be established. In the former case there arise further doubts. Is the presence of them known from *śrutis* or is it known by perception? It cannot be the first; since the *śruti* is interested in establishing non-duality not cognised by any other means, it cannot present anything else. In the second case difference, just like the things, is known by perception and for the same reason there will be no relevance for *śruti*.

Reply: There is no rule that in the case of things which are perceived directly, difference also should be perceived in the same way. It cannot be said that knowledge of difference is knowledge of the things themselves. Even those who consider difference as not different from the thing, do not consider knowledge of the thing and that of difference as the same. In fact, knowledge of the thing and that of difierence are entirely different. Such knowledge as that of the difference between jar and cloth is not competent to contradict *śruti* which reveals non-difference. On the other hand, it is better to hold that all knowledge of difference of the world comes to an end by the knowledge of *Brahman* obtained through the *śrutis* dealing with non-difference. There is no contradiction for the *śrutis* dealing with the sole single non-different *Brahman*, among themselves or with perception.

37. *Discussion on the meaning of the śruti 'one only', etc.*

Objection: The *śruti* 'an ocean is that one seer without any duality'[97] is there. In it the word ocean means only purity. This purity which is the state of lack of all impurities fits in *Brahman* also. The *śruti* 'O my dear son, in the beginning all this world was only one existence'[98] indicates time by the word 'beginning'. Then, in the *śrutis* 'that imagined'[99] and 'that emerged in name and form'[100] imagination and emergence into name and form are dealt with respectively. All these *śrutis* deal with the origin etc., of the false world. However, after having said the non-difference of the world and *Brahman* in the *śruti* 'O my dear son, in the beginning all this world was only one existence'; it is not proper to say in the very same *śruti* that *Brahman* is one without a second because it will result in the fallacy of *vyākhāta*. There is no meaning for the words 'that was existence' as that was non-existence.

Reply: The negation in the *śruti* means only negation of everything different from existence. This has been dealt with in details in the *ārambhaṇādhikaraṇa*.[101] It may be argued that if everything different from existence is said to be non-existent, the same will have reality in the form of existence. Let it be so; what is intended is the falsity of everything other than *Brahman*. All the six characteristic signs that help to decide the purport[102] support the *śruti* on non-duality and for the same reason duality should be explained to be false. Therefore, *śrutis* dealing with the origin etc., of the world deal with the same of the false world. Madhusūdana explains these things in his *Vedāntakalpalatikā*[103].

The *śrutis* 'one only without a second'[104] discards all kinds of difference in *Brahman*. It has no difference from other categories, its own categories and its own different parts, because it is the one without difference whatsoever. The three expressions 'one' 'only' and 'without a second' discard the three kinds of difference. It results in the falsity of the world.

Vyāsatīrtha quotes a number of *śrutis* and tries to establish that they do not deal with non-duality.[105] Infact, all the *śrutis*, 'there is no difference whatsoever',[165] 'the difference is only a name arising from speech'[107] etc., deal with non-duality and thereby the falsity of the world. For fear of inordinate length of discussion Madhusūdana does not try to explain all of them.

38. *Otherwise unfitness of the state of being discarded by cognition:*

The state of being discarded by cognition revealed by such *śrutis* as 'he who knows the self overcomes grief',[108] 'a wise man freed from name and form',[109] 'the fetter of heart is broken, all doubts are solved, all his deeds perish when he who is high and low has been beheld'[110] etc., and also by *smṛtis*, will not be correct if the world is not false. Therefore, that otherwise unfitness of the *śrutis* also is evidence for the falsity of the world. If the world is true it would not be discarded like *Brahman*.[111]

Everything that has come into being as a result of ignorance will be negated by knowledge of the same thing. Shell-silver has come into being as a result of the ignorance of the sea-shell. That shell-silver will be negated by the knowledge of that particular sea-shell. Similarly, the whole world has come into being as a result of ignorance of *Brahman* and the same will be negated by the knowledge of *Brahman*.

Objection: How can we deem that the reality of the substratum common to the knowledge of the sea-shell etc., is the correlate of the world which is to be negated by the knowledge of *Brahman*, because there is no evidence for the same. The shell-silver and the like can be negated otherwise also. *Śruti* is evidence, in general, only for the negation of the world in general and not in particular.

Reply: In the case of the knowledge of *Brahman* as well as in the case of the knowledge of sea-shell etc., knowledge of the substratum is that which negates those which are superimposed. There is no other way. *Śrutis* and *smṛtis* proclaim that ignorance is the cause of the world. And the same is bondage. The *śruti* says: 'know then, *prakṛti* as *māyā* and the great Lord as *māyin*'.[112] The *smṛti* also says: 'knowledge is enveloped by ignorance and thereby mortals are deluded'.[113] And ignorance can be eradicated only by knowledge.

There is also evidence of *śrutis* and *smṛtis* to the effect that the world is there before the origin of knowledge only and it comes to an end after the origin of knowledge. 'For when there is as it were duality, then one sees the other; . . . but when the self only is all this, how should he see another'?[114] 'What is night to all beings, therein the *sthitaprajña* is awake; where all beings are awake, that is the night of the sage who sees.'[115] Therefore, the falsity of the world can be well established by the evidence that it is negated by the knowledge of its substratum.

39. *Fitness of dṛṣṭisṛṣṭi*

Just like shell-silver, dream etc., the world also has come into being as a result of *dṛṣṭisṛṣṭi*. This evidences the falsity of the world. Otherwise, *dṛṣṭisṛṣṭi* will not fit in.

Dvaitins ask: What is meant by this *dṛṣṭisṛṣṭi*? Is it that *dṛṣṭi* and *sṛṣṭi* are the same? Or is it that there is no *sṛṣṭi* different from *dṛṣṭi*? Or is it that there is nothing other than *dṛṣṭi* to be created? Or is it the state of being created from the causal aggregate of *dṛṣṭi*? Or is it creation at the same time of *dṛṣṭi*? Or is it creation having the same status of reality as that of *dṛṣṭi*? Or is it difference from existence and non-existence? Or is it being different from non-existence and the three kinds of reality? Or is it the unknown absence of reality? Or is it existence that which is known alone? If it is the first, is it in the form of mental state or consciousness? In the former case *Brahman* which is subject to the final mental state also will have to be considered as that created by *dṛṣṭi*. In the latter case it will have to be said that creation is always there. If it is the second, the experience that 'I have seen what is created by Caitra' will not suit. It cannot be the third because it is against the experience that 'jar is known but not its knowledge'. For the same reason it cannot be the fourth too. It cannot be the fifth because in the case of jar etc., born at the same time of the origin of verbal knowledge, it will present the fallacy of establishing what is already established. Moreover, at other places it will cause *arthāntara* also. It cannot be the sixth because it fits in the presence of both whereby there arises the fallacy of establishing what is already established. It cannot be the seventh because that is what is called false and it is not correct to explain it for its own sake. It cannot be the eighth because apparent reality also is included in the three kinds of reality and therefore the world cannot be distinct from the three, since apparent reality also is there in the world. It cannot be the ninth because it suits *tuccha* also. It cannot be the tenth because it will present the fallacy of establishing what is already established in pleasure and the like and in other cases it will present *arthāntara* also.

Madhusūdana replies: What is meant by *dṛṣṭisṛṣṭi* can be taken to be existence that which is known alone or the unknown absence of reality or existence which is known alone born from *dṛṣṭi* deemed to be the locus or existence which is known alone and unknown to any other *draṣṭā* at the same time. Then there will not be any fallacy of establishing the established in pleasure etc., or *arthāntara*.

Objection: If this *dṛṣṭisṛṣṭi* is accepted it will contradict *advaitin's* concept that *jīva*, Īśa, pure consciousness, difference between *jiva* and Īśa, ignorance and combination of ignorance and consciousness are beginningless. Moreover, it will contradict portions of the *Brahma-*

ṣūtrabhāṣya, *Vārtika* and *Vivaraṇa* dealing with the existence of the world.

Reply: *Dṛṣṭisṛṣṭi* is accepted in the case of the world other than the six begnningless categories mentioned. Eventhough the world is resultant of *dṛṣṭisṛṣṭi* its existence in the form of its cause cannot be objected to. Therefore, there is no contradiction with what the *bhāṣya* etc., say too. Infact, texts of the earlier *advaitins* frequently deal with *dṛṣṭisṛṣṭi*.[116]

Madhusūdana deals with *dṛṣṭisṛṣṭivāda* in his other works also. *Siddhāntabindu* discards other schools of thought and establishes the authenticity of *dṛṣṭisṛṣṭivāda*.[117] *Vedāntakalpalatikā* also does the same thing.[118] *Yogavāsiṣṭa* and other authoritative texts also uphold *dṛṣṭisṛṣṭivāda*. Therefore, there is nothing that goes against the fitness of *dṛṣṭisṛṣṭi*.

40. *Fitness of imposition by the ignorance of only ane jīva*

The *draṣṭā* of the creation is only one, for, there is no evidence for his plurality.

Objection: How can it bo true that there is only one *jīva*? It will go against our experiences like 'I am pleasant', 'I am sorrowful', 'I am worldly', 'I am his lord' etc.

Reply: *Brahman* only is true. He runs this world by way of ignoance. That is what is called *jīva*. It is for him that in every body there is the conscience 'I'. In the body where there is the feeling 'this is pleasant' and 'this is sorrowful' there is no presence of *jīva*. Where there is the feeling of 'I', there, there is presence of *jīva* also. During the state of wakefulness it is for a single *jīva* that there is the feeling of 'I' in various bodies. There is no evidence for his plurality.

Objection: If *jīva* is only one when he dissolves in *suṣupti* all the world also should dissolve. However, it never happens so. While one is in *suṣupti* others may be in the state of wakefulness.

Reply: It is for the *jīva* who is proud of the individual ignorance that there is difference of sleep and wakefulness. The *jīva* who is proud of the aggregate of ignorance is always awake. Of these, the latter is the principal *jīva* whereas the former is only imposed. The principal *jīva* is not different from *Brahman* too.

Objection: If *Brahman* is *jīva*, bondage and liberation have to be considered as his and then *śrutis* dealing with the perpetual liberation of *Brahman* will have to be invalidated.

Reply: Liberation in the form of removal of the ignorance is

Brahman itself. Bondage is in the form of ignorance. Therefore, there can be no presence of it in *Brahman*. The desert will not be wet with the water of mirage.[119] Therefore, there is no harm for the *śrutis*.

Objection: In the *śruti* 'those who dwell in ignorance',[120] ignorance has been dealt with as belonging to many *jīvas*. The *śruti*, 'those whose conduct has been good, will quickly attain some good birth and those whose has been evil, evil birth,'[121] clearly mentions different *jīvas* who take birth. Similarly, a number of *śrutis* can be quoted.

Reply: The *śruti*, 'when the *jīva* sleeping as a result of beginningless ignorance wakes up,'[122] clearly uses the singular number which is evidence for the oneness of *jīva*. All other *śrutis* contradicting it have to be considered as *anuvādas* dealing with what is there as a result of ignorance.

Objection: If the *śrutis* having singular number can overwhelm those having plural number why cannot it be in the reverse form also? Moreover, the *śruti* quoted from *Māṇḍūkya*, if taken in the singular sense, will contradict its own beginning and end.

Reply: *Śrutis* are valid in the sense that they reveal new meanings and not in the sense that they retell anything. The plurality of *jīva* is there only in practical life of all people. The *śruti* cannot retell the same thing. And for the same reason there is no contradiction with its beginning or end too.

Objection: If the attainment of liberation dealt with in the *śrutis* can be taken to be valid, plurality of *jīvas* dealt with in them also can be taken so. 'Thus whatever *deva* was awakened he indeed became that, and the same with *ṛṣis* and men'.[123] 'There is one unborn being who loves her and lies by her, there is another who leaves her, while she is eating what has to be eaten'.[124] Similarly, *Bhagavadgītā* says: 'they who having resorted to this knowledge, have attained unity with me'.[125]

Reply: All these evidences are only *anuvādas* dealing with what we obtain as a result of ignorance in the practical world. Only the *śruti* dealing with the unity of *jīva* is authentic in the sense that it reveals unknown truth. Therefore, *jīva* who has ignorance as his adjunct is single.

41. *Definition of ignorance*

Dvaitins ask: What is this ignorance? Citsukha defines it as that which is beginningless, existent and at the same time negated by knowledge.[126] This definition has partial inapplication in the ignorance that conceals sea-shell because it has beginning. The definition is partially inapplicable in the ignorance which is the material cause of non-existence because it has not the part of the definition, existence.

Madhusūdana replies: Ignorance which is the cause of shell-silver is beginningless since it depends on the beginningless consciousness. Therefore, there is no fault of the partial inapplication of its definition in it. What is meant by the term 'existent' in the definition is only difference from non-existence. Since there is difference from non-existence in the ignorance that is the cause of non-existence, there also there is no partial inapplication of the definition of ignorance. Therefore, the said definition of ignorance is faultless.

Ignorance can also be defined as that which is the material cause of false. Ignorance is the material cause of the false world. *Brahman* is its substratum.

Objection: How can ignorance which is non-existent, be the material cause of the world which is existent?

Reply: Ignorance and the false world belong to the same category. Both are different from existent. Therefore, there is no harm in the former being the material cause of the latter.

Objection: If ignorance is the material cause of the world we should have experience also accordingly. Mud is the material cause of jar and accordingly we have such experience as jar is mud. Similarly, if ignorance is the material cause of the world we should have such experience concerning the world, as jar is ignorance and cloth is ignorance.

Reply: There is no rule that the material cause and effect should be experienced identically. Jar is the material cause of colour and the like in the jar. However, we do not experience that jar is colour. Any way, some sort of experience of the material cause is there in the effect. The experience of ignorance in the form of insentience is there in the jar etc. And insentience and ignorance are the same that conceals the true nature of the self.[127]

Ignorance can be defined as the state of being negated directly by knowledge being knowledge. This definition of ignorance was dealt with earlier in connection with the discussion on the third definition of falsity.[128] Therefore, ignorance can be well defined in any of the three forms mentioned herein. And for the same reason the arguments of the opponents have no locus standi.

42. *Fitness of the perception of ignorance*

Perception is evidence for ignorance. The general perception is as follows: 'I am ignorant, I don't know me and others'. Particular perception is in the form 'I don't know what you have said'. The reference of perception concerning *suṣupti* that 'so far I had been in pleasant sleep; I did not know anything' also is evidence for ignorance.

Objection: How can the perception 'I am ignorant' be taken as evidence for ignorance which is existent? *Advaitins* consider pure consciousness as the abode of ignorance. Here it is *jīva* that is mentioned as the same.

Reply: In such cases as 'I am ignorant' what happens is that in the consciousness which is the abode of ignorance the mind is imposed indiscriminately.[129] Therefore, 'I am ignorant' means 'I am the abode of the negation of knowledge'.

Objection: In such objects as pleasure, sorrow etc., and also apparent objects known by *sākṣin* alone, there is no presence of the existent ignorance. Therefore, how can there be the experience 'I am ignorant?'

Reply: The pleasure, sorrow etc., though known by *sākṣin* alone, dwell in oneself and in the apparent objects such as shell-silver there is no experience as 'I am ignorant'. Therefore, there is no harm for the experience 'I am ignorant'.

Objection: Why should we consider the experience 'I am ignorant' as evidence for existent ignorance? Let it be evidence for the absence of knowledge. The reason is that there is no difference caused by object between the experience of 'there is no knowledge in me' and that of 'I am ignorant'.

Reply: Of course, there is no difference of object in the experience of 'there is no knowledge in me' and that of 'I am ignorant'. However both experiences are considered as having the same object not because they are concerning the absence of knowledge but because they are concerning existent ignorance. If the experience 'I am ignorant' is concerning absence of knowledge it will have *vyākhāta* caused by the knowledge of its counter-correlate. Therefore, it is concerning existent ignorance itself.

Objection: It is not correct to say that there will be *vyākhāta* if the experience 'I am ignorant' is taken in the sense of the absence of knowledge because even though there is a general knowledge of the counter-correlate, in particular there is the absence of it. Otherwise, there will be no knowledge of antecedent negation, because there it is not possible to know its particular counter-correlate without the generality.

Reply: The said absence of particular knowledge is not possible because in the case of the absence of particular knowledge the counter-correlate is that which is qualified per proprium by the state of the particular knowledge and if it is known the particular also will be known whereby there will arise *vyākhāta* in the case of the absence of particular knowledge. Knowledge of antecedent negation has no harm at all. Knowledge of antecedent negation in the form of absence of knowledge having the counter-correlate as its qualification per proprium is not at all there.

Objection: If general property is not taken to be the qualification per proprium of the counter-correlate of particular absence, there will be no knowledge of antecedent negation.

Reply: There will be no knowledge of antecedent negation. There is no harm even if antecedent negation is not accepted.

In the same way particular perception and reference of perception about *suṣupti* also can be justified as evidences for the fitness of perception of ignorance. Madhusūdana's view-points concerning the experience of *suṣupti* are available in his *Siddhāntabindu* also.[130]

43. *Fitness of inference on ignorance*

Inference also is evidence for ignorance. *Vivaraṇakāra* has coined the inference.[131] The knowledge defined by mental state under dispute is along with another substance which belongs to its own place, which is different from its own antecedent negation, which veils it and which will be negated by it, because it illuminates a meaning hitherto unilluminated, like a light that appears first amidst darkness.[132] In this inference the term 'defined by mental state' is enjoined so as to avoid sublation of the valid knowledge of pleasure etc., which is in the form of consciousness defined by *sākṣin* and which does not negate ignorance. The term 'under dispute' is to exclude from the subject knowledge of the substratum defined by mental state which is in the form of 'this' and which is not capable of negating ignorance.

Objection: If the knowledge defined by mental state in the form of 'this' is not capable of negating ignorance it will not be acknowledging anything unknown and for the same reason it will not be proper to consider it as valid knowledge.

Reply: If the knowledge defined by mental state in the form of 'this' is capable of negating ignorance then the false knowledge and doubt which we experience will not suit. There is no false knowledge or doubt in the form of 'this'. Therefore, there is no evidence for assuming ignorance concerning the same too. What happens there, in fact, is that knowledge defined by mental state in the form of 'this' is considered valid since it is real like the knowledge of pleasure and the like. If the said ignorance which does not create false knowledge or doubt is accepted on the strength of experience, let it also be included in the subject; then the term 'under dispute' enjoined in the inference is not necessary. In this case the definition of ignorance should be the state of being capable to be the material cause of false knowledge.

One qualification of the probandum in the said inferenee is 'being different from its own antecedent negation'. This has been introduced so as to exclude the antecedent negation which is negated by valid knowledge. Another qualification is 'which veils it'. It has been introduced to avoid *arthāntara* in the *adṛṣṭa* which is capable of producing mental state. The third qualification is 'which will be negated by it'. It has been introduced so as to avoid over-applicability of the inferred ignorance in the *adṛṣṭa* capable of obstructing valid mental state.

Objection: Does the *adṛṣṭa* which obstructs the final valid cognition get extinguished by that final valid cognition itself or not? If it is the first then it will not be false. If it is the second *arthāntara* will be there.

Reply: If there is the presence of *adṛṣṭa* which obstructs the final valid cognition there is no final valid cognition at all. And for the same reason it need not be extinguished by the final valid cognition.

The fourth qualification is 'which belongs to its own place'. It excludes darkness from being the subject. And for the same reason there is no *arthāntara* also.

The probans of the inference is illumination of meaning hitherto unilluminated. It has no fault like unfamiliarity etc., as alleged by the opponents.

The example enjoined in the inference also has no fault at all. The probandum and probans of the inference fit in well in the example. Therefore, inference is valid evidence for ignorance.

Citsukha has coined two inferences for establishing ignorance.[133] Any number of inferences can be still coined too. Therefore, ignorance which is existent can be established beyond doubt by inference also.

44. *Fitness of śrutis dealing with ignorance*

Śrutis also are evidence for ignorance. *Chāndogya* says: 'As people who do not know the country, walk again and again over a gold treasure that has been hidden somewhere in the earth and do not discover it, thus do all these creatures day after day go into the world of *Brahman*, and yet do not discover it because they are carried away by untruth.'[134] This *śruti*, which depicts ignorance as *anṛta* that obstructs the knowledge of *Brahman*, is evidence for the existence of ignorance.

Objection: In such *śrutis* as 'there are two, drinking their reward *ṛta* in the world of their own deeds,'[135] the word *ṛta* is used in the sense of good deed and therefore, *anṛta* means only evil deeds and not ignorance.

Reply: After the *śruti* dealing with *anṛta*[136] there is another *śruti*: 'the self is free from sin, free from old age,[137] etc.' This *śruti* clearly says that the self has no sin and therefore the word *anṛta* cannot be taken in the sense of evil deeds. Moreover, if it is taken in the sense of evil deeds it will not suit in *suṣupti* because there is no deed at all in *suṣupti. Suṣupti* is existence of the individual self in causal form and this will not happen without ignorance. Above all, evil deeds cannot create veil on the substratum.

Only ignorance can be destroyed by knowledge and not evil deeds. The *śruti* 'there is further cessation of all ignorance in the end,'[138] is evidence for the same. It may be argued that here cessation denoted by the word *nivṛtti* is only a crossing over as mentioned in the *smṛti* 'they cross over this ignorance!'[139] Both cessation and crossing over mean destruction. Crossing over caused by knowledge can only be cessation and nothing else.

Objection: The word *māyā* need not necessarily mean ignorance. In the case of shell-silver and the like, we do not use the word *māyā*. Therefore, the word has no meaning of ignorance.

Reply: Even though we do not call diamond earth, it is earth itself. Thus *māyā* also has to be taken. Though the word is not used in the sense of shell-silver there is no harm in considering shell-silver as *māyika*. We often hear the word *māyā* in the sense of magic. If *māyā* is different from ignorance it will not be negated by knowledge. In this sense the words *nīhāra* and *tamaḥ* also can be used. Moreover, if *anṛta, nīharā* etc., are in the sense of evil deeds other *śrutis* dealing with them as the cause of the difference between *jīva* and *Īśa* and the like will have to be reversed. Therefore, the *śrutis* like 'they are carried away by *anṛta*,'[140] 'they are covered by *nīhāra*,'[41] 'in the beginning there was only *tamaḥ*'[142], '*prakṛti* is to be understood as *māyā*'[143], 'there is one unborn being red, white and black'[144], 'those who dwell in *avidyā*'[145], 'there is further cessation of all ignorance in the end'[146] and others are evidence for ignorance.

45. *Evidence of presumption on ignorance*

Presumption also is evidence for ignorance. In the absence of ignorance the non-illumination of the unsurpassed bliss of *Brahman* to *jīva* is unintelligible.

Objection: Since *jiva* is different from *Brahman* that non-illumination is suitable.

Reply: *Jīva* and *Brahman* are one and the same. This will be dealt with later.

Another presumption on ignorance is as follows: In the absence of ignorance the state of having a material cause of illusion is unintelligible. Mind cannot be taken to be that material cause because mind depends on the activity of cognitive mental state so as to produce knowledge and also it is not capable of producing knowledge in the case of shell-silver which is not subject to cognitive mental state. Moreover, since mind is having an origin, it cannot be the material cause of illusory series which have no origin. *Brahman* also cannot be the material cause since it is changeless.

Objection: Let *Brahman* be the material cause since it is the substratum for *vivarta* like sea-shell etc.

Reply: Material causality being the substratum of *vivarta* is not possible without any ignorance. Sea-shell etc., have no status of substratum as having the same as its qualification per proprium.

Objection: So as to explain the material causality of *vivarta* of the world in *Brahman*, ignorance which is real and different from *Brahman* is assumed. Similarly, so as to explain the material causality of ignorance in *Brahman*, some locus which is false and different from *Brahman* has to be assumed.

Reply: If *Brahman* is considered as the real material cause of the illusory world, change, impermanence etc., also will have to be admitted in *Brahman*. If *Brahman* is considered as the substratum, there is no such trouble. Therefore, no other substratum need be assumed.

Objection: The material cause of jar etc., is mud which is clearly known to everybody. Both the material cause and effect have the same status of reality too. This cannot be said in the case of

Brahman. Therefore, *Brahman* cannot be considered as the material cause of the world. Moreover, in the world, consciousness has not been known as the material cause of anything.

Reply: Bādarāyaṇa clearly says that it is only *Brahman* who through profound meditation on each thing created it as is known from his indicatory marks.[147] Saṅkara has made it more clear. He says that it is *Parameśvara* himself, abiding in the elements as their self, that creates every effect through profound meditation.[148] In the case of worldly objects like jar etc., also it is consciousness in the form of mud that is considered as the material cause.

The view of *Sāṅkhyas* that *pradhāna* comprising of its three *guṇās*, is the material cause of the world also cannot be accepted. Is this *pradhāna* true or false? If false, it is not different from ignorance. If it is true another question arises: Is it having components or not? In the first case the beginninglessness of *pradhāna* comes to an end because in the world we see that jar etc., which are having components have beginning too. If *pradhāna* is without components then it cannot be the changing material cause of the world like *Brahman*. Therefore, *pradhāna* cannot be considered as the material cause of the world. Thus it is established that presumption also is valid evidence for ignorance.

46. *Fitness of the knowledge of ignorance*

The said ignorance is known through *sākṣin* and not by pure consciousness. *Sākṣin* is the reflection of consciousness on *avidyāvṛtti*. Therefore, there is no scope for such adversities like the following: Ignorance has to be considered absolutely real since it is illuminated by pure consciousness. It is to be said that in liberation also there is the illumination of ignorance. It cannot be said that, then, since *avidyā* is destroyed there can be no illumination of it, because that which has its body only in knowledge cannot be said to disappear when there is the known.

It is aptly said that *avidyā* like *rāhu* is illuminated by the consciousness which it conceals. It need not be put as an allegation that, then, *avidyā* will have to be considered unilluminated sometimes, because it is acceptable to us. In *samādhi* it is the same.

Objection: *Avidyāvṛtti* is born of defects. Therefore, how can there be the same in consciousness?

Reply: *Avidyā* itself is the defect. There is also no presence of the unending process of dependence on *vṛttis* because *vṛtti* itself can be taken to be its illuminator.

Objection: Ignorance is not a subject to evidence because as you said, it is known through *sākṣin* and knowledge of *sāksin* cannot be taken to be authoritative. Therefore, discussion on the evidence on ignorance is useless. It cannot be said that it is for distinguishing it from the non-existent, because without ignorance it also is not possible.

Reply: It is ignorance distinct from the non-existents put forward by evidences that is known through *sākṣin*. Thus evidences are useful in distinguishing the non-existents.

47. *Fitness of the existence of ignorance in pure consciousness*

Pure *Brahman* is the locus of ignorance. Sarvajñātman says that undifferentiated consciousness is the locus as well as the object of ignorance and that all that come into being after ignorance can neither be the locus nor be the object of ignorance which exists prior to them.[148] The world is there only in *jīva* which is the reflection of *Brahman* and not in *Brahman*.

Objection: How can pure consciousness be the locus of ignorance? Ignorance and consciousness are like darkness and light respectively.

Reply: The knowledge that is contrary to ignorance is not consciousness alone: but it is that which is reflected on *vṛtti*. It is not the locus of ignorance and that which is the locus of ignorance is not contrary to it too.

Objection: It is not correct to say that pure consciousness is the locus of ignorance and that all that come into being after that can neither be the locus nor be the object of it because infact, through the *sākṣin* who acknowledges that 'I am ignorant', *jīva* is the locus of ignorance.

Reply: *Jīva* who comes into being through ignorance cannot be the locus of ignorance. Therefore, pure consciousness itself is the locus of ignorance. And for the same reason the knowledge 'I am ignorant' like 'I am fat' is the result of indiscriminate superimposition.

Objection: *Śrutis* depict pure consciousness as that which is without any defect. Therefore, it cannot be the locus of ignorance. *Jīva* is the locus of ignorance.

Reply: Pure consciousness being the locus of the defect ignorance is not against *śrutis*. In fact, ignorance can do no harm to pure consciousness, but it makes *jīva* who is the reflection in it defective. It is well known that medium and reflection belong to the same category. It cannot be said that there is no evidence for consciousness being the locus of ignorance and that there is the same for *jīva* being the locus of it because the *śruti*, '*prakṛti* is to be understood as *māyā* and Maheśvara as the *māyin*'[150] is evidence. It cannot be said that it contradicts the *śruti* '*Īśvara* is knowing and *jīva* is ignorant,'[151] because one can be called ignorant when one has the effect of ignorance even though one is not the locus of ignorance.

Objection: This ignorance should be considered on a par with that of sea-shell in all respects. Ignorance and the knowledge that dissolves it should be in the same locus. *Iṣṭasiddhi* says that illusion is for him who has ignorance and it is he himself who knows its reality also.[152] This is possible only in *jīva* because only he can be the locus of ignorance and knowledge of reality and not *Brahman*.

Reply: Pure consciousness itself can be the locus of both ignorance and the real knowledge by means of superimposition. There is no mutual dependency between ignorance and the knower because there is no rule that if there is the state of being the locus of two, those two should be mutually dependent.

Objection: There is a general rule that medium and reflection belong to the same category. This will be sublated if it is accepted that ignorance produces illusion belonging to its locus only.

Reply: The cause of the general rule is co-existence. It establishes instances beyond doubt. Therefore, there can be no special rule that is capable of contradicting the general rule in the said case.

Objection: What is meant by saying that medium and reflection belong to the same category? Is it by way of being responsible for reflecting the qualities? Or is it by way of reflecting the effects? Or is it by way of reflecting the qualities of the effects? Or is it veiling the object from the reflection? It cannot be the first because it will not suit *suṣupti*. It cannot be the second because the effects of the medium can be seen in the object that reflects too. It cannot be the third and fourth because the same cannot be seen in the case of mirror, jar etc.

Reply: The medium causes effects both in the object reflected and reflection. However, it is especially causative in the case of reflection. This is what is meant by saying that the medium and reflection belong to the same category. It is because of this that *Īśvara* who is reflected on various intellects need not be said to be more than one. All the differences are those concerning the medium.

Objection: Is this ignorance characteristic of pure consciousness or its qualification per accidens? If it is the first it will not be sublated at all like pure consciousness itself. If it is the second there arises another question. What is this medium of ignorance? If it is ignorance itself there is the defect of self-dependency. If it is something different from ignorance there will present any of the three defects of mutual dependency, circular dependency and infinite regress.

Reply: There is no harm in ignorance being the qualification per accidens. There is no self dependency, mutual dependency, circular dependency or infinite regress because it can be explained in the same way as difference being the cause of difference. Therefore, ignorance has pure consciousness as it locus.

48. *Fitness of ominiscient Brahman being the locus of ignorance*

Objection: If *Brahman* which is pure consciousness is the locus of ignorance its omiscience dealt with in the *śrutis* will be contradicted. It cannot be said that omniscience is in the qualified consciousness and not pure consciousness because the *śruti* 'the fourth is the cogniser of everything'[153] clearly says that pure consciousness is omniscient.

Reply: What is meant by 'the cogniser of everything' is the consciousness that which cognises everything and not the omniscience of the fourth. Therefore, omniscience is in the qualified consciousness. And that is not possible without ignorance. Citsukha says that omniscience is of two kinds: in its own form or through *pramāṇa* and that both come to be through ignorance.[154]

Objection: If omniscience is not in its own form there will be no relation with time etc., and it will result in the negation of omnipresence. Therefore, as by ignorance the relation of consciousness should be in its own form.

Reply: Relation of ignorance is not in its own form but by ignorance and for the same reason the posing of example as 'by ignorance' will not suit. Relation with time etc., can be by itself or otherwise and therefore, there is no negation of omnipresence or the sort. The *śruti* dealing with the lack of relation of any sort in *Brahman*[155] fits in the sense of the lack of relation in its own pure form. Therefore, Madhva's view that ignorance does not fit in the omniscient[156] is to be discarded. Ignorance is located at the pure consciousness alone.

49. *Fitness of jiva being the locus of ignorance*

Vācaspatimiśra considers ignorance as located in *jīva*.[157]

Objection: Is this ignorance located in *jīva* consciousness reflected in it or qualified by it? Is *jīva* difference assumed by ignorance? In that case there is mutual dependency.

Reply: Is this mutual dependency in origin or cognition or existence? It cannot be the first because both are beginningless. It cannot be the second because even though ignorance is illuminated by consciousness, consciousness is self-luminous and therefore it has no dependence on ignorance. It cannot be the third too because in that case mutual dependency should be either by being locus mutually or by having mutually dependent existence. In both cases, eventhough, ignorance has dependence on consciousness, consciousness has no dependence on ignorance and for the same reason there is no mutual dependency.

In fact, dependence of ignorance and *jīva* is similar to that between jar and ether both being imposed. It may be argued that if *Īśvara* is assumed by *Īśvara* and *jīva* by *jīva* there is self-dependency and if *Īśvara* is assumed by *jīva* and *jīva* by *Īśvara* there will be mutual dependency too. Pure consciousness cannot be the assumer, for, in this case ignorance is not in pure consciousness but in *jīva*. However, this argument has no locus standi because ignorance located in *jīva* is that which assumes both *jīva* and *Īśvara* and for the same reason there is no harm in ignorance being located in *jīva*.

50. *Fitness of the object of ignorance*

There is no harm in pure consciousness being the object of ignorance. It is only consciousness that is the object of ignorance. Since it is not something assumed there is no mutual dependency. Since it is self-luminous there is ample scope for ignorance to create veil on its light. Nothing else can be the object because everything else is a product of ignorance and as has no light, there is no scope for the function of veil too.

Objection: What is this function of veil? Is it the absence of evident light? Is it the non-origin of non-evident light? Is it the object's lack of contact with existent light? Is it counter to the effect known as *prākaṭya*? Is it the practical experience to the effect that 'there is not' and 'illumines not'? Is it the lack of practical experience to the opposite effect? Is it capability of being experienced as 'there is not' etc.? Is it capability of being experienced as 'there is' etc.? It cannot be the first and the second because the self-luminous can never have the absence or non-origin of light. It cannot be the third because it is natural to knowledge to have contact with the object. It cannot be the fourth because there can be nothing of that sort besides light. It cannot be the fifth because in that case, in *suṣupti* where there is no practical experience of objects, it will have to be said that there is no veil too. It cannot be the sixth because there can be no practical experience to that effect. It cannot be the seventh and the eighth because they also, being superimposed, do not fit in without veil.

Reply: The practical experience to the effect that 'there is not' and 'illumines not' is quite common. The lack of practical experience to the contrary also can be considered as the function of veil. The veil is the capability for the same which is connected with ignorance and which lasts till the realisation of *Brahman*. Therefore, there is veil in *suṣupti* and there is not in liberation. The argument that in the seventh and eighth cases they also being superimposed, do not fit in without veil, is baseless because the veil in the form of contact of ignorance being beginningless and illuminated by consciousness does not depend on itself in its origin, cognition or existence.

It is the pure consciousness that illumines. However, it does not illumine in its completeness. That happens only in liberation. It is due to the veil created by ignorance that *Brahman* which is complete is not experienced as existing or illumining.

Objection: The veil can be of two kinds: that of the subject and that of the object. The first type of veil conceals objects which are larger. It is just like small fingers concealing greater objects. The second type conceals objects smaller than itself. Here the veil created by ignorance is of the object and therefore, how can it conceal *Brahman*?

Reply: The answer is that which is already given. What is meant by veil is the causality of such practical experience as 'there is not' and 'illumines not'. It is not concealment of the type done by cloth. Therefore, the form, locus and object of ignorance can be well explained.

51. *Fitness of the meaning of 'I' being non-self*

It is as a result of ignorance that *ahaṁkāra* and the sort originate.

Objection: The meaning of *ahaṁ* is *Ātman*. How can it originate from ignorance? Nothing other than the self-luminous *Ātman* can be established to be the meaning of *ahaṁ*. The same *Ātman* is referred to in the reference on the perception of *suṣupti*: 'I had a pleasant sleep; I did not know anything'.

Reply: *Ahaṁkāra* is known in the form of desire. In *suṣupti* there is no desire and the like. Therefore, then how can there be the experience of *ahamartha*? It may be argued that there is no rule that *ahamartha* is experienced along with desire and the like. However, it is not correct because the qualitied can be experienced oly along with its qualities. Otherwise, it will have to be admitted that jar is known without its qualities such as colour. It can be said that lack of knowledge of jar without colour etc., is because of the non-existence of such jar; but it is not right. In the moment when the former colour has been destructed and further colour has not yet been produced and also in the first moment of production, such jar is available. Therefore, it has to be admitted that it is the qualityless *Ātman* who is grasped in *suṣupti*. And for the same reason *ahaṁkāra* is different from the *Ātman* grasped in *suṣupti*. In the reference to *suṣupti ahaṁ* is not a part of the memory.

Objection: If there is no grasping of *ahamartha* in *suṣupti* and also if there is no reference to it in the memory, the question arises: who is that who underwent sleep, *ahaṁ* or some one else? In fact, it is *ahaṁ* himself who slept.

Reply: The reference 'I myself slept' is as a result of indiscriminate superimposition of *Ātman* grasped in *suṣupti* on that in the waking period. There is no scope for such doubt as 'I am I or not?' It is because of the indiscriminate nature of superimposition. After having superimposed indiscriminately Devadatta on Caitra yesterday, one mentions him today as Devadatta himself.

Vyāsatīrtha still persists in his view that in *suṣupti ahaṁ* is grasped. He says that as is said of *Ātman*, ignorance also referred to in 'I did not know', is different from that of *suṣupti*.

Reply: It is sheer ignorance to say so. In fact, knowledge of *sākṣin* is not contrary to ignorance. As already said *ahamartha* is not grasped in *suṣupti*. The *śruti*, 'in truth he thus does not know himself that he is'[158] also is evidence for the absence of the experience of *ahamartha* in *suṣupti*.

Objection: The *śruti* '*prājña* comprehends neither himself nor others, neither truth nor falsehood, but that *turīya* is for ever everything and the witness'[159] clearly deals with particular ignorance. Similarly, let the *śruti* 'in truth he thus does not know himself that he is'[160] also deal with particular ignorance; but why should it contradict the experience of *ahamartha*?

Reply: There is no contradiction in the *Chāndogyaśruti* being evidence for the absence of the experience of *ahamartha*. Infact, there is no similarity between the quoted *śrutis* of *Māṇḍūkya* and *Chāndogya* as alleged by the opponent.

Brahman is distinct from *ahaṁkāra*. *Brahman* is omnipresent. It is on *Brahman* that everything cognisable is superimposed. The *śruti* 'where one sees nothing else, hears nothing else, understands nothing else, that is the infinite; where one sees something else, that is the finite'[161] is ample evidence for the same.

Objection: It is well known that the beginning and conclusion deal with the same thing. Therefore, the concluding *śrutis* 'he is indeed all this',[162] 'the self is all this'[163] etc., and the beginning *śrutis* 'he is indeed bellow'[165] 'the self is below' etc.[166] denote the omnipresence of *Ātman* and not *sarvātmatā*. The *smṛti* 'thou pervadest in all, wherefore, thou art all'[167] also evidences the same. Therefore, there is no logic in the word *ahaṁ* being in the sense of *ahaṁkāra*. Omnipresence is being in many and not in a single one. In short, the *śrutis* in between cannot be taken in the sense of *ahaṁkāra*.

Reply: Sanatkumāra asks the question: 'sir, in what does the infinite rest?'[168] Is it only a locus that is intended? Or is it the absolute substratum? If it is the first, then the answer is that which the same *śruti* gives: 'in its own greatness or not even in greatness.'[169] If it is second, the answer is 'he is indeed below.'[170] This is in accordance with the previous *śruti:* 'One rests in something else.'[171] There is no harm in taking the second case in the sense of *sarvātmatā*. The *smṛti* quoted deals with *sarvātmatā* about which Madhusūdana elaborates in his *Gītāgūḍhārthadīpikā*.[172] The *śrutis* in between dealing with *ahaṁkāra* cannot be posed as a defect because it is with the specific purpose of establishing the unity of *Brahman* with *ahaṁkāra* whereby the direct cognitive nature of *Brahman* also is established.

Objection: The *śrutis* 'what is it by whose departure I shall depart, and by whose staying I shall stay?',[173] 'he created *prāṇa*'[174] and others clearly say that in the cause of the world there was *ahaṁkāra* even before the origin of *prāṇa* and mind. Here is another *śruti* that reveals beyond doubt the fact that *ahaṁ* is *Ātman*: 'that *Brahman* knew self only as I am *Brahman*.'[175] Therefore, non-self can never be the meaning of 'I'.

Reply: In the *śrutis* cited what is intended is not the selfhood of *ahaṁkāra*, but by implication *ahaṁ* is intended as the pure consciousness without any *ahaṁkāra*. In *śrutis* like 'therefore this *ahaṁ* is the self'[176] also implication should be taken in the main. Wherever the qualified is to be taken in the meaning of the substrate there is application of implication.

52. *Fitness of the superimposition of agency*

Objection: If agency is a property of non-self how can it be grasped in *Ātman*? It cannot be said that the agency of mind is superimposed on *Ātman* like the red colour of the China-rose on the mirror and that therefore, it is not real, on the ground that it will contradict *śrutis* dealing with the changelessness of *Ātman* and that in *suṣupti* there is no agency since there is no mind there. If agency is the property of mind there should be the experience 'mind is agent' at least sometimes, just like the experience 'the flower is red' and also the experience 'consciousness is agent', just like the experience 'the mirror is red'.

Reply: Since the mind qualified by agency is superimposed on consciousness indiscriminately, there is no experience as said. Moreover, what is said by the opponent is not correct because there is no experience of superimposition of flower on mirror indiscriminately.

Superimposition is of two kinds: that along with extraneous adjuncts and that which is natural. The superimposition, 'I am the agent', is quite natural. In fact, what happens here is that an agency distinct from that of the mind is produced on *Ātman*.

In the case of superimposition of China-rose on the mirror there is the sense of distinction that China-rose is different from mirror. In the case of superimposition of the mind there is no such distinction because such sense is contrary to indiscriminate superimposition.

Objection: Is it that the agency of mind is superimposed on *ahamartha* or that the agency of *ahamartha* is superimposed on *Ātman*? In the first case it will have to be said that there is nothing evil even superimposed in *Ātman* and that *Ātman* is not the substratum of bondage or release. In the second case even without superimposition the experience 'I am the agent' will have to be admitted and then there will be no relevance for superimposition.

Reply: *Ahaṁkāra* is in the form of a knot of the conscious and the unconscious and thus it has two parts. There is agency in the unconscious part of it. However, in the conscious part, the same is superimposed. Therefore, superimposition is necessary. Without superimposition the cognition, 'I am the agent', is not possible. Therefore, agency is superimposed on the self.

Objection: In the *adhikaraṇa* of 'soul as agent'[177] the agency of the mind alleged by the *sāṅkhyās*, has been refuted and the same established in the soul. Here what is said is on the contrary. If it is said that agency of the soul is as a result of ignorance the same rule can be applied to the connection of *saṅkhyās* too. And then why should their view be discarded?

Reply: What is said in the *adhikaraṇa* of 'soul as agent' has been misunderstood by the opponent. There, the opponent's view is that agency is of the mind and that enjoyment is of consciousness. Refuting this it is said there that agency and enjoyment are in one and the same locus. Over and above this the *adhikaraṇa* has no intention to establish the non-agency of mind or natural agency of *Ātman*. In the *adhikaraṇa* that immediately follows[178] the opponent's question is whether the agency of *Ātman* is natural or caused by extraneous adjuncts. And the answer given is that it is caused by extraneous adjuncts.

Opponent: Inference is evidence for the agency of *Ātman*. *Ātman* has the agency of the means of liberation since he is the enjoyer of the results like the well known agent. Ignorance and knowledge belong to the same substratum since ignorance is destroyed by knowledge like the antecedent negation of knowledge. Enjoyment of pain etc., is in the very same substratum of liberation, since it is bondage like the well known cases of the same.

Reply: In the first inference, is it the agency common to real and superimposed ones that is intended or the real agency? If it is the first *advaitins* also have no objection. In the second case there is inconstancy in the agency and enjoyment in connection with *jāteṣṭi* and *pitṛyajña*. In the second inference also the same kind of problem arises. If the existence of agency is common in the substratum of real and superimposed knowledge *advaitins* have no objection. In case it is connected with real knowledge only, there is presence of extraneous adjuncts. In the third inference also similar are the options and answers. Therefore, agency is that of mind and it is superimposed on *Ātman*.

53. *Discussion on the superimposition of unity of Ātman and the body*

Objection: If *ahamartha* is non-self, perceptions like 'I am a Brahmin' and 'I am blind' cannot be taken to be evidence for superimposition of unity of *Ātman* and the body and the organs because

Ātman is not a subject of the knowledge of unity.

Reply: As said earlier *aham* has got two parts. As in the case of the superimposition of the unity of mind along with its agency etc., on the conscious *aham*, in the present case also the body and organs along with Brahminhood and blindness respectively are superimposed on *aham*. Therefore, the superimposition of the body and organs on *Ātman* fits well.

It cannot be said that the perception of the unity of the body and *Ātman* is repudiated by inference and *śrutis* because the authority of inference and *śrutis* is greater and therefore, perception has to be explained in accordance with them. They reveal difference of *Ātman* and the body and for the same reason the perception of the unity of *Ātman* and the body is not correct.

Objection: It is not proper to say that the body, organs etc., which are definitely known as separate are superimposed indiscriminately on *Ātman* at the same time. Tin and silver known to be separate are not superimposed on sea-shell at one and the same time indiscriminately.

Reply: There are separate perceptions like 'organs are different from the body' and 'the body is different from the organs'. Therefore, there is no superimposition of unity as 'I am organs and the body'. However, eventhough there is no knowledge of difference as 'the blind is different from the Brahmin' and 'the Brahmin is different from the blind', there is superimposition of unity as 'I am a blind Brahmin'. Therefore, the knowledge of difference is contradictory only when the qualifications are the same.

Objection: In our view cognitions such as 'I am a Brahmin' and 'I am a man' are true because Brahminhood and humanhood exist in *Ātman* qualified by the body. Therefore, how can they be considered to be superimpositions?

Reply: If humanhood etc., exist in *Ātman* qualified by the body how can they be cognised by eyes? *Ātman* qualified by the body is not subject to the eyes. Therefore, Brahminhood, humanhood etc., are superimposed on *Ātman*.

Objection: Superimposition of Brahminhood etc., on *Ātman* presupposes some other relation too. And the same cannot be admitted by you. Therefore, Brahminhood etc., are not superimposed.

Reply: In the case of superimposition the relation also is superimposed because other practical relations do not apply to *Ātman*. It cannot be conjunction because *Ātman* is all-pervading and as a result, is already in conjunction with bodies of all kinds. It cannot be the relation of owner and the owned because it is common to cow and the like. In short, no relation other than the superimposed one is possible and necessary. In fact, everything is dependent on superimposition. Śaṅkara says that cognisership and the sort are effects of superimposition.[179] Superimposition of the unity of *Ātman* with the body is perceptible. That is why it is said pointing to the body with the finger that 'this is I'. That is why the *śrutis* negating the unity of *Ātman* and the body also fit in; otherwise, it will have to be said that they negate what is irrelevant. It cannot be said that they negate the wrong views of evil schools of thought because there is no such school of thought which denies perception. Therefore, based on the cognition, 'I am white' common to people of all walks of life, it is established that the mind is superimposed on *Ātman* as one and the same with it and subsequently the body and its properties are also superimposed.

54. *Definition of indefinability*

Objection: Let there be ignorance and its resultant superimposition. However, how can it be established to be indefinable? There is no definition or evidence for indefinability. What is this indefinability? Is it the absence of explanation? Or is it the absence of knowledge of the instrumental cause of such explanation? Or is it the absence of the instrumental object for such explanation? Or is it the absence of the generality of instrument for explanation? If it is the first, there is *vyākhāta* because indefinability itself is an explanation and 'this is silver' another. In the second case, since there is the result explanation there is no logic in assuming the absence of its instrument. For the same reason the third case also is not correct; moreover, the object is not the instrument of explanation. Since there is the result, the fourth case also is not acceptable. It cannot also be said to be difference from existent and non-existent at the same time because there is no harm in it being existent and non-existent. For the same reason difference from existence and non-existence also cannot be said to be the definition. Thus there is no definition for indefinability.

Reply: There is definition for indefinability. Difference from existent, non-existent and existent non-existent at the same time can be taken to be the definition. It can also be incapability of being described as existence and non-existence and also existence-non-existence at the same time. It can further be defined as being subject to sublation at the very same locus where it seems to be.

Objection: What is this existence? What is this non-existence too?

Reply: What are meant by existence and non-existence are the same as those intended by the opponents. It should be noted in this connection that *advaitins* accept this only for the time being and not as fundamental tenets of *Advaita*.

Discussion on the definition of indefinability continues. The *dvaitins* ask whether the absence of existence etc., in the world is apparent or having the same status of reality as that of the propertied or practical? Madhusūdana replies that what is intended by the absence of existence is that having the same status of reality as that of the propertied. As the object that is superimposed its status of reality is also superimposed and therefore unreal.

Objection: The apparent and practical world can have no absolute reality. Therefore, it results that indefinability is the absence of absolute reality. Absolute reality is the absence of the state of being sublated. Then let unsublatedness be the definition of indefinability.

Reply: In the said case the qualification of sublatedness does not apply to the qualified. Therefore, it cannot be the definition. It can be argued that the *śrutis* and inferences discard difference whatsoever and therefore, difference from existent and non-existent or its pervaded cannot be the definition of indefinability. However, this argument is out of place. The indefinability established also is of the nature of falsity. Therefore, there is nothing unfit in indefinability having a definition applicable to shell-silver and the world alike.

55. *Inference on the indefinability*

Perception, inference, verbal testimony and presumption are evidences for the indefinability of ignorance.

Perception is in the form of cognition that the silver shone was false. The word false is not in the sense of non-existent because non-existence common to 'human horn' etc., cannot be said to be in the silver that is known, though apparently.

Inference is as follows: The thing under dispute is different from the existent, non-existent and the existent-non-existent at the same time because it is subject to sublation or because it seems to be as a result of defect; what is not like this, is not like this as *Brahman*. The opponent alleges a number of fallacies in this inference. However, all of them are discarded by Madhusūdana.

Objection: Out of the three parts of the probandum put forward by the said inference, difference from non-existence is accepted by *dvaitins* also. Therefore, part of the probandum is already established whereby there arises the fallacy of partial establishment of what is already established.

Reply: This was explained earlier:[180] Where all the parts of the probandum are intended together there can be no fallacy of establishment of what is already established eventhough any part is already established.

Objection: Since existence and non-existence are in the form of mutual absence the probandum presents the fallacy of *vyākhāta*.

Reply: It need not necessarily be in the form of mutual absence. Moreover, the absence of existence and non-existence is not absolutely real. Therefore, there is no presence of the fallacy of *vyākhāta*.

Objection: Let there not be existence as that of *Brahman* in the world. However, the world can be existent. Therefore, there need not be indefinability in the world. Thus the inference presents the fallacy of *arthāntara*.

Reply: There is no evidence for the existence of the world. Since the world is non-existent, existence in it will be subject to sublation. And for the existence of *Brahman*, otherwise presence of nihilism is ample evidence.

Objection: The inference presented has resemblance with the following pseudo-inference: The thing under dispute is in the form of existent and non-existent since it is subject to sublation unlike *Brahman*. Moreover, the inference has an opponent too: The thing under dispute is non-existent since it is not a substratum for existence like human horn.

Reply: There is no resemblance with pseudo-inference or presence of opposite inference. The reason for the same is that otherwise unfitness of cognition and sublation repudiates the opposite. This will be dealt with in detail later.[181]

It cannot be said that the indefinable has no difference from the non-existence of human horn because it is better to conclude the non-existence of human horn based on this than to conclude the *tucchatva* of the indefinable based on that. Therefore, inference is ample evidence for indefinability.

56. *Otherwise unfitness of cognition and sublation*

Presumption in the form of otherwise unfitness of cognition and sublation and the like is also evidence for indefinability. The shell-silver etc., under dispute are indefinable because if they were existent they would not have been sublated, if they were non-existent they would not have been cognised. In fact, they are being cognised and sublated. Therefore, they are different from existent and non-existent whereby their indefinability is established.

Objection: What do you mean by the existent? Is it the generality of existence? Or is it causation of fruitful activity? Or is it the state of being unsublated? Or is it having evidence? All these options are unacceptable to us. It can, therefore, be taken to be the state of not being sublated during the period of practical activity. Then it will contradict the *śruti* 'there is in it no diversity'.[182] The world which is not subject to sublation during the period of practical activity will lose indefinability too.

It can be argued that since *Brahman* is self-luminous consciousness no evidence can proceed in its case and that therefore, concomitance of having evidence and unsublatedness cannot be established. It may further be argued that therefore, it is better to say that if it were existent it would have been sublated rather than if it were existent it would not have been sublated. However, this is not correct. Eventhough *Brahman* is self-luminous, evidence can proceed in its case so as to destroy the veil created by ignorance. For the same reason there is no comcomitance between sublatedness and having evidence. Such concomitance is inconstant in *Brahman*. That which reveals reality cannot be said to reveal unreality.

Unsublatedness also can be taken to be the meaning of existence. Unsublatedness means not being the counter-correlate of negation for all the three periods of time.

Objection: By unsublatedness difference from non-existent also can be established in the world like that from existent. That will result in indefinability and for the same reason all other arguments for the establishment of indefinability are futile.

Reply: Both unsublatedness and cognisability establish difference from existent and non-existent. However, there is no harm in allotting each a separate domain of operation. Therefore, there is no problem of futility. The said form of presumption can be split into two separate presumptions establishing indefinability too. They will be then otherwise unfitness of sublation and otherwise unfitness of cognition of apparent reality.

Otherwise unfitness of the state of being the object of practical activity can also be taken to be evidence for indefinability. It can be argued that there is no causal aggregate for the origin of such object, but it is not so. In the case of superimposed silver it is the part 'this' that is cognised as silver. Everything forming part of the superimposition is superimposed too.

Objection: Presumption is depended upon for establishing the difference from existent and non-existent. In the same way it can be depended upon for establishing the being of existent and non-existent at the same time too. Therefore, presumption is not evidence for indefinability.

Reply: Being existent and non-existent at the same time cannot be established through presumption. Existence cannot be considered to be the cause of cognition. Similarly, non-existence cannot be considered to be the cause of sublation too. Therefore, otherwise unfitness of cognition and sublation evidences indefinability.

57. *Otherwise unfitness of being the counter-correlate of negation*

Some hold that sublation is unfit in the existent as well as the non-existent. They, therefore, consider the state of being sublated as indefinability.

Objection: There is being the counter-correlate of destruction in that which is part and non-existent at the present time. Similarly, there can be being the counter-correlate of absolute negation in the absolute non-existent too. Then it will result that sublatedness is not contrary to absolute negation.

Reply: Existence at one time is not useful for existence at another time. The state of being the counter-correlate of destruction is accepted in the existing jar etc., since there is the experience: 'the non-eternal jar is there'. The state of jar's being the counter-correlate of destruction is not at the time of destruction because then there is no jar at all. It may be said that then there will be no cognition of the jar being the counter-correlate of destruction; but it is not so. Otherwise, the cognition, 'jar has colour' also will not be there. Since colour is there in the jar as long as the jar is there, there is no harm for the cognition, 'jar has colour'. Similarly, the cognition, 'jar is the counter-correlate of destruction' also has no harm. Infact, at the time of destruction also there is the cognition that the jar is destructed whereby its being the counter-correlate of destruction is established. Thus it is also established that indefinability is causative of being the counter-correlate and the sort.

Objection: Let existence itself be causative of being the counter-correlate and the sort since it is parsimonious than the difference from non-existent. Then, though there is indefinability, there need not be being the counter-correlate and the sort.

Reply: Of course, existence in the form of unsublatedness for some time is causative there. It is not unsublatedness throughout the three periods of time, for, then it will present prolixity. It may be asked: How is then unsublatedness unfit in the existent? Answer: It is not so in simple existent, but in absolute existent. Thus there is no harm for indefinability.

Objection: Then how can the non-existent be the counter-correlate of difference from the non-existent? How can the negation of non-existence in the beginning found in the *śruti*[183] be fit?

Reply: What is meant by non-existence is the absence of any particular form. The difference from it is to have some form and the same has no counter-correlate also.

Objection: In such cognitions as 'there is no rabbit-horn' the rabbit horn's being the counter-correlate of non-existence is perceptible. How can this being counter-correlate be in the non-existent?

Reply: Negation is perceptible only there where nothing suitable is obtained. In the case of rabbit-horn and the sort suitability is defective. Therefore, there can be no unobtainability of it.

Objection: Unobtainability of that which is contrary to the counter-correlate of existence is the causal aggregate of negation. It is there in the case of rabbit-horn also.

Reply: If this is accepted, such assumptions as 'if the pillar were goblin it would have been obtainable' also will have to be accepted. However, there is no assumption that if there were rabbit-horn it would have been obtained.

Objection: In the cognition 'there is no jar' the subject is the absence of contact of the jar and not the negation of jar.

Reply: The contact of jar presents the existence of it. Therefore, if there is no contact that will mean the negation of it. Therefore, otherwise unfitnesss of being the counter-correlate of negation also is evidence for the existence of indefinability.

58. *Presumption of śrutis like 'there was no non-existent' etc.*

Śrutis like 'then there was neither non-existent nor existent'[184] etc., presume indefinability. Therefore, they are also evidence for it.

Objection: The words existent and non-existent in the *śruti* are in the sense of the five elements. In the *Bhagavadgitā* we see such usage as 'it is not said to be existent or non-existent'[185] in the sense of elements. In another *śruti* it is said that 'everything except air and sky is material'[186] and that 'air and sky are immaterial'.[187]

Reply: When the well-known sense is there, there is no need to resort to other senses. The words existent and non-existent are not well-known in the sense of matter. They are well-known in the sense of real and unreal respectively.

Objection: Then it will have to be said that the *śruti* 'there was neither non-existent nor existent'[188] rejects what is irrelevant.

Reply: It is not correct. Since by 'nor existent' the difference from existent is said, non-existent also is relevant and therefore, rejection of non-existent by 'neither non-existent' is quite relevant. It cannot be said that the word 'then' in the *śruti* is useless because by 'there was neither sky nor heaven beyond'[189] sky is negated whereby the word gets application. The sky etc., have not always non-existence.

Objection: There is no need of negating sky etc., separately because by the negation of the existent the same also will be negated.

Reply: In the expression 'there was no existent' what is meant by existent is absolute reality. Therefore, negation of sky etc., of practical reality will not present.

Objection: The *śruti* says: 'that one breathed by itself without breath'.[190] By this *Brahman* also can be said to be indefinable like ignorance which is said to be so by the *śruti* 'there was darkness'.[190]

Reply: The total sense of the hymn ends in it that then there was only one existent *Brahman* which was not different from existent or non-existent. Otherwise, there will be contradiction with other *śrutis*. Therefore, presumption of *śrutis* reveals the existence of indefinability.

59. *Refutation of asatkhyāti*

Thus it can be concluded that in superimposition what is relevant is *anirvacanīyakhyāti* because evidence is for the same. There is no evidence for holding it to be *asatkhyāti* or *anyathākhyāti*. It cannot be said that the perception 'the silver shone was non-existent' is evidence for cognition of non-existent because it is in the sense of difference from existent. Moreover, the perception is not of non-existent because *dvaitins* consider that the existent is being cognised as non-existent.

Objection: The form of non-existence of superimposed objects can be established by inferences. The thing under dispute is non-existent since it is not substratum for existence like rabbit-horn. The invalid cognition under dispute is of non-existence since it is of a subject which is not the substratum for existence, like the imperceptible knowledge originated from the sentence 'human horn is non-existent'.

Reply: As per the reason already presented, the said inferences are sublated. In the first inference the state of being known from words alone is extraneous adjunct. In the second inference imperceptibility is extraneous adjunct. Moreover, if *asatkhyāti* is accepted it will result in the acceptance of the *Bauddha* school of thought. It cannot be said that there is difference caused by the relation of existent because even then there is no change for *asatkhyāti.*

Objection: *Advaitins* also admit the cognition of the non-existent through such sentences as 'rabbit-horn is non-existent'. Therefore, they will also have to accept *asatkhyāti.*

Reply: We do not accept the cognition of non-existent through such sentences as 'rabbit-horn is non-existent'. In fact, such things as 'rabbit-horn' are *vikalpas* that rest simply in words without having any object to be known at all. Therefore, *asatkhyāti* cannot be admitted.

60. *Refutation of anyathākhyāti*

Anyathākhyāti also is not correct. According to *anyathākhyāti* silver at another place is that which shines on the sea-shell. As in the case of the absolute non-existent, in the case of thing at another place also the absence of relation necessary for perceptual cognition is the same. It cannot be said that the defects of impression and recollection act as relation because even then without the relation of organs and object it is not possible to admit the perception of silver.

Objection: Relation of organs with object is necessary only in the case of valid worldly cognitions.

Reply: It is better to advise about this division to your own disciples because in our view it will create prolixity. Moreover, the same is not applicable to *nirvikalpaka* perception. Cognition of silver having silverness as its adjunct originated as a result of the relation between the organs and silver cannot be false too. In the false knowledge 'these are tin and silver' there is relation with silver. However, it does not create knowledge of silver because in that case silver existing somewhere else will also have to be considered subject of knowledge as in inference. If thus inference is born as a result of direct contact with the object it will be perception. If it is said that owing to the seriousness of defect, relation with silver produces knowledge of tin and relation with tin produces knowledge of silver, then since the knowledge of silver is not born of relation with silver it will lack perception. Therefore, it has to be admitted that the knowledge of 'these' alone is born of relation of organs and that knowledge of 'tin and silver' is in the form of recollection. The same is to be admitted as a projection of ignorance and also *anirvacanīya.*

61. *Fitness of the origin of silver from ignorance*

The indefinable silver originates from the material cause of ignorance. And it is destroyed by the knowledge of reality.

Objection: If so, such cognitions as 'silver originated' and 'silver is destroyed' will have to be admitted. Moreover, there would not have the cognition of negation applicable to all the three points of time.

Reply: Do these cognitions of origin and destruction happen at the time of the false knowledge? Or do they happen at the time of the destruction of such false knowledge? If it is the first, it will not suit because knowledge of the same as not distinct from that of the sea-shell only is competent to create contradiction. Moreover, since there originates no knowledge contrary to that of sea-shell, silver will not be destroyed. It cannot be the second too because knowledge of absolute negation only, as in the case of knowledge of the counter-correlate, is competent to obstruct such cognitions. Never and nowhere can one have coginitions of origin and destruction at the very same locus where absolute negation is cognised.

Objection: How can the origin, destruction and absolute negation of silver be admitted in the sea-shell? Do they not contradict?

Reply: What we do is to assume cause as per the effects and not vice-versa. Since the silver is cognised through perception its origin is accepted. Since it is destroyed later by knowledge of the sea-shell, destruction also is admitted. Since silver is absolutely non-existent in the sea-shell its absolute negation also is admitted. Or else it can be said that the silver is originated and destroyed apparently. Its negation is absolutely.

Objection: At the time of apparent perception of silver on the sea-shell it is absolutely real. Therefore, it cannot be absolutely negated, in the same way as apparent silver cannot be negated absolutely.

Reply: Absolute reality perceived at the time of apparent perception is also apparent. Therefore, what is negated is not absolute reality, but absolute reality in the form of superimposed silver. And for the same reason there is no contradiction with our experience too. Or else, it can be said that what is negated in the sea-shell is not apparent silver; but practical silver. The practical silver is relevant in the sea-shell in the form of apparent silver. And the same is considered to be the origin of indefinable silver in the sea-shell. Ignorance is its material cause.

Objection: Ignorance cannot be said to be the material cause of apparent silver because the object is perceived in the form of its material cause and in the case of shell-silver no such perception is available. What is perceived in the sea-shell is 'this silver' and not 'ignorance-silver' as in the case of 'mud-jar'.

Reply: As per positive and negative reasonings the causality of shell-silver has to be assigned to ignorance of the sea-shell itself. Let that causality be material also. No other cause of the shell-silver is available too. Moreover, the knowledge of the sea-shell destroys ignorance as well as the shell-silver. It will not be fit unless ignorance is the material cause of the shell-silver. Destruction of the instrumental cause is not capable of destroying the effect. There is no rule that the object should be perceived in the form of its material cause.

Objection: If ignorance is the material cause of superimposed object there will be no knowledge of ignorance and pleasure by the *sākṣin* as superimposed absence of knowledge and absence of pleasure respectively.

Reply: Eventhough ignorance is known by *sākṣin*, opposition or difference of it is not known by *sākṣin*. Therefore, there is nothing unfit if *sākṣin* does not have superimposed knowledge or absence of knowledge in ignorance or absence of pleasure in pleasure. In short, ignorance is the material cause of superimposed objects like shell-silver. It has also to be admitted that the shell-silver originates for the time being. It is also absolutely real for the time being. At the destruction of ignorance everything caused by it also come to an end.

62. *Fitness of two vṛttis in illusory knowledge*

At the places of superimposition two *vṛttis* are there. In the case of the substratum it is the *vṛtti* of mind while in the case of the superimposed object it is the *vṛtti* of ignorance. Since the superimposition is, in total, indiscriminate there is no relevance for *akhyāti* as advocated by the *prābhākaras*.

Objection: In the superimposition of silver on the sea-shell since the portion 'this' also is superimposed there also two *vṛttis* have to be admitted. In the cognition 'this is silver' three *vṛttis* have to be admitted. In the cognition of silver in dream four *vṛttis* also will have to be accepted.

Reply: Even if 'thisness' also is superimposed the cognition 'this' need not have two *vṛttis* because the substratum of 'thisness' is self-luminous. Moreover, we do not accept two *vṛttis* at all places. Two *vṛttis* are accepted there where for the cognition of the substratum *vṛtti* of mind is necessary. And for the same reason in the cognition 'this is silver' there are not three *vṛttis*. There is no relevance for any doubt regarding the number of *vṛttis*. There, both 'this' and 'silver' are superimposed on the consciousness qualified per proprium by ignorance.

Objection: If the knowledge of silver on the sea-shell is not visual perception it will be contrary to our experience in the form of 'I see silver'.

Reply: There, the silver is an evolute of the ignorance qualified per proprium by the *vṛtti* of *idaṁ* which is visual. The same visuality is imposed on the silver too. We see such usage as 'I see the self' where the self is evidently not subject to visuality.

Objection: Shell-silver is superimposed and known through the *vṛtti* of ignorance. Since everything that is known through superimposition is known through the *vṛtti* of ignorance only, the *vṛtti* of ignorance needs another *vṛtti* for being known and that *vṛtti* needs still another and so on. Thus there presents an infinite regress.

Reply: What is said about the necessity of *vṛtti* of ignorance is true; however, there will be no presence of infinite regress. The *vṛtti* of ignorance is illuminated by consciousness. Thus, *vṛtti* of ignorance itself being an extraneous adjunct does not need another *vṛtti* for being known.

Objection: If the knowledge of shell-silver is an evolute of ignorance why should we assume the evolution of the very same ignorance into shell-silver also? Knowledge can occur even without object as in the case of the knowledge of objects of the past.

Reply: If knowledge without object is accepted it will result in the *vijñānavāda* of the Buddhists. It cannot be explained like the knowledge of objects of the past because then it will lose its state of perception.

Objection: If two *vṛttis* are accepted the knowledge 'this silver' will lose its unity.

Reply: When there is superimposition of unity of objects, naturally there will be superimposition of the unity of their knowledge too.

Objection: So long as there is unity of knowledge there is no need for accepting two *vṛttis* in the knowledge 'this silver'.

Reply: In that knowledge, in the case of 'this' there is relation of organs; but there is no such relation in the case of silver. Therefore, two *vṛttis* are necessary for the knowledge of both.

Vṛtti of ignorance is not capable of destroying ignorance. For it *vṛtti* of mind in the form of 'this' itself is needed. It is consciousness reflected on it that illuminates the sea-shell. It is the absolutely real consciouness that is the substratum for all superimpositions and resultant knowledges. Superimposed knowledge is of two kinds: practical and apparent. Accordingly, there are three kinds of reality too: absolute practical and apparent.

63. *Fitness of three kinds of existence*

Objection: The division of existence into three is not fit because a fourth category which is lower than apparent and a fifth category which is higher than practical also are there. Shell-silver seen in dream is example for the former and the cessation of ignorance is example for the latter.

Reply: There is no evidence for considering things seen in dream to be lower in existence than the apparent. Apparent existence means existence for the period of shining alone. And it is the same for apparent objects of dream and waking period alike. In both cases the substratum is consciousness qualified per proprium by ignorance. There is also no need to consider the cessation of ignorance as a fifth division because its existence also includes in practical existence. Or it can be said that the cessation of ignorance has no existence at all and that there is no harm in excluding it from the division of existence. In fact, the cessation of ignorance is *Brahman* itself and is indefinable.

Objection: If the division of existence is real, *Advaita* will be in danger and if it is not real the trinity of existence will be lost.

Reply: We have no objection in considering it unreal because as far as we are concerned everything other than *Brahman* is unreal. There is no collapse of trinity of existence because reality of the trinity is only practical.

Objection: In the divisions of existence do you mean difference caused by the time-length taken for sublation and otherwise of the practical and the apparent which seem to be as a result of the absolute or difference of existence itself? It cannot be the first because in the absence of existence there can be no knowledge of existence as per your view which holds that there is no knowledge of silver without silver. It cannot be the second because there is no generality common to the existence of real and superimposed ones. And if practical is a particular of the absolute, there is no need of objection as far as we are concerned too.

Reply: The second option is agreeable to us. The state of not being sublated is generality common to the real and the superimposed alike. Though the superimposed is subject to sublation afterwards, it has the state of not being sublated for the time being. If there is no generality common to the real and the superimposed alike, action will be impossible. Sarvajñātman has made it clear.[192] One form of reality is present in ether etc., which are practical. Another form of reality is present in *Atman* which is absolutely real. A third form of reality is in a blend of the two. Usually it is the last that is taken as the meaning of the word real.

In the apparent silver the reality behind it is known. In the practical silver the reality behind it is not known. The state of silver is common to both these superimposed and real silvers. Eventhough the practical world has a particular existence it is not distinct from superimposed. Since existence of the same is admitted there is nothing unfit in its origin etc., also.

Objection: If the state of being sublated is common to the practical and apparent alike what is their difference? It cannot be said that one is the creation of *māyā* and the other that of *avidyā* because both *māyā* and *avidyā* are the same. It cannot be said that the difference is created by causality to fruitful action and otherwise because in the case of jar etc., of dream there is fruitful action like fetching of water in the dream itself.

Reply: Eventhough both the practical and the apparent are alike subject to sublation, there is difference. One is sublated by indeterminate knowledge while the other by determinate. One is sublated by the knowledge of pure *Brahman* while the other is sublated by other knowledges. One is sublated by the knowledge originated from *mahāvākyas* while the other is not so. One is sublated by the knowledge which sublates itself while the other is not so. What is meant by pure existence is the propertyless substratum. All the world superimposed on it as a result of ignorance is unreal.

Since the cognisable world is false all the *śrutis* which reveal the impartite knowledge of *Brahman* reveal absolute reality alone. All other means of partite knowledge reveal unreality. Of the practical and apparent realities one is originated as a result of the defect of organs while the other is not so, though both in ultimate sense are unreal. Therefore, there is nothing unfit in the concept of the three kinds of existence.

Thus the first *pariccheda* of *Advaitasiddhi* of Madhusūdana comes to a close. Having established the falsity of the world Madhusūdana ascertains the absolute reality of *Brahman*. In accordance with the same sense Madhusūdana adds two verses as an epilogue of the first *pariccheda* of his book. He depicts *Hari* as the sole substance of all the *śrutis*. *Hari* is all in all, beginningless pleasure, released from all cognisable entities, self-luminous and without end. As if having obtained the realisation of *Brahman* Madhusūdana considers himself as *Hari* who is absolutely real throughout the three periods of time and who is devoid of the difference of the three kinds.

REFERENCES

[1]Vide, Madhusūdanasarasavati, AS, ed., Anantakṛṣṇaśāstri, N.S., (Delhi, 1982), pp. 1-2.

[2]Vide, Danielou Alain, *Viṣṇu the Pervader*, ALB, Vol. XVIII, Pt., 3-4, pp. 333-34.

[3]Of, Śaṅkara, AB, 9.

[4]Vide, anon., AGK, p. 101.

[5]Vide, Gauḍapāda, MK, I. 17.

[6]Vide, AB, 48.

[7]Vide, Vyāsatīrtha, NA, ed. Yogīndrānanda, Svāmi, p. 1.

[8]Vide, Kālidāsa, *Raghuvaṁśa*, I., 3.

[9]Vide, Gotama, NS, 1, 2, 1-3.

[10]Vide, Udayana, NK, ed., *Padmaprasādaupādhyāya avoid* and Ḍhunḍhirāj-śāstri, (Benares, 1957), p. 29.

[11]'Idaṁ ca vipratipattipradarśanaṁ tārkikarītyaiva' Vide, Vyāsatīrtha, NA, p.3.

[12]Vide, Ānandabodha, ND, ed., Balaramaudaseenmandalika, (Benares, 1907), p.l.

[13]Ibid. Ānandabodha deals with the inference in his *Nyāyamakaranda* and *Pramāṇamālā* also.

[14]Vide, NA, p. 10.

[15]Vide, Padmapāda, PP, ed., Srirāmaśāstri, S. and Kṛṣṇamūrtiśāstri, S.R., (Madras, 1958), p. 23

[16]Vide, NS, I, 2, 9.

[17]Ibid., I, 2-8.

[18]Ibid., V, 2, 7.

[19]Vide, Prakāśātman, PPV, ed., Śrīrāmaśāstri, S. and Kṛṣṇamūrtiśāstri, S.R., (Madras, 1958), pp. 174-75.
[20]Vide, BU, IV, 4, 19.
[21]Vide, PPV, p. 192.
[22]Vide, TU, II, 1, 3.
[23]Vide, PPV, p. 179.
[24]Ibid.
[25]Vide, BUBV, IV, 4, 497.
[26]Vide, Citsukha, TP, ed., Yogīndrānanda, Svāmi, (Benares, 1974), p. 67.
The actual words of Citsukha are as follows:
sarveṣāmapibhāvānamāśrayatvenasammate
pratiyogitvamatyantābhāvampratimṛṣātmatā.
[27]Vide, CU, VI, 2, 1.
[28]Ibid.
[29]Vide, ND, p. 1.
[30]Vide, NA, p. 45.
[31]Vide, ND, p. 1.
[32]Ibid.
[33]Ibid.
[34]Vide, TU, II, 1, 6.
[35]Vide, BU, III, 8, 8.
[36]Vide, TP, p. 69.
[37]Vide, Bādarāyaṇa, BRS, II 1, 14.
[38]Vide, NS, V, 2, 7.
[39]Vide, NA, pp. 88-89.
[40]Vide, Annaṁbhaṭṭa, TS, ed., Virūpākṣānanda, Svāmi, (Madras, 1980), p. 119.
[41]Vide, supra, chapter III.
[42]Vi(e- Viśvanāthapañcanana, NSM (Benares, 1972), pp. 209-13.
[43]Vide, Jaimini MS, I, 2, 10; I, 2, 47.
[44]Ibid., I, 2, 2,
[45]Ibid., I, 4, 23-28.
[46]Vide, CU, VI, 8, 7.
[47]Vide, Sadānanda, VS, ed. with Eng. Tr., Nikhilānanda, Svāmi, (Calcutta, 1968) pp. 111-112.
[48]*Paurvāparye pūrvadaurbalyam prakṛtivat*, Vide, MS, VI, 5, 54.
[49]*Vipratiṣedhāt vikalpaḥ syāt*, Vide, MS, VI, 5, 51.
[50]Vide, BRS, II, 1, 11.
[51]Vide, PPV, p. 227.
[52]Vide, BU, IV, 4, 19 etc.
[53]Vide, RV, II, 7, 3 etc.
[55]Vide, RV, II, 7, 3.
[56]Ibid., VIII, 1, 17.
[57]Vide, IU, 8.
[58]Vide, BG, XVI, 8.
[59]Vide, BRS, II, 2, 28.
[60]Ibid., II, 2, 29.

[61]The name of the *adhikaraṇa* is *Nābhāvādhikaraṇam.*
[62]Vide, PP, p. 100.
[63]Ibid., p. 101.
[64]Vide, BRS, II, 1, 14.
[65]Vide, Vācaspatimiśra, *Bhāmati*, Pt. I, ed., Ḍhuṇḍirājaśāstri, (Benares, 1935), p. 4.
[66]Ibid.: p. 228.
[67]Vide, Sarvajñātman, SS, I, 319.
[68]Ibid., I, 331.
[69]Vide, BRS, III. 4, 26.
[70]Ibid., I, 1, 2.
[71]Vide, TU, III, 1, 2.
[72]Vide, BRS, I, 1, 5.
[73]Vide, CU, VI, 2, 3.
[74]Vide, BRS, II, 3, 14.
[75]Vide, *tadabhidhyānādeva tu tulliṅgātsaḥ*, BRS, II, 3, 13.
[76]Ibid., II, 1, 14.
[77]Vide, Śaṅkara, comm. BRS, II, 1, 14.
[78]Vide, SU, VI, 1.
[79]Vide, CU, VI, 2, 1.
[80]Vide, *Mahābhāṣya* of Patañjali on PS, I, 1, 39.
[81]Ibid.
[82]Vide, PS, I, 1, 24.
[83]Ibid., VII, 1, 72.
[84]Ibid., VII, 1, 20.
[85]Ibid., I, 1, 42.
[86]Ibid., I, 1, 61.
[87]Vide, Vācaspatimiśra, op. cit., Pt., I, p. 4.
[88]Vide, TU, II, 1, 1.
[89]Vide, CU, VI, 8, 7.
[90]loc. cit.
[91]Vide, RV, VIII, 6, 11.
[92]Vide, MB, I, 251.
[93]Vide, MS, I, 4, 3.
[94]Vide, BRS, I, 1, 22.
[95]Vide, CU, I, 9, 1.
[96]Vide, supra, chapter V, 21.
[97]Vide, BU, IV, 3, 32.
[98]Vide, CU, VI, 2, 1.
[99]Ibid., VI, 2, 2.
[100]Ibid., VI, 3, 3.
[101]Vide, BRS, II, 1, 14.
[102]Vide, Sadānanda, VS, loc. cit.
[103]Vide, VKL, pp. 170-75.
[104]Vide, CU, VI, 2, 1.
[105]Vide, NA, pp. 438-47.
[106]Vide, KU, IV, II.

[107]Vide, CU, VI, 1, 4.
[108]Ibid., VII, 1, 3.
[109]Vide, MUU, III, 2, 8.
[110]Ibid., II, 2, 8.
[111]For more about the state of being discarded by cognition see, supra, chapter V, 8.
[112]Vide, SU, IV, 10.
[113]Vide, BG, V, 15.
[114]Vide, SU, IV, 5, 15.
[115]Vide, BG, II, 69.
[116]Vide, Sarvajñātman, SS, I, 338.
[117]Vide, SB.
[118]Vide, VKL.
[119]Vide, Sarvajñātman, SS, III, 25.
[120]Vide, KU, II, 5.
[121]Vide, CU, V, 10, 7.
[122]Vide, MK, I, 16.
[123]Vide, BU, I, 4, 10.
[124]Vide, SU, IV, 5.
[125]Vide, BG, XIV, 2.
[126]Vide, TP, p. 97.
[127]Vide, SS, I, 322.
[128]Vide, supra, chapter V, 8.
[129]Vide, PPV, p. 220.
[130]Vide, SB, pp. 119-125.
[131]Vide, PPV, p. 85.
[132]Ibid.
[133]Vide, TP, *pariccheda* I.
[134]Vide, CU, VIII, 3, 2.
[135]Vide, KU, III, 1.
[136]Vide, CU, VIII, 3, 2.
[137]Ibid., VIII, 7, 1.
[138]Vide, SU, I, 10.
[139]Vide, BG, VII. 14.
[140]Vide, CU, VIII, 3, 2.
[141]Yide, RV, VIII, 3, 17.
[142]Ibid., VIII, 7, 17.
[143]Vide, SU, IV, 10.
[144]Ibid., IV, 5.
[145]Vide, KU, II, 5.
[146]Vide, SU, I, 10.
[147]Vide, BRS, II, 3, 13.
[148]Vide, Śaṅkara, comm. BRS, II, 3, 13.
[149]Vide, SS, I, 319.
[150]Vide, SU, IV, 10.
[151]Ibid., I, 9.
[152]Vide, IS, p. 193.
[153]Vide, MK, I, 12.

[154]Vide, TP, p. 578.
[155]Vide, BU, IV, 3, 15.
[156]Vide, NA, p. 580.
[157]Vide, Vācaspatimiśra, op. cit., pt. I., p. 114.
[158]Vide, CU, VIII, H, 1.
[159]Vide, MK, I, 12.
[160]loc. cit.
[161]Vide, CU, VII, 24, 1.
[162]Ibid., VII, 25, 1.
[163]Ibid.. VII, 25, 2.
[164]Ibid., VII, 25, 1-
[165]Ibid., VII, 25, 1.
[166]Ibid., VII, 25, 2.
[167]Vide, BG, XI, 40.
[168]Vide, CU, VII, 24, 1.
[169]Ibid.
[170]Ibid., VII, 25, 1.
[171]Ibid., VII, 24, 2.
[172]Vide, GGD on BG, II, 18.
[173]Vide, PU, VI, 3.
[174]Ibid., VI, 4.
[175]Vide, BU, I, 4, 10.
[176]Vide, AU, II, 1, 2.
[177]Vide, BRS, II, 3, 33.
[178]Ibid., II, 3, 40.
[179]Vide, Śaṅkara, *Adhyāsabhāṣya* on BRS.
[180]Vide, supra, chapter V, 6.
[181]Vide, infra, chapter V, 56.
[182]Vide, BU, IV, 4, 19.
[183]Vide, RV, X, 129, 1.
[184]Ibid.
[185]Vide, BG, XIII, 12.
[186]Vide, BU, II, 3, 2.
[187]Ibid., II, 3, 3.
[188]loc. cit.
[189]Ibid.
[190]Ibid., X, 129, 2.
[191]Ibid., X, 129, 3.
[192]Vide, SS, I, 178.

CHAPTER VI

Pariccheda–2

The first *pariccheda* dealt with the falsity of the world. The world is bondage. Now the means of severing the false bondage is to be dealt with. Impartite knowledge of *Brahman* is the means. However, *Nyāyāmṛta* refutes the definition of impartite knowledge held by *advaitins*. The second *pariccheda* opens with the substantiation of the definition of impartite cognition.

1. *Impartite cognition*

Impartite cognition is valid cognition produced by words which are not synonymous and tainted by relation. It can also be defined as valid cognition produced by stem alone of words without reference to relations.[1] *Pañcapādikā* says the same things.[2] *Tattvapradīpikā* also vouchsafes the same. That has been said: 'This production by words of a valid cognition untainted by relation is what is called impartite sense, or in other words it is the sense of stems alone without reference to relations'[3].

Impartite cognition is of two kinds. One is that produced by words and the other is that produced by sentence. Each of them is further divided into two types namely ordinary and scriptural. Scriptural impartite cognition produced by words itself is of two kinds: that produced by the word 'that' and that produced by the word 'thou'. The *śruti* 'reality, knowledge, infinitude is *Brahman*'[4] etc., is example for the former and 'he who is within the heart, surrounded by the *prāṇas*, the person of light'[5] etc., is example for the latter. 'The moon is full of light'[6] etc., are examples for ordinary impartite cognition produced by words. The *śruti* 'that though art'[7] is example for impartite cognition produced by scriptural sentence. And 'this is that Devadatta' is example for impartite cognition produced by ordinary sentence.

Objection: In the impartite cognition there is no relation of qualification and the qualified. Then how can there be difference of the qualifieds?

Reply: Even if there is no such difference at one place there can be the same at another place. 'Water has cold touch', 'fire has hot touch' etc., are sentences revealing different qualifieds.

In the definition of impartite knowledge the portion 'words which are not synonymous' has been included so as to avoid overapplicability in such sentences as '*ghaṭa* is *kalaśa*' which reveal relation. What is intended is joint revelation of meaning by all the words. Therefore, there is no overapplicability of the definition in such compounds as '*dhavakhadirapalāśāḥ*'.

The second definition also has no fault. There, what is intended by the word 'alone' is the stem-sense's being the subject of mental state qualified per proprium by a single property. The singularity of the object is not intended.

Objection: What is meant by not being synonymous is having different objects as meaning. That is not possible in the case of words such as reality, consciousness, infinitude and the sort because all those words mean pure *Brahman* alone. Therefore, the definition of impartite cognition does not apply to *vedāntavākyas*.

Reply: In the case of words such as reality, consciousness and infinitude difference of objects in meaning is intended. They reveal pure *Brahman* by implication.

Objection: In pure *Brahman*, since there is no relation how can implication be applicable?

Reply: There the relation is not real. In the case of shell-silver we assume implication of sea-shell by the relation of superimposed silver. Since pure *Brahman* is the substratum for all superimpositions there is no harm in assuming relation in *Brahman*.

2. *Fitness of impartite sense of secondary sentences like 'reality' etc.*

After having defined impartite cognition Madhusūdana proceeds to present evidence for the same. The sentence beginning with 'reality' is of impartite sense or it produces the stem-sense of *Brahman* alone since it is a definitive sentence or since it is an answer to a question regarding *Brahman* alone like the sentence 'moon is profound in light'. This inference is the evidence for impartite sense of words. Inference on impartite sense of sentence is as follows: Sentences like 'that thou art' produce impartite sense or they produce cognition about the essential nature of *Brahman* alone because the cognition produced is not with regard to any matter of cause-effect relation alone and at the same time the sentence denotes one and the same substratum or because it is a sentence in answer to a question regarding *Brahman* alone like the sentence 'this is he'.

Objection: Valid cognition untainted by relation can never be—

established because all means of valid knowledge beginning from perception produce cognition of a specific relation.

Reply: Valid cognition untainted by relation is quite possible. It is well known that indeterminate knowledge is that apprehending no relation. Thus it is known that validity of cognition can exist in cognition without relation. The cognition 'moon is profound in light' is example.

Objection: The specific quality is considered as definition. In impartite knowledge there is no specific quality at all. Therefore, how can it be defined?

Reply: In the definition by essential nature there is no need of specific quality. In the impartite cognition of *Brahman* the words 'reality' etc., denote essential nature and not qualification per accidens.

Objection: Definition which is essential quality and impartite cognition which is essential nature are contradictory. In fact, all definitions reveal partite knowledge only.

Reply: There is no rule that all definitions should be partite in sense. Infact, all definitions end in essential nature. Though essential quality is contrary to impartite sense essential nature is not so.

Objection: A general knowledge of the essential nature of *Brahman* is already there for us. Therefore, definition by the essential nature of *Brahman* is not necessary for the knowledge of *Brahman* in general.

Reply: Depending up on the different forms of mental state both can be explained. It is just like having veil and otherwise. If this is not accepted the difference of definition as that by essential nature and by qualification per accidens will not be fit.

Vyāsatīrtha now alleges a number of fallacies in the inference on the impartite cognition put forward by *advaitins.* Madhusūdana ably refutes them all.

Objection: The inference on impartite cognition is subject to sublation because lack of probandum is certain in the *śruti* 'reality' etc. This is caused by the otherwise unfitness of the fact that the discussion on *vedānta* has been intended as a means of attaining determinate cognition which is capable of doing away with determinate doubt etc., regarding the knowledge of the qualified and also which is cause of liberation.

Reply: Here the probandum is otherwise established. By the *śruti* 'reality is *Brahman*' the doubt whether *Brahman* is false or not, get itself extinguished. Determinate knowledge is not always necessary to expel doubt. Therefore, there is no presence of sublatedness.

Presence of antithetical reason, *sādhyavaikalya* etc., alleged by the opponent also are refuted by Madhusūdana.

Objection: Since *Brahman* is having extraneous adjuncts how can there be reality in the form of not being the subject of negation for all the three periods of time, in *Brahman*?

Reply: What is meant by reality of *Brahman* is that the word reality can be grasped in its sense as a result of its relation with the pure one. The same thing is said by Sarvajñātman: One form of reality is present in the ether etc., another form is present in the self and the third is a blend of the two. Of these three, it is the last that is the primary sense of the word *satya*.[8]

Then comes the discussion on *abhihitānvayavāda* and *anvitābhidhānavāda*. Madhusūdana says that a word having secondary implication cannot be *anvayānubhāvaka*. And the secondary implication here is of the non-exclusive type.

Objection: Let it be so if the secondary implication is of the non-exclusive type. How will it fit in if the same is of the exclusive type? *Sarvajñātman* has made it clear: Just as in the sentences, 'the boat makes noise', 'the iron burns', and 'in front of you there is the rope bearing poison', the words convey the multitude of men, fire and the serpant respectively, what objection can there be if the words *aham* and *Brahman* of the *śruti* '*aham brahmāsmi*', which primarily signify the intellect and ignorance respectively, convey the supreme self through exclusive secondary implication?[9]

Reply: In the case of exclusive secondary implication *anvitābhidhānavāda* cannot be accepted. And for the same reason there is no fault of the sort alleged. If secondary implication of the exclusive-non-exclusive type is accepted both *anvitābhidhānavāda* and *abhihitānvayavāda* can be substantiated. Sarvajñātman himself has said the same: In the *abhihitānvaya* the two words give rise, through secondary implication, to two cognitions regarding the self. These cognitions are similar to recollection. In the *anvitābhidhāna* the two words give rise to two cognitions which are of the nature of recollection.[10] Citsukha admits *abhihitānvayavāda*. In either case there is nothing detrimental to *Advaita*.

3. *Impartite sense of sentences like 'that thou art'*

Inference establishing the impartite sense of *mahāvākyas* like 'that thou art' also is faultless. *Mahāvākyas* like 'that thou art' reveal impartite sense or the stem-sense of *Brahman* alone because they are with regard to no matter of cause-effect relation only and at the same time they have words having one and the same substratum like the sentence 'this is that Devadatta'.

Objection: The example 'this is that Devadatta' has no probandum.

Reply: It is not correct because no qualified non-difference can be established. For, is it qualifiedness of this place and this time qualified by that place and that time that is intended? Is it the qualifiedness of that place and that time in that which is qualified by this place and this time? Or is it that the qualifications are one and the same? Or is it that the qualifieds are one and the same? It cannot be the first because the qualifiedness of that place and that time is not intended as probandum since the same is not perceptible. Moreover, it will have to be said that that place and that time are present now too. It cannot be the second because then it will have to be said that this place and this time are present then too. It cannot be the third because it is subject to sublation. And for the same reason it cannot be the fourth too. The qualifieds are different since the qualifications are different. Thus, since both the qualifications are left and since the non-different substrate alone is cognised, the impartite sense is established. Sarvajñātman has made it clear: When two qualified entities resulting from the two unopposed qualifications cannot be possibly identical, it is highly improbable that the qualified entities characterised by contradictory qualifications could be identical.[11]

Objection: The recognition 'this is he' cannot be of any impartite sense because there is no secondary implication of the *vṛtri* of verbal testimony in that perception. Besides, there indeterminacy is refuted by perception of thatness and thisness.

Reply: Even if there is no dependence on *vṛtti* the perception there, is of non-difference of the qualifieds. And therefore, the is no presence of sublation. What is intended is only the non-difference of essential nature? And non-difference is not a determinent because what is important is the essential nature. Thatness and thisness also are not determinents since they are not counter-correlates of non-difference cognised. In short, there is no harm for the probandum the inference. As the sense of the sentence 'this is that Devadatta' is impartite the sense of *mahāvākyas* like 'that thou art' also is impartite.

Objection: If the non-difference of pure consciousness from pure consciousness is what is intended we have no objection. If it is negation of difference, then there results the negation of what is irrelevant because non-difference is the essential nature as per your view. If it is said that non-difference is not cognised, then the *mahāvākyas* will be futile.

Reply: Eventhough the consciousness is always established beyond doubt the cognition of the essential nature of it indicated by omniscience etc., which negates ignorance is what is intended here. Therefore, there is no problem of futility of *mahāvākyas*.

In the sentence 'that thou art' the word 'that' denotes what is qualified by omniscience etc., and the word 'thou' denotes what is qualified by partial knowledge etc. All these differences are negated by impartite cognition. Thus all *vedāntavākyas* are evidences for the qualityless impartite *Brahman* and also the knowledge of *Brahman* accordingly.

Madhusūdana concludes the discussion on the impartite sense of sentences like 'that thou art' with a powerful hit at the opponent. He says that the ignorant opponent, *dvaitin*, is prattling many things in his eagerness to retort the well founded views of *Advaita*. Therefore, Madhusūdana expresses the hope that there is no harm even if those prattlings are not refuted. No lion will roar on hearing the bark of the village dog.

4. *Fitness of qualityiessness of Brahman*

Brahman is qualityless because *śruti* deals with the qualitylessness of *Brahman*.[12]

Objection: How can it be said that *Brahman* is devoid of any quality? There are *śrutis*, *smṛtis* and inferences to establish the qualities of *Brahman*. *Śruti* says that great are his qualities!'[13] Similarly *smṛti* says that *Brahman* is full of the qualities of *Brahmā*, *Īśāna* and such other *devas*. Inference also is there: *Brahman* is having qualities because it is a substance.

Reply: *Śrutis* do not establish quality of *Brahman*. The *śruti* cited is that which belongs to the context of *upāsana* and therefore, it is to be taken only in praise and not in literal sense. The same is the case of *smṛtis* also. Inference also is not capable of establishing qualities in *Brahman*.

Vyāsatīrtha exhibits seven inferences so as to establish quality in *Brahman*. Madhusūdana points out fallacy in all of these inferences and discards them all.

Objection: The *śruti* 'he who knows *Brahman* as non-existing becomes himself non-existing'[14] clearly mentions non-existence in *Brahman.* If it is not a quality it results in voidness.

Reply: How can voidness be the supreme human goal? Moreover, it will contradict the concept of liberation in the form of achievement of supreme bliss.

Objection: Such *śrutis* as 'this is the eternal greatness of the *Brāhmaṇa*'[15] deal with the eternality of knowledge of *Brahman* whereby *Brahman* is said to be with quality.

Reply: Knowledge etc., in *Brahman* are the essential nature of *Brahman* and not qualities. All those other than the essential nature exist until the final realisation. And for the same reason eternality is imposed on them. Therefore, the *śruti* cited does not reveal eternality as a quality of *Brahman.*

The most important thing is that only by knowing *Brahman* without any quality one can attain liberation. All the *śrutis* become fully reconciled only when they are accepted as dealing with *Brahman* without quality whatsoever.

Objection: Since there are various kinds of *śrutis* there is possibility of contradiction among them. So as to solve such contradictions, Jaimini has made necessary provision. Different agencies have been employed.[16]

Reply: When there is contradiction between two *śrutis* or *śāstras* the same should be reconciled. Bādarāyaṇa also has made it clear.[17] However, it never goes against the principal theme of all *śrutis* being *Brahman.*

If the qualities of *Brahman* which have only practical reality are taken to be eternal, *śrutis* dealing with its absence of quality will go against them. In fact, *Brahman* is 'reality of the real'.[18]

Objection: The determinate knowledge of *Brahman* is that which causes liberation. *Śruti* says: 'In that vast *Brahma*-wheel, in which all things live and rest the bird flutters about, so long as he thinks that the self is different from the mover. When he has been blessed by him he gains immortality'.[19] *Śmṛti* also says: 'On knowing me, the lord of all sacrifices and austerities, the Great Lord of all worlds, the friend of all beings, he goes to peace'.[20] Therefore, it is clear that *Brahman* is the abode of qualities.

Reply: The sole means of liberation is the indeterminate knowledge of qualityless *Brahman.* Purification of mind and the like are useful in creating such knowledge. Any number of *śrutis* and *smṛtis* can be cited in this regard. The *śruti* and *smṛti* cited may be explained accordingly. All qualities that appear to be in *Brahman* are superimposed.

Now the opponent says that even for superimposition some qualities should be there in *Brahman* because in pure *Brahman* superimposition is not possible. To this Madhusūdana replies that there is no harm in superimposition on the qualityless *Brahman*. It is as a result of the relation of the beginningless ignorance in *Brahman*. Therefore, it is established that *Brahman* is qualityless.

5. *Evidence for the qualitylessness of Brahman*

Brahman is not only qualityless but also particularityless.

Objection: What is evidence for the particularitylessness of *Brahman*?

Reply: What use is expected of evidence? Is it for establishing *Brahman* itself or for eradicating ignorance? In the former case no evidence is necessary because *Brahman* is self-evident. In the latter case all *Upaniṣads* are evidence. And for the same reason there is no relevance for such questions as whether it is perception or inference?

Objection: How can *Upaniṣads* be evidence? Since there is no generality, quality, action and the sort the principal *vṛtti* cannot act in the case of the sentences of the *Upanisads*. Subordinate *vṛtti* also cannot be accepted without any principal one. It cannot be secondary implication also because it can proceed only if there is an express principal sense. In short, *Upaniṣads* are not evidence on *Brahman* either by means of words or by means of sentences. The lack of relation also is cause for the same.

Reply: It is true that the principal *vṛtti* or subordinate *vṛtti* is not possible. However, there is nothing that prevents secondary implication. There is no rule that only sentences which have relation are evidence. Vārtikakāra has established the fact that sentences can be evidence even without relation.[21]

In the case of secondary implication also the overapplicability is to be excluded by means of the non-grasping of the particular purport. Relation with the express sense is possible at many places. And the grasping of the particular purport depends on particular persons and not on all. The particularity of the person is purity of mind which amounts to lack of hindrance. Sin is hindrance. At the lapse of hindrance even without any relation *Atman* can be realised from *śruti*. Madhusūdana deals in detail with this in his *Gītāgūḍhārthadīpikā*.

Objection: Discussion on a *dharmin* is intended for some who have no certainty about it. Then, the knowledge originated from the discussion cannot be indeterminate.

Reply: Discussion should result in knowledge capable of eradicating doubt. It can originate from *dharmin* also. And for that, determinacy also can be applied. It cannot be said that then there will be prolixity because if evidence is there, prolixity cannot be considered as a defect.

Thus, since there is no probans for having quality in *Brahman* and since there is sublator for the same and also since there is no either in its qualitylessness *Brahman* is qualityless.

6. *Formlessness of Brahman*

Brahman is formless also. However, *dvaitins* cannot agree with this too.

Objection: *Śrutis, smṛtis* and inference establish formfulness of *Brahman*. 'I know that great person of sunlike lustre beyond the darkness.'[22] 'When the seer sees the lord of the world, *Brahman* in brilliant colour, then he is wise.'[23] These and the sort are *śrutis*. *Smṛtis* are 'O, son of Pṛthā, see my heavenly forms by hundreds and thousands' etc.,[24] 'With hands and feet everywhere, with eyes and heads and mouths everywhere, with hearing everywhere that exists enveloping all' etc.,[25] and others. Similarly inference is there. *Brahman* is formful since he is the creator, protector and preacher.

Reply: The *śruti* about the great person of sunlike lustre does not deal with the form of *Brahman*. It deals with the essential nature of self-luminousness which is different from ignorance. It can also be explained in tune with meditation. It cannot be said that since it is described as that which is beyond darkness it cannot be explained in tune with meditation because what is intended is that which is beyond the darkness which is *upalakṣaṇa* of the body of that which is to be meditated upon. Qualification by colour is not intended.

Objection: Since the *śruti* 'this is that golden person who is seen within the sun'[26] says about *Brahman* as existing and also subject to perceptible knowledge it cannot be said that form is imposed.

Reply: Meditation is of two kinds: symbolic and formful. In either case the meditator or the medium does not make formless *Brahman* otherwise. The other *śrutis* and *smṛtis* also have to be explained on the same lines. The inference presented has the fallacy of establishing the established. Bādarāyaṇa's aphorism 'if it be argued that *Brahman* cannot act on account of absence of organs, that was answered earlier'[27] makes it clear that the supreme and sublime *Brahman* is to be known from the *Vedas* alone and not from reasoning. It also establishes that eventhough all distinctions are denied in Brahman, there can have the accession of all powers owing to the presence of a variety of aspects conjured up by ignorance.

If *Brahman* has form there arise a number of questions. Is the form of *Brahman* mortal or immortal? If immortal whether it is *māyika* or not? If not *māyika* whether it is different from *Brahman* or not? Are the mortal and the *māyika* earned by own deeds or by others' deeds? If it is the first, *Brahman* will also be wordly. The second option is acceptable to us. If it is different from *Brahman* that will cause *apasiddhānta* to the opponent himself. It will contradict the *śruti* 'this is not, this is not'[28] too. The *śruti* 'grasping without hands, hasting withoot feet'[29] will also go against. If form which is immortal, not *māyika* and non-different from *Brahman* is accepted not only the *śrutis* will go against but also there will present the doctrine of *Cārvākas* and also lack of evidence. In fact, *Brahman* is formless and *jīva* is formful.

7. *Fitness of Brahman being consciousness etc.*

The topic begins with a couplet in praise of Lord Kṛṣṇa. Madhusūdana says that he does not know a reality other than Kṛṣṇa.

Objection: If *Brahman* is without any particularity or form it cannot be considered the only one in the form of consciousness, bliss, non-duality, eternality and supreme *sākṣin*. What is this consciousness? Is it a particular generality? Or is it the causality of direct activity? Or is it contrariness to materiality? Or is it difference from materiality? Or is it contrariness to ignorance? Or is it the ability to illuminate objects? Or is it that accepted by others? It cannot be the first because eventhough it is fit to the pseudo-cognition of reflection on the *vṛtti*, it will not be fit to the impartite knowledge of *Brahman*. It cannot be the second because it is not there in *suṣupti* and also in liberation. It cannot be the third because since self-knowledge is eternal the material contrary to, will never be released. It cannot be the fourth because it will go against the *śruti* 'reality, consciousness, endless' etc.[30] It cannot be the fifth because then ignorance will have eternal sublation. It cannot be the sixth because there is no feeling of other objects in liberation. It cannot be the seventh because *advaitins* do not accept generality, causality of activity etc., admitted by others.

Reply: Ability to illuminate objects can be taken as the definition of consciousness. Therefore, there is no harm in *Brahman* being consciousness. In the world state consciousness is along with its object. At the state of emancipation the same consciousness follows eventhough the objects are sublated.

Now Vyāsatīrtha puts the definition of bliss to test. Is bliss a particular generality? Or is it the state of being known favourably? Or is it favourable knowledge? Or is it simple favourableness? Or is it the form of knowledge? Or is it contrariness to pain? Or is it the essential nature indicated by the absence of pain? Or is it that held by others?

Reply: Bliss is enjoyment without any extraneous adjunct. Wordly enjoyment is not of that type. At the state of emancipation eventhough there is no longing for enjoyment, joy is there. Pure joy without any object is bliss of *Brahman*.

Then follows discussion on non-duality. Is non-duality that which is qualified by the absence of a second? Or is it that indicated by the same? To these questions of the opponent Madhusūdana answers in the affirmative. Therefore, there is no harm for the nonduality of *Brahman* too.

Now it is the discussion on eternality. Vyāsatīrtha holds that eternality also cannot be defined. What is this eternality accepted by *advaitins* in *Frahman*? Is it relation with all periods of time? Or is it the absence of time as qualification per proprium? Or is it not being the counter-correlate of destruction. Or is it the absence of initial and final point?

Reply: There is no harm in considering absence of initial and final points as the definition of eternality. Not being the counter-correlate of destruction also can be considered the definition of eternality. *Brahman* has no initial or final point and it is not the counter-correlate of destruction too. Therefore, *Brahman* is eternal.

Finally, it is the discussion on *sākṣitva*. The opponent objects to *Brahman* being the *sākṣin*.

Objection: *Sākṣitva* is there only in him who directly visualises the thing or whatever concerned.[31] *Brahman* does not directly visualise anything. *Brahman* is infact *dṛk* and not *draṣṭā*. Then how can there be *sākṣitva* in *Brahman*?

Reply: *Sākṣin* is consciousness reflected on ignorance or its objects. Therefore, *dṛk* can be *draṣṭā* also on account of extraneous adjunct. Now, it may be asked: To which category does *sākṣin* belong? Does it belong to the category of *jīva*? Or does it belong to the category of *Īśvara*? Or does it belong to both? Consciousness different from pure *Brahman* as well as *jīva*, having intellect as its extraneous adjunct is considered as *sākṣin*. In fact, it is consciousness reflected on the *vṛtti* of ignorance. In short, *Brahman* is consciousness, bliss, non-duality, eternality and *sākṣin*.

8. *Material causality of Brahman*

Objection: If *Brahman* is without any particularity how can that *Brahman* be the material and efficient cause of the world at the same time? Only a cause which is subject to change can be the material cause. *Brahman* is not subject to change. Otherwise *śrutis* dealing with the changelessness of *Brahman* will contradict.

Reply: Of course, *Brahman* is not the material cause of evolution, but it is the material cause of illusory modification. And to be the material cause of illusory modification means to be subject to ignorance which is the cause of illusory modification. It cannot be said that material cause has no definition because there is definition. The definition of material cause is to be the cause of creation of effect in itself. And this definition is applicable to material cause which is subject to change and which is not.

Objection: Is *Brahman* alone the material cause or is ignorance also there? In the former case, since the material cause is real the world also will have reality and therefore, it will contradict the assumption of ignorance as the material cause of the world. In the latter case there arise a number of further questions. Is the material causality of *Brahman* and ignorance equal as that of two yarns which make the rope? Is it then that the *śruti* dealing with the changelessness of *Brahman* pertains to pure *Brahman* alone? Or is *Brahman* along with the power of ignorance the material cause? Is it then that the *śruti* dealing with the changelessness of *Brahman* pertains to *Brahman* excluding ignorance? Or is *Brahman* the material cause through ignorance? Is it then that the *śruti* dealing with the changelessness of *Brahman* pertains to negation of change without any intermediary?

Reply: Material causality is accepted without deeming the change of both. Ignorance is the material cause of the world. That material cause has evolution. Even in the presence of ignorance *Brahman* does not evolve, but only modifies itself illusorily. Even if the world is evolute of the material cause ignorance, it will not be real because reality in the sense of having the same status as that of the material cause is what is intended in the evolute. And the evolute world has not the same status of reality as that of *Brahman* whereby evolution of *Brahman* is discarded. Since *Brahman* is not cause of the evolution into something having the same status of reality there is no harm for the changelessness of *Brahman* too.

Objection: The generality of smoke is not there in the real smoke and illusory one alike. Similarly, material causality cannot be there in the real *Brahman* and illusory ignorance alike.

Reply: As already said what is meant by material causality is being the cause of creation of effect in itself. Even when there is difference in particular aspects, we see generality in contrary objects. Therefore, there is no harm in material causality being in the real *Brahman* and illusory ignorance alike.

Objection: Why should ignorance be considered the material cause of the world? Material causality of *Brahman* is enough to explain the world of illusion and of practical reality.

Reply: We see that jar, ear-ring etc., evolve from mud, gold etc., respectively. There the material cause also undergoes change. Similarly material cause of ether etc., also has to be assumed as something which undergoes change. Ignorance is that material cause which evolves.

Objection: That which has change is the material cause. The change intended here is that which is common to illusory and real alike. Let *Brahman* be the material cause of illusory evolution. Evolving ignorance is not at all necessary.

Reply: Shell-silver born as an evolute of the ignorance existing in the sea-shell is illusory. Similarly, so as to consider ether etc., as illusory in *Brahman* also ignorance will have to be admitted as a rule. Since *Brahman* and ignorance are there, both are assigned material causality. *Brahman* is material and efficient cause of the world.

9. *Brahman's agency of the world*

Objection: Agency is the possession of an immediate knowledge of the material cause, a will to act and also action as these are found in the potter who is agent for the origin of the jar. This will not suit if the effect is illusory because we see that the agency of the potter is not of illusory jar. Moreover, we do not find agency in anyone as regards the illusory shell-silver etc.

Reply: In jar etc., which are the effects of the potter we do not grasp any absence of illusoriness. Having no agency of shell-silver etc., is not established too. In fact, in such cases *sākṣin* is the agent. We cannot do away with agency on the simple ground that the same is not seen. In that case, in your view also the omniscient will lose his agency.

By what has been said, the objections raised by Vyāsatīrtha against the meaning of substratum also have been refuted. Being substratum is not agency because then, since there is no material causality other than being substratum, the concept that agency and material causality have the same locus, will contradict. Being substratum is not being *draṣṭā* of superimposition also because then, one who has such *draṣṭṛtva* of superimposition has no agency of superimposition along with imagination to that effect. Creating fantacy like a magician also is not agency because without seeing *jīva*, to whom fantacy is to be created, there can be no creation of fantacy; if he is seen it will be superimposition and in that case, since creating fantacy is also superimposed, there will be mutual dependency. Moreover, the *śruti* 'let me assume name and form'[32] will become unfit. The magician does not create anything after imagining his creation, but simply shows after imagining to show. In all these cases, the view of *advaitin* that the *janmādisūtra*[33] deals with the creator of the world and that the *śāstrayonitvasūtra*[34] has been enjoined to express the omniscience of of that creator, will be refuted since the creator has no omniscience because of being the substratum of illusion. Action etc., connected with the material cause also cannot be admitted because it will not be fit in that which is imposed. Therefore, the agency of *Brahman* attributed by *advaitins* has no locus standi.

Madhusūdana refutes all these allegations of the opponent. Agency is the possession of an immediate knowledge of the material cause, a will to act and also action. There is no harm in the *draṣṭṛtva* of *jīva* being superimposed. Lack of experience of agency of the magician along with imagination cannot be established. There is also no harm for the *advaita* view that *śāstrayonitvasūtra* has been enjoined to express the omniscience of the creator indicated by the *janmādisūtra*. *Brahman* is the substratum for the ignorance which evolves into the form of the world. Thus *Brahman* is omniscient. Therefore, *Brahman's* agency of the world is established.

10. *Evidence for Brahman's non-different material and efficient causality of the world*

The *śruti* 'that from which these beings take birth'[35] etc., reveals

Brahman's material causality of the world. The means of proof of direct statement[36] is there in the *śruti* as evidence for the same. *Pāṇini* says that the prime cause of the agent of the verb *jan* meaning to be born, is called *apādāna*.[37] And the ablative case is used in the sense of *apādāna*.[38] In the *śruti* cited there is the use of ablative case which can be taken as direct statement which evidences for material causality. *Liṅga* also is evidence for the same.[89] The *śruti* 'that by which they exist and into which they enter at their destruction'[40] depicts *Brahman* as the substratum of existence and dissolution. And it is *liṅga* for the material causality of *Brahman*. Since the *śruti* 'it imagined, let me become many'[41] mentions *Brahman* as the locus of imagination etc., its agency also is established.

Objection: In the commentary on Panini's *sūtra*, it has been said that what is meant by the prime cause is only general causality and not material causality, since the ablative case is used in the sense of non-material cause as in 'pleasure is born from son.'[42] *Nyāsa* also vouchsafes the same.[43] Patañjali has opined that the *sūtra* prescribing *apādānatva* of the agent of *jan* itself is unnecessary since the same purpose is served by the *sūtra* defining *apādāna*.[44] Kaiyaṭa also has followed suit.[45] In short, the material cause need be considered as only the limit from which effect originates.

Reply: The general injunction that prescribes animal as the instrument of the sacrifice does not contradict the later injuction which prescribes the particular animal goat as instrument. Similarly, though the *śruti* 'that from which these beings take birth'[46] reveals general causality, it does not contradict in any way the *śruti* that reveals the particular material causality.

Objection: The *śruti*, 'he brooded over himself, after having brooded, he created all this-whatever is there, having created he entered into it, having entered he became *sat* and *tyat*'[47] reveals that becoming *sat* and *tyat* happens only after his creation of the world and his entrance into it. Therefore, becoming *sat* and *tyat* is not something that happens afterwards. The expression 'after having entered into it' can be explained like 'after having opened the mouth'. Thus *Brahman* is the material cause of the world.

Objection: The *śruti* 'he desired'[48] is not in the sense of illusory modification of *Brahman*. What is meant is the imagination of the supreme *Atman* to become in infinite forms.

Reply: In the *śruti* it is clearly said: 'I shall become' whereby it is established that it is the future existence in different forms and not mere imagination. It is just like the experience 'I shall enjoy'. Therefore, the *śruti* is evidence for *Brahman's* illusory modification in the form of the world. Other *śrutis* like 'it imagined, let me become many'[49] etc., also are evidence for the same.

Inference also is evidence for the material causality of *Brahman*. *Brahman* is the material cause of the world because it is *sat* in essence and also the effect of *sat*.

The opponent puts forward other inferences as to discard *Brahman's* material causality of the world. *Brahman* is not the material cause of substance since it is consciousness like Caitra. The world has not bliss as its material cause since that nature does not follow in the world; that the nature of which does not follow in one thing cannot be the material cause of it just like jar which is not the material cause of cloth since the nature of jar does not follow in cloth.

Madhusūdana replies that the inferences put forward by the opponent are not competent to contradict that which establishes the material causality of *Brahman*. In fact there is much stronger inference for the causality of *Brahman*. The world has *Brahman* as its material and efficient cause at the same time since the world is an effect born out of some one's imagination like pleasure, pain etc. Therefore, it is established beyond doubt that *Brahman* is the material as well as the efficient cause of the world.

11. *Fitness of the definition of Brahman's self-luminousness*

Objection: The material causality of *Brahman* has to be said to be due to its being the substratum for the ignorance which evolves in the form of the world. Something that is not capable of being known cannot be the substratum. If for the knowledge of *Brahman vṛtti* of mind is accepted there will be mutual dependency. It may be said that *Brahman* is self-luminous and that being substratum is the resultant one. Then arises the question: what is this self-luminousness?

The opponent himself puts forward five possible definitions of self-luminousness and discards them all. Madhusūdana replies that the fifth definition is valid.

Reply: Self-luminousness is not being the locus of absolute negation of the capability of being subjected to empirical usage as perceptible and incognisability at the same time. This definition fits in *Brahman* very well. At the stage of emancipation also there is no defect of partial application of this definition because not being the locus is the essential nature which is there in emancipation.

Objection: The said capability of being subject to empirical usage as perceptible qualified by incognisability also is illusory according to *advaitins*. Therefore, the absolute negation of the same also has to be considered so. *Brahman* is the locus of absolute negation of such capability.

Reply: What is meant is absolute negation and said capability in contra-position. An object which exists on a particular locus cannot be contradictory to the same locus. Therefore, there is no harm in *Brahman* not being the locus of the said capability.

Objection: The said definition of self-luminousness has overapplicability in such practically real objects as jar etc., which are known by *vṛtti* and also in such apparent objects as shell-silver etc., which are capable of being perceived directly.

Reply: Jar etc., are subject to the consiousness qualified per proprium by them. Shell-silver etc., are directly perceived by *sākṣin* since they are not subject to *vṛtti* of the mind. Therefore, there is no over-applicability of the definition as alleged by the opponent. It cannot be said that the definition has over applicability in negation because what is intended is practice governed by *vṛtti* of mind and the same is not there in the case of negation.

Objection: The capability of being subjected to empirical usage is not with regard to all, because Maitra has no empirical usage with the knowledge Caitra has. It is also not with regard to cognition because it is not subject to practical usage. It is also not with regard to the locus of cognition because cognition is not the locus of consciousness in your view.

Reply: The capability of being subjected to empirical usage is with regard to any cogniser. And the cogniser well-known is *ahamartha*. Now, let us take what is said about Maitra's lack of empirical usage with the knowledge Caitra has. What do you mean by this? Is it that Maitra has no empirical usage having the knowledge Caitra has, as its efficient cause? Or is it that Maitra has no empirical usage having the knowledge Caitra has, as its subject? In the first case, eventhough, Maitra has no empirical usage with the knowledge Caitra has, he can have direct perceptible empirical usage of *Brahman* and jar with his own knowledge. In the second case there is no harm even if there is no such empirical usage. In fact, *vṛtti* is not self-luminous. As far as Maitra is concerned, it is true that there is no such direct empirical usage having the knowledge Caitra has, as its subject. In our view consciousness only is self-luminous and not consciousness qualified per accidens by *vṛtti* which is called knowledge of Caitra.

Objection: Whether self-luminousness of *Brahman* is real or false? If it is real *Advaita* will be in danger. If it is false it will have to be said that *Brahman* is not self-luminous. And that will invalidate the inference which is put forward for establishing the self-luminousness of *Brahman*.

Reply: As already said self-luminousness is the essential nature of *Brahman*. This will not be acceptable to *dvaitins* who do not admit an essential nature which is against being known.

12. *Self-luminousness of realisation*

It cannot be said that there is no evidence for the self-luminousness of *Brahman*. Negative inference is there as evidence for the same. Realisation of *Brahman* is self-luminous since it is a realisation unlike other realisations.

Objection: In the inference there is fallacy of non-establishment of probandum. It may be said that the inference, the capability of being known is the counter-correlate of absolute negation, existing in something since it is a property, generally establishes the capability of being known. However, it is not enough, for, though the inference establishes the capability of not being known, the probandum qualified by the same is not established.

Reply: There is no defect in the inference that establishes self-luminousness in the form of the essential nature of the subject based on realisation. In it the capability of being known is being the subject of consciousness itself. The subject is that which exists only in that which is other than consciousness. The probandum is being the essential nature of the counter-correlate of absolute negation. The state of being subject to consciousness reflected on *vṛtti* is only in jar etc., and not in *Brahman*. There is no inconstancy in being the counter-correlate of absolute negation being the counter-correlate of absolute negation because being the counter-correlate of absolute negation is false and therefore, being the counter-correlate of absolute negation can be there only in the counter-correlate of absolute negation.

Objection: Thus it comes that even if *Brahman* is subject to consciousness there is absolute negation of being the subject of consciousness on it whereby there presents *arthāntara*. Moreover, the said probandum is there in jar etc., whereby there presents the defect of the probans called *asādhāraṇa anaikāntikatva*.

Reply: The probandum intended is in the form of being the counter-correlate of absolute negation which is contradictory to being the subject of consciousness. Therefore, there is no presence of *arthāntara* or *asādhāraṇatā*. They coexist in jar etc., and therefore, there is no contradiction, but in *Brahman* they do not coexist and therefore, there is contradiction. It cannot be said that there is non-establishment with regard to the portion of contradiction because there can be establishment based on the inference that the capability of being known is the counter-correlate of absolute negation which is contradictory since it is counter-correlate of absolute negation like jar. If in the former inference self-luminousness, in the form of incapability of being known and capability of direct practical usage at the same time, is the probandum, then capability of being known in the form of concomitance with the result is the subject and being the counter-correlate of absolute negation existing in something which is capable of direct practical usage is the probandum. Thus, since incapability of being known existing in the very same locus of capability of being subject to practical usage is generally established, there is no presence of non-established qualification or *asādhāraṇatā*.

Objection: The inference put forward for establishing the incapability is having a counter inference: This is not the locus of being different from not being the locus of capability of being known and being different from this jar at the same time since it is an object.

Reply: The inference put forward for establishing incapability is more powerful than the just cited inference because the former has the support of favourable reasonings of the *śrutis* too.

It cannot also be said that there is non-establishment because the generality of realisation can be there in pure *Brahman* also based on imposed difference of individuals. There is no rule that generality should be dependent on the individuals having the same status of reality as that of the qualified because then there will be prolixity. In short, it is established that realisation is self-luminous.

13. *Fitness of self-luminousness of Ātman*

Ātman is not distinct from consciousness. Self-luminousness of *Ātman* should be established on the strength of its being consciousness. Consciousness of *Ātman* cannot be discarded. It was stated earlier and will be done further too. The inference is as follows: *Ātman* is self-luminous since it is consciousness.

Objection: The *śruti* 'there is no other cogniser but he'[50] etc., deals with *Ātman* as the cogniser. Then how can *Ātman* be consciousness?

Reply: The *śruti* cited deals with *Ātman* as the substratum for cognition in the form of *vṛtti.* If it is not taken in that sense a number of other *śrutis* will contradict. Vidyāsāgara has coined inferences like the following: 'The knowledge under dispute pertains to different subjects because it is a knowledge like other knowledge.'[51] This he has done in imitation of *naiyāyikas* and others. In our view there is no generality of knowledge in the self-luminous *Ātman.* Vidyāsāgara's inference 'the knowledge under dispute is not having its locus as its subject since it is a quality like the hotness of fire' also is on similar lines because there is no quality, in our view, in knowledge.

Objection: Eventhough *Ātman* is consciousness you do not deny it the subjecthood and locushood of ignorance. Similarly, let it be the same for knowledge also. Otherwise there will be non-efficiency.

Reply: There is no non-efficiency because favourable counter-argument is there. If *Ātman* is knowable, then, it will be subject to doubt and misconception at the state of ignorance. *Ātman* is not subject to doubt because, no one doubts 'whether I am or I am not'. *Ātman* is not subject to misconception also because no one has the knowledge 'I am some one else'. In fact, if *Ātman* is not self-luminous there will be sublation.

Objection: It is right that no one has doubt or misconception regarding the meaning of 'I'. But that is not *Ātman* in your view. In your view, it is only from *śrutis* that *Ātman* is known. And there can be doubt and misconception regarding that *Ātman.*

Reply: In our view *Ātman* is beyond doubt. *Ahamartha* is in the form of a knot of conscious and unconscious. In that, regarding the portion of unconscious qualified per proprium by *ahaṁtva* there can be doubt.

Śrutis like 'there the person is self-luminous'[52] are evidences for the self-luminousness of *Ātman.* There, the question is regarding the light of man. 'When the sun has set, O Yājñavalkya, and the moon has set and the fire has gone out and the sound hushed, what is the light of man?'[53] And in answer to this question the self-luminousness of *Ātman* has been dealt with. 'The self indeed is his light, for, having the self alone as his light, man sits, moves about, does his work and returns'.[54]

Objection: The *śruti* 'sound indeed is his light'[55] makes it clear that the word light has been used in the sense of articulate sound which is capable of producing knowledge. Therefore, in the *śruti* which you cited also, the word light should be in the sense of the means of knowledge and not in the sense of knowledge.

Reply: The word light is used by convention in the sense of worldly light. The same word has been used in the case of articulate sound as the means of knowledge. Like that it can be used in the sense of that which is contrary to ignorance like its contrariness to darkness.

Vivaraṇakāra has coined five inferences on the self-luminousness of *Ātman*. *Ātman* is self-luminous because it has no difference in its existence from light like the knowledge of light. *Ātman* is self-luminous because it illuminates objects like light. *Ātman* is self-luminous because it is the locus of the illumination of object like light. *Ātman's* light is unborn because light is the property of *Ātman* like sun who has also light as his property. *Ātman* is self-luminous because it is not subject to organs and at the same time is perceptible like knowledge.[56]

Vyāsatīrtha alleges a number of deficiencies in these inferences, but all of them are ably refuted by Madhusūdana. Madhusūdana says that self-luminousness is not in the form of being subject to itself. Self-luminousness is not being capable of being known and being capable of practical usage at the same time. This self-luminousness is there in *Ātman*.

14. *Fitness of Brahman not being the express sense of words*

Brahman has no property and is not capable of being known too. For the same reason *Brahman* is the sense of secondary implication of words like bliss and not their express sense. There is no ground to consider *Brahmrn* as their express sense.

Objection: Take the word *avācya*. If *Brahman* is expressed by the word *avācya* it has to be considered the express sense of that word. How can there be secondary implication without the principal sense in the form of express sense? If there is the express sense it cannot be said that *Brahman* is not the express sense. In fact, it is the express sense like the shore. If it is said that even without the principal sense the word *avācya* can imply secondarily *Brahman* it also has to be said that the word jar secondarily implies jar.

Reply: The word *avācya* has not a principal sense. However, the word *vācya* pronounced along with the negative prefix a denotes the absolute negation of *vācyatva* whereby it ends in secondarily implying *Brahman*. The word *nirviśeṣa* also is like this. It is only in the case of the secondary implication of impartite words that there arises the necessity of principal sense invariably.

Objection: If *Brahman* is said to be *lakṣya* then it becomes the express sense of that word. And thus *Brahman* is not the sense of secondary implication.

Reply: It is so. In fact *Brahman* has no property at all. Therefore, it is apt to say that it is not the subject of secondary implication also.

Objection: If *Brahman* is not subject to secondary implication it will have to be said that it is the express sense.

Reply: Secondarily, express sense also can be admitted. Words like *satya*, *jñāna* etc., which expressly denote imposed properties, secondarily imply the individual in the form of *Brahman* and therefore, there is no harm for their impartite sense.

Objection: If *Brahman* is not the secondarily implied sense being the locus of properties like existence etc., it will happen to be non-existent like a person who is not palanquin though he has relation with palanquin and is the implied sense of it.

Reply: In the superimposed generality of moon there is absence of not being moon because it has identity with the real individual moon. Similarly, in the case of *Brahman* also it will not happen to be non-existent.

In fact, *Brahman* is not the meaning of word though it is secondarily implied by word. It is impartite too though it is the sense of sentences. In the *anvitābhiddhānavāda* secondary implication is accepted, in the case of words which served their purpose of express sense also, so as to denote their essential meaning. It cannot be said that then *avācyatva* will be lost because there is nothing which prevents *avācyatva* which has been sought as the means of realisation of impartite *Brahman*. *Śrutis* like 'he who knows the bliss of that *Brahman*, from which all speech, along with the mind turns away'[57] and 'he who has perceived that which is without sound, without touch'[58] etc., also can be cited in this regard. As in the case of the word *avācya* there is no defect in the case of the word *aśabda* also.

Objection: Why should the principal sense be discarded in the case of a number of words like bliss etc.? Let there be secondary implication in the case of the single word *nivartante* because that will do.

Reply: *Brahman* has no property. Therefore, there in no potency in it and for the same reason the plurality of words is non-efficient in its case. It is through the sense contrary to that which is express that the impartite sense is intended. Therefore, whether it be in the case of a number of words or in the case of a single word the contrariness to *vācyatva* is there unaltered.

Objection: If *Brahman* is not express it cannot be implied too. Implied sense is that which is related to express sense. And the knowledge of *Brahman* cannot be from something other than words because it is known only from the *Upaniṣads*. It cannot be said that it is self illuminated because then since the same is eternal, words will be futile. The secondary implication of the word *avācya* itself needs express sense and thereby presents an infinite regress.

Reply: Konwledge is useful in presenting the object. Since *Brahman* is self-luminous it is already present by itself and therefore, there is no need of knowledge for its presence. It cannot be said that then words will be futile because they have use in creating mental state which does away with the veil of ignorance. And for the same reason there is no presence of infinite regress too.

Brahman is *avācya* and *nirviśeṣa*. Since *Brahman* is *nirviśeṣa* there is no difference between *Brahman* and *jīva*; there is nothing that differentiates. One who considers such *Brahman* as *vācya* has no shyness to do anything at all.

15. *Refutation in general of difference in Brahman*

Objection: It is not proper to deny difference in *Brahman* because difference in it is established by evidence. If it is said that difference is non-established, there arise a number of questions. Is it that there is no cognition of difference at all? Or is it that difference is not born of any cause? Or is it that the subject of difference is subject to sublation? In the first case all the differences in knowledge will have to be denied. In the second case since difference not born of any cause is eternal no one will aspire for liberation in the form of refutation of difference. It cannot be the third also because there is no reliable argument for the same.

Reply: We do not deny the essential form or cause of the cognition of difference. What we say is that the cognition of difference has a subject which is subject to sublation. Difference is sublated by *śruti*, *smṛti* and reasoning. It cannot be said that non-difference also is thus subject to sublation because both sublation of difference and non-difference operate in different fields. *Śrutis*, *smṛtis* and reasonings that refute difference do so with reference to the absolute reality of it. The practical reality of difference is not refuted. It cannot be said that if difference of *Brahman* from the false world is absolutely refuted *Brahman* will become false because we do not see the jar becoming superimposed when its difference from a superimposed jar is denied.

It cannot be said that non-difference also can be thus absolutely refuted because in that case it will end in nihilism. Moreover, even when we deny difference we do not accept any unity other than *Brahman*. Otherwise *śrutis* will contradict.

Objection: In our view also there is no difference other than jar because when it is denied it will contradict perception.

Reply: Perception is not capable of revealing absolute reality. Therefore, perception need not contradict the refutation of the absolute reality of difference.

Objection: The evidence which sublates difference cannot subject difference because then it will establish difference instead of sublating it. It cannot subject non-difference also. Thus the knowledge which sublates difference subjects the meaning of the negative particle which is different from it and is either contradictory to it or is its negation. And in all cases difference is inevitable. If the meaning of the negative particle is not different from difference it cannot be either contradictory to or be the negation of, difference.

Reply: The knowledge which subjects the negation of difference absolutely is that which sublates difference. There is no inevitability of difference because practical difference itself explains its practical contradiction as well as its absence. It is only proper to hold that the knowledge of the substratum of superimposed difference sublates the superimposed difference.

Objection: The knowledge, 'there is no difference here' does not discard all difference.

Reply: If there is difference elsewhere, difference from it is necessary here and therefore, the knowledge 'there is no difference here' discards difference at all places.

Objection: It has to be said that the difference of *Brahman* from false etc., is not sublated by the knowledge of *Brahman* because the difference from voidness of jar etc., which are not void, is not sublated by the knowledge of jar.

Reply: *Brahman* and jar are different since the former is the substratum and the latter is superimposed. Since the false is superimposed, difference from it also should be similar.

Objection: If the difference of the false world also is false difference from superimposed shell-silver also has to be considered superimposed. Then there will be no separation of superimposed knowledge and the knowledge which sublates it.

Reply: The superimposed and its sublation can be differentiated by the means of not being born from the sight of the particular and being born from that respectively. And therefore, there is no harm for being superimposed.

In fact, it is ignorance that illustrates everything that is different, in the eternal non-different *Brahman*. There is no point in alleging any impropriety in ignorance because it has been introduced in *Advaita* so as to explain away all improprieties. Thus difference is subject to sublation and non-difference not. And it is generally established that there is no difference in *Brahman*. Our dislike for difference is not unfounded because *śrutis*, *smṛtis* and reason discard it and establish non-difference.

16. *Refutation in particular of difference in Brahman*

Objection: Your concept is that *Brahman* is independent in all respects; but it is not suitable. Eradication of ignorance and identity of *jīva* and *Brahman* are non-different from *Brahman* in your view. Both of them are not independent. Dependence of *Brahman* can well be established. It is said that '*Brahman* exists'. Here existence is dependent on time whereby it results that *Brahman* is dependent.

Reply: We do not deny the apparent dependence of eradication of ignorance and identity of *jīva* and *Brahman*. However, this illusory dependence cannot contradict the actual independence of *Brahman*. In such cases as '*Brahman* exists' the dependence of existence on time is not eternal.

Objection: If identity is independent, *śrutis* dealing with the meaning of 'that' and 'thou' such as 'reality, consciousness'[59] etc., and 'he who is full of knowledge'[60] etc., will not fit in as one sentence and will not go hand in hand with those revealing identity of *Brahman* and *jīva*.

Reply: Identity is not different from the self-luminous *Brahman* and there is no dependence in its existence or knowledge. However, in the case of the production of mental state necessary for the eradication of the illusory difference between the meanings of 'that' and 'thou' dependence of objects is there and therefore, those *śrutis* will fit in as one sentence and will go hand in hand with those revealing identity. Since there is dependence on the counter-correlate in the form of difference, it is accepted that there is practical usage accordingly.

Objection: In such cases as 'jar is not cloth' the difference which is the meaning of the negative particle is that which negates identity. That is the contradiction there.

Reply: If identity is the essential characteristic of the substratum itself, there is no dependence of difference on identity. If identity is non-different from the substratum dependence of difference is there and therefore, there is no need of further dependence.

Objection: What is meant by the difference of jar from cloth? Is it jar's unfitness of being identical with cloth? Or is it not being the subject of the cognition of their identity? Or is it contradiction to the superimposition of identity? Or is it not being the locus of any property existing in what is not the locus of any of the properties existing in itself? Of is it being the locus of some property which does not exist in the locus of some property which does not exist in itself?

Reply: All these options are irrelevant because the essential nature of object can never be dependent on anything else. If it is something different there will be an infinite regress. Moreover, it will result in the identity of absolute negation and mutual negation. If difference is the essential nature of jar its counter-correlate, cloth, also will have to be considered as the essential nature of jar. In fact, jar is not in the only form of difference; but it is in the form of difference having cloth as its counter-correlate.

Objection: The counter-correlate can never be the correlate. The counter-correlate of difference fits in the essential nature subsidiarily. Otherwise, in the eradication of pain being *puruṣārtha*, pain also will become *puruṣārtha* because there, eradication of pain and pain are the same as per what is said earlier. Similarly, if difference from the false and eradication of ignorance are not different from *Brahman*, falsity and ignorance also will have to be considered not different from *Brahman*. In the same way if eradication of ignorance is not different from liberation itself, ignorance also will have to be considered liberation itself.

Reply: The arguments have no base at all. *Advaitins* do not consider difference from counter-correlate as the essential nature of the correlate. Difference from cloth is not the essential nature of jar. Thus, pain will never be *puruṣārtha*, ignorance will never be *Brahman* too, eventhough eradication of ignorance is liberation and liberation is *Brahman* itself.

Objection: There is evidence for difference being the essential nature of objects. There is knowledge that jar is not in the form of cloth just like the knowledge that jar is mud.

Reply: The knowledge 'jar is not cloth' subjects mutual negation and not difference and non-difference. Otherwise, knowledge like 'jar is blue' will have to be considered that subjecting non-difference of colour. Therefore, difference is not the essential nature of objects.

Objection: Difference will not exist in either the different or the non-different; but will exist in the object capable of being its substratum. The capability is to be inferred from the cognition of difference.

Reply: Without difference capability cannot be said so. And in the non-different, there will never be capability of difference. Therefore, difference exists in the different itself. There is no difference in *Brahman* which is non-different.

17. *Refutation of the particular*

Objection: In our view difference is not the essential nature of objects; but is mutual negation. And that mutual negation is non-different from particular objects. Therefore, there is no presence of infinite regress etc., as alleged. Since there is the particular as representative of difference, there is no synonymity etc. And the particular remains in non-different objects too.

Reply: If a particular which is different from the essestial nature and which can create real cognition of synonymity etc., is admitted that itself being different, difference cannot be said to be difference of property. And the difference of the particular also has to be considered non-different from that which has the particular. Then the presence of infinite regress is inevitable.

Objection: Presumption is evidence for the particular. *Śrutis* like '*Brahman* is knowledge and bliss'[61] do not deal with difference or difference and non-difference jointly as their impartite sense because then other *śrutis* like 'it is to be known in one way only'[62] will contradict. Therefore, the meaning of non-synonymity etc., of the particular which is representative of difference has to be necessarily accepted on the evidence of presumption.

Reply: If difference is accepted the *śruti* dealing with non-difference will contradict. The same trouble is there in the acceptance of the particular also. Non-synonymity has relevance since there is difference in the express sense though there is no difference in the implied sense. Let there be non-synonymity caused by knowledge, bliss etc., in your view also; why should we accept the particular?

Objection: It cannot be so because the *śruti*, 'as rain-water that has fallen on a mountain-ridge runs down the rocks on all sides, thus does he, who sees a difference between qualities, run after them on all sides,'[63] discards all differences even in qualities. Therefore, there cannot be difference between knowledge and bliss also.

Reply: In that case the particulars also will have the same thing applicable because they are also qualities dependent on some locus. Therefore, the *śruti* forbidding difference of qualities cannot be posed as evidence against the non-synonymity of knowledge, bliss etc.

Objection: Knowledge and bliss cannot exist in one and the same locus because the locus of knowledge which is in the form of illumination of objects should also be in the form of illumination of objects and the locus of bliss which is in the form of being subject to aspiration without any extraneous adjunct should be in the form of aspiration without any extraneous adjunct.

Reply: Knowledge, bliss etc., are considered as generality and not as anything alleged by you. Therefore, there is no harm in their having one and the same locus.

In fact, qualities are not eternal. Therefore, we need not worry about the plurality of them. The *śruti*[64] only restates this fact and the same is in order to be discarded.

Objection: If quality and that having the same are non-different the particular has to be admitted so as to explain the non-cognition of whiteness etc., at the time of cognition of jar etc. If they are different and non-different at the same time the particular should be admitted to explain the same. If they are entirely different the particular should be admitted so as to explain the unsublatedness of such practical usages as 'inherence is a relation', 'generality is existent' 'that which is finally particular is different from everything', 'time is there always' and 'space is everywhere'. If the particular is not admitted the existence of negation also cannot be explained.

Reply: The said problems can be there even after the particular is admitted. In fact, everything has to be explained in accordance with the particular nature of everything.

Objection: Thus it results that you also admit the particular.

Reply: No; what is meant by the particular nature is nothihg different from everything, but everything itself. Inherence and the sort also have particular nature of themselves not different from themselves.

Madhusūdana concludes the discussion on the particular with a scornful verse which hits at the *dvaitins* who still argue for admitting the particular. Madhusūdana says: O my friend, *dvaitin*, the particular has no evidence. However, you need not worry because our ignorance will explain everything.

18. *Refutation of the validity of perception on the five differences*

Thus difference evidenced by perception itself has been refuted. Then what is the state of the difference between *Īśa* and *jiva* which is not subject to perception? *Īśvara* is not subject to perception. Then how can we cognise difference having him as subject or counter-correlate?

Objection: Perception of difference having the qualified *Īśvara* as its subject may not be possible for *jīva*. However, *jīva* can have perception of difference having himself qualified as the subject of it because we have such experiences as 'I am not omniscient' and 'I am not without pain'. It cannot be said that having suitable counter-correlate is necessary for the perception of negation because even-though it is the case with relative negation on the evidence of such perception as 'the pillar is not devil', in the case of mutual negation suitability of the locus is necessary. In fact, in the case of relative negation also it is not right because if so, it will have to be admitted that there is the negation of suitable earth in the atoms of water. Therefore, it is better to admit that if the existence of something is contrary to perception of something anywhere, there the negation of that is perceptible and that thus the suitability of negation everywhere is governed by the locus. The same is present in the case of difference of *Īśvara* perceived by *jiva*. Otherwise, *śrutis* dealing with non-difference will have to be considered as those negating irrelevant difference. *Śrutis* dealing with difference will not be dealing with re-statement of difference perceived, unlike held by *advaitins*. In the case of perception of difference having *Īśvara* as the qualified, there is evidence inferred from such words of the Lord himself as 'O Arjuna, all these I know, but you do not'[65] and 'distinct is the highest spirit spoken of as the supreme self'.[66]

Reply: The said experiences subject only consciousness limited by the mind. They therefore, govern difference having the consciousness not qualified per proprium by the mind as its counter-correlate and not difference having pure consciousness as the qualified and painlessness etc., as the counter-correlate. *Śrutis* also restate difference qualified per proprium by the consciousness of mind. *Śrutis* dealing with non-difference negate difference made relevant by inference etc.

Objection: 'I, who slept and who has ignorance, the world etc., am not painless'. This experience evidences that there is no difference between the consciousness qualified per proprium by the mind and that dependent on ignorance etc., in *suṣupti*. The difference in question is not with regard to pure consciousness and consciousness qualified per proprium by mind but with regard to the locus of the world and that which is not.

Reply: It is clear from this that difference is only there in consciousness qualified per proprium by ignorance and not in the pure. It is not correct to say that there is being not qualified per proprium by ignorance in *suṣupti* though there is being not qualified per proprium by mind because ignorance is there in *suṣupti* also. The facts that there is difference between consciousness and consciousness, is acceptable to us. We consider non-difference in consciousness by nature which you do not admit. You also admit that the consciousness of Caitra, Maitra etc., are not identical. And the consciousness qualified per proproium by mind is not pure consciousness.

Objection: Maitra who knows Caitra without any doubt perceives the difference clearly as 'I am not Caitra'. Similarly, he perccives that 'Jar is not *Brahman*', 'jar is not cloth', 'I am not jar' and 'I am not *Brahman*'. All these five perceptions reveal difference.

Reply: Perceptions like 'I am not Caitra', deal with difference qualified per proprium. Perceptions like 'jar is not *Brahman*', 'jar is not cloth', 'I am not jar' and 'I am not *Brahman*' deal with difference which is superimposed. Therefore, absolutely real difference cannot be established on the evidence of the said five perceptions of diffrence.

19. *Refutation of inference on the difference between jīva and Brahman*

Dvaitins put forward inference as evidence for the difference between *jīva* and *Brahman*. Madhusūdana discards the same too. Vyāsatirtha coins seven inferences to prove the difference between *jīva* and *Brahman*. Madhusūdana examines and rejects all of them.

1. *Jīva* and *Īśvara* are different because they are loci for contradictory properties, like fire and ice. Here, the probans is unestablished because absolute difference is not known anywhere. Locus for pain etc., is the mind only. Moreover, to be locus for contradictory properties is not evidence for the difference in locus because we see that one and the same locus is having contradictory properties according to different qualifications per proprium. If it is said that the inference establishes difference in general, then the fallacy of esta-

blishing the established will be present. If the difference intended is absolute one then the example will lack probandum. Therefore, this inference is not valid.

2. *Brahman* is different from *jīva* absolutely because it is omniscient unlike *jīva*. Here, there is fallacy of having a non-established qualification. Moreover, if it is said that *Brahman* has difference having equal status of reality as that of itself there will be the fallacy of *asādhāraṇatā*.

3. *Ātmatva* exists in different individuals because it is a generality like earthness. As far as *advaitins* who do not admit different *Ā*tmans are concerned this inference has a non-established probans. If it is said that the difference is superimposed, then there is the trouble of establishing what is already established.

4. Pain, being a subsidiary generality of quality, depends on equal generality and therefore, is dependent on different loci because it is a quality like colour. This inference has inconstancy in sound. Moreover, there is establishment of what is already established since pain etc., are properties of the mind.

5. The bodies under dispute have an equal number of *Ātmans* also because they are bodies like the established bodies. This inference has inconstancy in the body of *Yogin*.

6. *Ātman* has difference having *Ātman* which has the same status of reality as that of the qualified, as its counter-correlate because it is a substance like jar. This inference also is invalid since its probans is non-established. Moreover, a pseudo-inference of the same kind can be coined in the case of Caitra whereby this inference will go invalid.

7. *Ātmans*, depending on the generality which is pervaded with substancehood, are different because they are loci of particular qualities which are not subject to hearing, like jar. This inference also has the same defects as the inference dealt with immediately before, has.

The inferences coined by later *ācāryas* also can be invalidated in the same manner. *Īśvara* has absolute difference having *jīva* as its counter-correlate because he is omnipotent, omniscient, omnific and independent unlike *jīva*. *Jīva* has absolute difference having *Brahman* as its counter-correlate because he is less potent, less knowing, less creative and dependent on the world unlike *Brahman*. In these and similar inferences there is sublation.

Objection: If all inferences are invalid, that establishing the unity of *jīva* and *Ātman* also will go invalid and then unity of *jīva* and *Ātman* held by *advaitins* cannot be established.

Reply: *Advaitins* do not object to what has been said. *Ādvaita* is established by *śrutis* and not by inference. Inference only discards the superimposition of reality on difference.

20. *Refutation of inference on difference among jīvas*

Inference cannot be put forward as valid evidence for difference among *jīvas* also.

Caitra has difference which will not be sublated by the knowledge of the propertied which has Maitra as its counter-correlate or Caitra does not have absolute non-difference having Maitra as its counter-correlate because he is not able to recognise the pains suffered by Maitra, because he does not recollect all that Maitra has recollected and because he does not experience all that Maitra has experienced, like jar. In the first option of the inference the probandum has the fallacy of establishing the established presented by the word propertied. In the second option of the inference the probandum has the same fallacy because absolute non-difference and unreal difference are the same. *Arthāntara*, non-establishment of proof etc., are also present in the inference.

The destruction of bondage under dispute exists in that which has difference which will not be sublated by the knowledge of the counter-correlate which has the locus having qualification per proprium by the essential characteristic of its own counter-correlate as its counter-correlate because it is the destruction of bondage like other established destruction of bondage. *Jīva* is worldly or the locus of the destruction of the world, *jīva* has difference having *jīva* who is not subject to sublation by its own knowledge as its counter-correlate or has difference which is not sublated by its own knowledge having worldly counter-correlate or has difference which has the locus of the destruction of the world which is not subject to sublation as its counter-correlate because he is a substance like jar. These and other similar inferences are not valid because they have defects such as *arthāntara* and *asaṁbhava*. Destruction exists in time etc., which have difference having bondage as its counter-correlate. Moreover, a generality of bondage is not possible.

Dvaitins put forward many other inferences for proving difference among *jīvas*. Madhusūdana discards all of them in the above mentioned manner.

21. *Refutation of favourable reasoning for difference among jīvas*

Objection: If the unity of *Ātman* is accepted, one Caitra will have to remember all pains experienced by all.

Reply: This need not happen because the lack of such experience can be explained by the difference created by extraneous adjuncts.

Objection: Difference created by extraneous adjuncts, is not enough to explain the lack of such experience because hands, feet etc., have such experience though there is difference created by extraneous adjuncts. It cannot be said that difference created by extraneous adjuncts existing in different bodies is the cause of such lack of experience because then it will have to be said that the child in the womb of the mother experiences its mother's pleasure etc.

Reply: We do not say that any extraneous adjunct can explain the lack of experience. Difference created by extraneous adjuncts in the form of mind or by ignorance is cause thereof. That difference is there in Caitra and Maitra and that is why there is lack of experiences of all.

Objection: If the consciousness existing in Caitra and others is one and the same, difference created by extraneous adjuncts in the form of mind will not be cause to it like the difference of organs.

Reply: As said earlier, difference created by mind is the cause of the lack of experience and not difference of external organs. The mind is indiscriminately superimposed on the consciousness.

Objection: Difference created by ignorance cannot be cause to the lack of experience because in one and the same person there can be a number of antecedent negations of knowledge and they are not cause to the lack of experience.

Reply: Difference of the extraneous adjuncts that differentiates *jīva* and non-difference of the same are causes respectively to lack of experience and experience. The extraneous adjunct that differentiates *jīva* is not antecedent negation or absence of knowledge which equals in number to knowledge, but ignorance which is destructed by the final mental state.

In fact, it is the mind which is the extraneous adjunct that creates difference of *jīvas*. All differences like the the bonded and the released are due to difference of mind.

Objection: Is this mind the extraneous adjunct of pure consciousness? Or is it so of consciousness which is qualified per accidens? In the first case there is the fallacy of *vyākhāta*. In the second case there is the defect of self-dependency. If the extraneous adjunct and qualification per accidens are separate there will be mutual dependency. If a third extraneous adjunct is accepted there will be circular dependency and if fourth, fifth etc., are admitted there will be infinite regress.

Reply: The extraneous adjunct makes the absolute qualified per accidens. Extraneous adjunct is not qualification and it does not need a different individual too. Therefore, there is no presence of self-dependency, mutual dependency, circular dependency or infinite regress.

In fact, there is no real difference among *jīvas*. This fact has been persistently substantiated by *Śaṅkara* in his works. Therefore, no reasoning can be favourably put forward for establishing difference of *jīvas*.

22. *Refutation of inference on the five differences*

There is no evidence for real difference between the material and *Īśvara* and also the material and *jīva*. *Dvaitins* however, hold the same. Vyāsatīrtha has coined inferences to that effect.

Brahman or *jīva* has difference which is not subject to sublation by knowledge of the propertied having *anātman* as its counter-correlate because they are substances like jar. *Brahman* or *jīva* has difference which is not subject to sublation by knowledge of the propertied having jar as its counter-correlate because they are connected with time which is not connected with jar or they are connected with place which is not connected with jar or they are not born from the creator of jar, like cloth. *Brahman* or *jīva* has difference which is not subject to sublation by knowledge of the propertied having the material as its counter-correlate because they are not material; whatever is like this is like this, like one of the two trees standing at a distance.

All the above mentioned inferences are defective. They are not capable of establishing their probandum. They have finiteness, materiality and origin as extraneous adjuncts respectively.

Objection: If jar and *Brahman* are one and the same, then *Brahman* will be established by the establishment of jar and the whole of *Vedānta* will be of no use. Moreover, *Brahman* will be material and non-eternal. It will also have to be said that *jīva* who has the same locus as that of bondage and release is destructed like the material. Knowledge like 'I am white' will have to be considered valid too.

Reply: *Brahman* is self-luminous and is subject of all knowledges. Therefore, there is no need of *Vedānta* there. However, Vedanta is useful in creating knowledge which is capable of eradicating ignorance. This has been persistently illustrated by us. In the jar etc., though there is no difference unassumed by other imposed individuals, there is no imposed individuality too. Similar is the case of phenomenality. Jar etc., will not be sublated by the simple sight of the particular. In them there is no knowledge of unity of them and other imposed individuals. Thus, here in the case of imposed materiality also there is no presence of it. Inference is not capable to prove difference between one material and another also. Difference between one *jīva* and another and also difference in general cannot be established by inference. Therefore, any of the five differences is not subject to inference. The five alleged differences are, as already dealt with, that between *Īśvara* and *jīva*, between *jīva* and *jīva*, between *Īśvara* and the material, between *jīva* and the material and between the material and the material.

23. *Śrutis on difference being restatements*

Objection: There are *śrutis* as evidence for difference being real. 'Two birds, inseparable friends, cling to the same tree',[67] 'he who dwells in the self',[68] 'there is one eternal among the non-eternal who is conscious among the conscious many'[69] and 'there is one unborn being who loves her and lies by her; there is another who leaves her, while she is eating what has to be eaten'[70] are the *śrutis*.

Reply: In the first *śruti* which begins with 'two birds' etc., difference is not the subject dealt with in the first half of the verse because difference is not the meaning of either word or sentence there. Duality invariably has the same locus as that of the difference which has its own locus, as its counter-correlate.

Objection: Duality dealt with in the *śruti* will not be suitable without difference. Therefore, the difference presented by the presumption of the *śruti* also will have to be considered *śrauta*.

Reply: Difference need not necessarily be real. As in the case of the cognition 'there are two moons', superimposed duality will do. Real difference is not expected in the *śruti*. Therefore, the second half of the *śruti* verse also does not ideal with real difference. In fact, in the *Paiṅgirahasyabrāhmaṇa* the duality of the *śruti* has been explained as that of mind and *jīva*. Thus, the *śruti* does not evidence difference between *Īśvara* and *jīva*.

In the *śruti* 'he who dwells in the self' the relation of locus and attribute can be explained taking difference to be only superimposed.

also. In the *śruti* 'there is one unborn being' also the difference dealt with can be considered to be superimposed. The *śrutis* do not end in absolute difference because in that case other *śrutis* will contradict. In fact, *śrutis* revealing difference are only restatements of difference perceived in the world. Therefore, they are comparatively weaker in validity than those dealing with non-difference.

Objection: The *śrutis* dealing with difference cannot be taken to be restatements in the same manner as 'no living being is to be killed'. Eventhough there can be killing qualified per proprium by Brahminhood, there can be no such killing qualified per proprium by all beings. Therefore, there is no doubt even of restatement in the case of such prohibitions as 'no living being is to be killed'.

Reply: Difference from *Īśvara* can be perceived in *jīva*. In the perception of difference capability of the correlate for the same is cause. In the difference where *Īśvara* is counter-correlate, *jīva* which is correlate is subject to perception. Therefore, difference where *Īśvara* is the propertied and *jivatva* is the qualification per proprium, is directly perceived. In the prohibition of killing there is no doubt of restatement because prohibition of killing of Brahmin and the same of all beings are different.

In fact, in the *śrutis* cited earlier there is no word which denotes difference eternally. They are, therefore, to be taken as restatements of difference experienced by us in the world.

Objection: *Brahman* known from *śrutis* alone cannot be perceived by other means. Therefore, difference having *Brahman* as its correlate or counter-correlate also cannot be perceived in the world. Then how can *śrutis* be restatements of difference experienced in the world?

Reply: In the perception of negation, only knowledge of the correlate and counter-correlate will do. That knowledge may be in the form of recollection too. Therefore, difference can be perceived. It is true that difference having *Īśvara* as the propertied is not perceived. However, it can be presumed from the difference of *Īśvara* which has the perceptual *jīva* as the propertied. It is like the scriptural nature of that which is established by scriptural presumption.

24. *Fitness of śrutis dealing with the difference of practical reality*

There is no harm even if *śrutis* dealing with difference are not considered as restatements because they can be explained as those dealing with difference of practical reality alone. It cannot be said that those *śrutis* will lose authority then, because they can be substantiated like eulogies. We have no objection in *śrutis* dealing with seeming reality, being invalid as a result of their contradiction with *śrutis* dealing with absolute reality. The difference that seems to us in the *śrutis* should necessarily contradict with non-difference which is the final purport of the *śrutis*.

Objection: If so, *śrutis* dealing with non-difference also will have to be considered to be invalid since they contradict perception. Being known by other means and contradiction are alike causes of invalidity.

Reply: In the case of contradiction, that which is contradicted also is a means; but in the case of *śrutis* which are restatements, such state of affairs is not there. Perception is subject to sublation. It cannot invalidate *śrutis* dealing with non-difference. Moreover, all the six principles which determine the purport of *śrutis* namely harmony of initial and concluding passages, repetition, novelty of what is taught, fruitfulness, eulogy in other passages, and consistency in reasoning show that *śrutis* dealing with non-difference are more valid.

Objection: All the six principles determining the purport can be exhibited in the case of difference also. 'One of them eats the sweet fruit', 'the other looks on without eating', 'one is perfect', 'the other is imperfect' etc., are reasonings. 'Difference is truth, difference is truth, difference is truth'. This is repeated in *śrutis* whereby it is clear that the principle of repetition also is there.

Reply: 'Eats', 'imperfect' etc., are concerned with *jīva* and not with difference. They denote *jīva's* perfect form of *Brahman*. 'Difference is truth' is not repetition of difference because this sentence is invalid. Even if it is taken as valid it will end in non-difference because its substratum is the very same as that of sublation.

Objection: *Śrutis* dealing with difference are more valid because they go in tune with perception and because they are first advanced and complete.

Reply: Since *śrutis* dealing with non-difference are there, those dealing with difference are already contrary. Being in tune with perception is not enough because perception itself is subject to sublation. Perception cannot invalidate any *śruti*. *Śrutis* dealing with difference are not complete because they deal only with practical reality and not absolute.

It cannot be said that difference has no practical reality but absolute because it is there even in liberation as evidenced by *śrutis* and *smṛtis*, for, that liberation cannot be taken to be absolute.

Objection: *Bhagavadgitā* says that they who having resorted to the knowledge of *Brahman* have attained unity with it, are neither born in the creation nor disturbed in the dissolution.[71] Here, creation and dissolution are negated. *Śruti* says: 'He who khows this supremely immortal *Brahman*, as existing in the heart, destroys here the knot of ignorance.'[72] Here, fruit of the knowledge of pure *Brahman* has been dealt with. *Ṣrutis* like 'for him there is freedom in all the worlds',[73] 'he becomes five, he becomes seven' etc., deal with difference clearly. *Sūtra* also says that the released soul gets all the divine powers except that of running the universe.[74] Another *sūtra* says that the fathers and others come as a result of the will alone because the *Upaniṣads* say so.[75] Still another *sūtra* says that from the indicatory mark in the *Upaniṣads* about the equality of experience alone, it is known that the liberated souls do not get unfettered powers.[76] Therefore, difference is real and it is there in absolute liberation too.

Reply: The evidences presented can be explained in the sense of non-difference. Difference is not at all relevant in the final liberation. All the *śtutis* can be interpreted accordingly. This does not mean that there are no *śrutis* dealing with difference. There are such *śrutis* and they all deal with difference of practical reality alone and not absolute.

25. *Refutation of difference in words etc., as evidence for difference in Ātman*

Objection: In the second chapter of Jaimini's *sūtras* six evidences for difference in deeds have been dealt with. They are difference in words, repetition, number, name, quality and difference in context.[77] The same evidences can be cited for establishing difference between *Īśvara* and *jīva* also.

In such sentences as 'this does acknowledge *jīva*' and 'from this originates *jīva*' there is express difference of words. 'The supreme is eternal, *jīva* is eternal' etc., present repetition. 'Two birds' etc., have number denoting difference. 'Not sound' and 'without eating' have quality that denotes difference. 'From where words reverse themselves' etc., are contexts revealing difference. Similarly, names such as *jīva* and *Īśa* clearly demarcate difference.

Reply: Of course, difference in words and the sort are evidences which reveal difference and they belong to the same category as that of perception. However, they are not competent to contradict absolute non-difference. You,*mīmāṁsakas* alone, consider evidences like difference in words etc., which are valid only in the case of deeds or texts, as applicable to *Ātman* also. It is quite unseen elsewhere. Evidence capable in one case need not necessarily be capable in other cases also. Otherwise, one qualification capable of establishing diffe-rence in the qualified will have to be accepted as that capable of establishing difference in the substrate also. In such sentences as 'Devadatta stands up', 'Devadatta teaches his pupil', 'Devadatta offers sacrifice', 'Devadatta gives', 'Devadatta places the sacrificial object to the fire' etc., Devadatta, though one and the same, will have to be taken as different. Really it is the same Devadatta who performs all the said deeds. Therefore, difference in words etc., can-not make any difference in the agent. *Ātman* is not different at all.

26. *Refutation of the six principles of purport in ihe śrutis dealing with difference*

Objection: *Śrutis* dealing with difference do so based on the six principles which determine the purport. How can, then, difference established by them, be invalid? Presence of the six principles can be exhibited. In the *Muṇḍaka* which belongs to *Atharvaveda* there are the beginning 'two birds'[78] and the conclusion 'he reaches the highest similarity'.[79] 'One of them',[80] 'one without eating'[81] and '*Īsa*, the other'[82] are repetitions. There is the principle of novelty also. Difference which has *Īśvara* who is known only from the *śāstra*, as its counter-correlate and which is not subject to sublation through all the three periods of time, cannot be known from other sources than the *śastra* itself. And it is the novelty. Fruitfulness is clearly mention-ed in the *śruti* as 'having shaken off good and evil'.[83] Eulogy, here, is in the form of praise. 'His glory'[84] etc., praise *Īśa*. 'One eats' and 'the other without eating' etc., are evidences for consistency of reasoning. In such sentences as 'all this duality is only an illusion',[85] the word denoting two has been used in the sense of difference. Therefore, the beginning is in favour of difference. The conclusion also is in favour of difference. Similarity means having difference from it and many of its properties at the same time and not simply to be the substrate. We experience that 'this is not himself, but is like him' and 'this is not like him, but is himself' Here, similarity and identity have been placed as being mutually exclusive. Thus, repeti-tion etc., are also present.

Reply: In the first *Muṇḍaka* we come across the question put by

Śaunaka to Aṅgiras: 'Sir, what is that through which, if known, everything else becomes known?'[86] Angiras told him that 'two kinds of knowledge are to be known.'[87] After introducing this and having dealt with the lower knowledge of *Ṛgveda* etc., Aṅgiras explains the higher knowledge. The higher knowledge is that by which *Brahman* is apprehended; '*Brahman* is not to be seen, not to be seized, has no family, has no caste.'[88] Thus, non-difference is that which is introduced here for discussion. Moreover, in the second *Muṇḍaka* it is said, towards the middle, that '*puruṣa* is all this'[89] and '*Brahman* alone is all this, it is the best.'[90] At the end of the third *Muṇḍaka* it is said that 'they all become one in the highest imperishable'[91] and that 'he who knows that highest *Brahman* becomes *Brahman*.'[92] Thus, it is clear that the *Upaniṣad* deals with non-difference in all its three chapters. Therefore, sentences like 'two birds' etc., which come in the *Upaniṣad* also should be explained absolutely in the sense of non-difference. Otherwise, they will go against the whole purport of the text.

Objection: The *antaryāmibrāhmaṇa* of the *Bṛahadāraṇyakopaniṣad* has all the six principles which determine the purport, in evidence of difference. Initial passage is as follows: 'Dost thou know, Kāpya, that inner thread?'[93] The conclusion is as follows: 'He is thy self, the thread within all.'[94] The same sentence has been repeated twenty-one times in the *brāhmaṇa* whereby the principle, repetition, is assured. Since being the thread within all is something still unachieved there is the principle of novelty also. The sentence 'he knows *Brahman*'[95] mentions the fruit. Here is eulogy in the form of condemnation: 'If thou, O Yājñavalkya without knowing that string and the thread within, drivest away those *Brahma*-cows, thy head will fall off.'[96] Reasoning is as follows: 'He who dwells on the earth and within the earth, whom the earth does not know, whose body the earth is.'[97]

Reply: The first four chapters of the *Bṛhadāraṇyakopaniṣad* deal with the same *brahmavidyā* as is mentioned in the *śruti* 'let men worship him as self, for all these are one in the self'.[98] The initial passage deals with non-difference: 'Verily in the beginning this was *Brahman*; that *Brahman* knew self only as I am *Brahman*'.[99] It should also be remembered that this passage follows the promise that by knowing only one, everything else can be known, as evidenced by the *śruti* 'this self is the foot-step of everything, for through it one knows everything'.[100] Then, in the end of the fourth[101] chapter, in the *maitreyībrāhmaṇa*, the conclusion is as follows: 'When the self only is all this, how should he see another'[102] etc. Thus, all the four chapters deal with non-difference in general and therefore, the *antaryāmibrāhmaṇa* which comes in the third chapter, cannot be taken in the sense of difference in its absolute form. In fact, as exhibited, the principles that determine purport, agree with difference. They are to be explained in tune with the superimposed difference. Therefore, they are not against absolute non-difference too. It is in this way that the *sūtra* 'the followers of both the recensions read of this one as different whereby the embodied soul also is not the internal ruler'[103] and Śaṅkara's commentary thereon, fit well.

27. *Fitness of the essential nature of unity*

Objection: What is this unity? Is it the essential nature of *Ātman* or something else? It cannot be the first because if *Ātman* and unity are one and the same only one of the term will be enough. Moreover, conditional unity can never be the essential nature of unconditional *Ātman*. It cannot be the second also because then arise two questions: Is this unity real? Is this unity unreal? If it is real *Advaita* will be in danger. If it is unreal it will have to be said that *śrutis* like 'that thou art' deal with unreality.

Reply: The first is correct. Though consciousness and bliss are identical with *Brahman* those terms are used separately, because they deal with superimposed consciousness etc. Similar is the case here also. Unity is unconditional and therefore there is no contradiction with unconditional *Ātman* as alleged. There is no point in scolding *advaitins* on the basis of the second option because they never admit the same.

Objection: If unity is something other than *Ātman*, is it singular in number? Is it having all the properties *Ātman* has or is it having the essential characteristic of *Ātman*? Any of these cannot be admitted because *Ātman* has no property as held by you. It cannot also be considered to be lack of difference because difference is in the form of lack of unity and for the same reason there will be mutual dependency. It cannot also be not being the locus of any property of *Ātman* because then voidness also will have to be considered to be *Ātman*.

Reply: These allegations are summarily rejected because unity is the essential nature indicated by not being the locus of properties which do not exist in *Ātman*. Since voidness has no form it cannot be the form of unity.

Objection: By saying about 'properties which do not exist in *Ātman*' it is said that there are properties in *Ātman* because negation of a particular thing will result in the admission of the rest.

Reply: This admission of the rest is not a rule because nowhere it can be seen so. Otherwise, by negating blue colour in air it will result that there is white colour in it.

Objection: If unity is one and the same with *Ātman* there arise further questions: Does *Ātman* have unity, absolute reality, difference from non-existent etc., in reality or not? In the first case it will result in having a second. In the second case unity will be lost.

Reply: All this can be there in any form other than that of absolute reality. Therefore, there is no harm for non-duality. And for the unity of *jīva* and *Ātman śrutis* like 'that thou art'[104] 'this *Ātman* is *Brahman* itself'[105] etc., are evidence.

28. *Evidence for the unity of jīva and Ātman*

Objection: How can the *śrutis* cited evidence unity of *jīva* and *Ātman*? *Ātman* is omniscient and *jīva* is not so. Therefore, their unity is impossible.

Reply: Unity can be said as in the case of such experiences as 'this is that'. Because of the unintelligibility of the two being one, all the contradictory qualifications are dropped and the substrate, which is also the purport, alone is taken. Similarly, in the case of *jīva* and *Ātman* only the pure consciousness is taken in the sense of unity.

Objection: How is the contradiction solved? Is it simply by not intending? Is it by taking *jīva* in the sense of non-eternal? Or is it that *jīva* is illusory? It cannot be the first because even though some of the properties are not intended, contradiction will not be rectified. We can see this in the case of *śrutis* such as 'in the beginning this was non-existent'[106] and 'all this is *Brahman* itself'.[107] There, simply because of non-intention unity of *Brahman* with voidness or materiality cannot be said though non-intention of existence and voidness or consciousness and materiality, is quite possible. The second also cannot be admitted because then the use of the present tense will be unfit. 'That thou art' will have to be taken in the meaning of 'you will be that'. You do not admit of the existence of non-difference and difference depending on difference in time. You consider independence of *Īśa* and dependence of *jīva* as eternal. It cannot be the third also because the contradictory properties revealed by the *śrutis* and *sākṣin* cannot be considered to be illusory.

Reply: All sorts of contradictions can be solved by simple non-intention of them. The contradictory properties are omitted. Omission means not being subject in the experience of *Brahman* and not lapse because it is possible only by the final realisation of *Brahman*. Thus, omniscience and non-omniscience are not capable of creating difference in the locus just like 'thatness' and 'thisness' are not capable of creating difference in Devadatta. Non-intention is for the purpose of substantiating the prime purport of the *śrutis*.

Objection: There is no omission of 'thatness' and 'thisness' because both can be admitted in different times in the case of such experience as 'this is that Devadatta'.

Reply: Eventhough they can be admitted with reference to different times, since they are qualifications, omission is necessary for fear of their being one and the same. In the case of *śrutis* such as 'that thou art' and 'this was non-existent' there is no trouble of *Brahman* being void or material because the contradictory forms of void and existent or conscious and material are omitted. Moreover, they have no constant form as those of *jīva* and *Brahman*. In fact, non-existent has no form and material has being subject to sublation as its essential nature. Therefore, *śrutis* are ample evidence for the unity of *jīva* and *Brahman*.

29. *Negation of contradiction of śrutis on unity with the evidence which is being depended*

Objection: What kind of unity do you intend to be imparted by the *śrutis* on unity? Is it that after having restated *jīva* who is established to be by perception, his *Brahmatvam* is imparted by the *śrutis*? Is it that after having restated *Brahman* who is established to be by the *śrutis*, its *jīvatvam* is imparted? Is it that after having restated both, their non-difference is imparted? In all these cases there is contradiction with the evidence which is depended on. Perception shows that *jīva* is different from *Brahman*. *Śrutis* also acknowledge that *Brahman* who is omniscient etc., is different from *jīva* who is just the opposite. Inference also cannot be put forward as evidence for the same because in that case also contradiction with the evidence which is depended on is there. In short, unity of *jīva* and *Ātman* is not possible.

Reply: It is true that in the matter of determining the significative potency of words there is dependence on perception. However, there is no dependence in deciding the object signified. Vācaspatimiśra has said the same thing: 'That which is depended on is not subject to sublation and that which is subject to sublation is not depended on.'[108] If it is said that the state of being depended on is somehow, then, in the case of the knowledge 'this is not silver', the knowledge, 'this is silver', will also have to be considered as that which is depended on.

Objection: If, of two, one is there only when the other also is there and when one is destructed the other also is destructed, we can say that the one is dependent on the other. In the present case that which acknowledges the propertied is that which does the validity of it also and therefore, in its sublation, that itself will be sublated. Where that which is subject to negation is presented, this is not the case.

Reply: It is true. However, that which has omniscience etc., is not the propertied, but the essential nature of *Brahman*. Validity of the knowledge of the propertied is not necessary for the validity of the knowledge of unity; what is necessary is the validity of the knowledge of the essential nature alone. Otherwise, it will come that the knowlege, 'this is silver', also is valid since it is a knowledge of the propertied and is being depended. In fact, though the knowledge that negates is valid, this knowledge is not so. Omniscience etc., are non-efficient for the propertied as silverness itself.

Objection: If *Brahman* is not intended as having the qualification per proprium of omniscience and such essential characteristics, how is it then intended? Is it based on general characteristics or on its essential nature? In the first case we have no objection because we do admit the unity of *Brahman* with such general characteristic as consciousness. In the second case unity of *Brahman* will not be established.

Reply: Do you mean by *Brahman* that which is along with omniscience etc? If so, we have no objection. We hold the unity of *Brahman* and *jīva* secondarily implied by the words 'that' and 'thou' respectively.

As far as *śrutis* dealing with non-difference are concerned there is no contradiction with the evidence which is being depended on. On the contrary, *śrutis* dealing with difference have contradiction with those dealing with non-difference and for the same reason they have to be explained in accordance with the *śrutis* on non-difference. *Śrutis* like 'that thou art', therefore, establish the unity of *jīva* and *Brahman*.

30. *Discussion on the meaning of the sentence 'that thou art'*

Objection: *Advaitins* admit, secondary implication on both the words 'that' and 'thou' of the sentence 'that thou art'[109] In our view, secondary implication is needed in the case of only one word.

In the *śruti*, 'two birds, inseparable'[110] *jīva* is said to have concomitance with *Brahman*. Therefore, based on concomitance with *Brahman jiva* can be denoted as 'that'. Pāṇini has said that 'the affix *ṭak* comes in the sense of who studies or who knows, after the words *vasanta* etc.'[111] Here the word *vasanta* is used in the sense of a book related to *vasanta*. Patañjali also has vouchsafed the same.[112] On the same lines, here also the word 'that' is used in the sense of that which is related to that namely *jiva*. There is *śruti*; 'All these creatures, my son, have their root in the existent; they dwell in the existent.'[113] This shows the relation of *jīva* with *Brahman*.

Based on having 'that' as the locus also *jīva* can be denoted by the word 'that'. Pāṇini says that 'a rule which relates to complete words is to be taken to apply to those words the senses of which are connected'.[114] Patañjali says that what is intended by the usage 'complete words' is that which is related to those words.[115] Since *jīva* is originated from *Brahman* he can be called by the word 'that'. Similarly, since *jīva* is dependent on *Brahman* he can be called by the word 'that'. Finally, based on *jīva's* similarity in form with *Brahman* also it is fit to denote the former by the word 'that'. Jaimini has said that similarity in form is one of the bases of figurative description.[116] The sacrificial post is praised as the sun accordingly. Bādarāyaṇa also says: 'But the soul comes to have such appellations because of the dominance of the modes of that intellect; this is just as in the case of the supreme self'.[117] Brahmadatta as well as one who is similar to Brahmadatta can be called Brahmadatta.[118] Therefore, 'that thou art' means 'thou art like that'.

Reply: Once the purport of the *śruti* is decided based on the six principles that determine the same, other things should be explained accordingly. The purport of the *śruti* is non-difference. Therefore, admitting secondary implication on both words is not at all a demerit. It is not proper to get rid of the purport in order to save one secondary implication. Since the purport can be known based on exclusive-non-exclusive implication there is no point in depending on concomitance and the sort.

The *śruti* 'two birds inseparable' does not deal with *jīva's* relation to *Brahman*. In fact, *jīva's* concomitance with the intellect is dealt with in the *śruti*. The *śruti* 'all these creatures etc'., also does not deal with dependence of *jīva* on *Brahman*, for, by the word creature *jīva* is not mentioned. For the same reason based on being born from it also, the word 'that' cannot be explained. Bādarāyaṇa's *sūtra* intends to say that *jīva* is minute like *Brahman* and not that *jīva* has *Brahman's* properties. In short, the *śruti* deals with non-difference and nothing else.

The opponent interprets the *śruti* 'that thou art' in many ways so as to avoid its meaning of non-difference. He quotes a number of reasonings from Jaimini, Pāṇini, Patañjali and Bādarāyaṇa. His contention is that the *śruti* means by 'that' and 'thou' 'thou of that'. He assumes the compound to be *ṣaṣṭītatpuruṣa*. Madhusūdana rejects all the arguments of his opponent. He says that where the meaning is clear without any compound there it is not necessary to assume any compound. 'That' and 'thou' of the *śruti* 'that thou art' are two separate words and there is no problem of any compounding.

Madhusūdana examines the meaning of the *śruti* with reference to the whole of the sixth chapter of the *Chāndogyopaniṣad* where it occurs. All the six principles which help to determine the purport are in favour of non-difference of *jīva* and *Brahman*. The initial passage states that *Brahman* is 'one only without a second'.[119] Thus is the conclusion also: '*Ātman* is all this world'.[120] In the sixth chapter the sentence 'that thou art' has been repeated nine times so as to clear Śvetaketu's doubts one by one. In the very same chapter it has been established that *Brahman*, the one without a second, is not knowable from any other source than *śruti*. The same is novelty. And the result is mentioned in the *śruti*: 'The man who has got an *ācārya* knows *Brahman*. He has to wait only till he is delivered from the body; then he becomes united with *Brahman*.'[121] Eulogy in the form of praise is as follows: 'By that instruction one hears all that one has not heard'[122] Reasonings also have been exhibited in detail. The examples of mud and jar, gold and ornaments and iron and nail-cutter are reasonings in support of the unity of *jīva* and *Ātman*.

31. *Meaning of the śruti 'I am Brahman' and a number of other śrutis and smṛtis*

In the *Bṛhadāraṇyaka* it is said: 'In the beginning this was verily *Brahman*. That *Brahman* knew only itself as I am *Brahman*'[123] This *śruti* deals with the non-difference of *jīva* and *Brahman*. It does not occur in any context of meditation.

Objection: The remaining portion of the *śruti* is as follows: 'Thus, whatever *Deva* was awakened indeed he became that; and the same with *Ṛṣis* and men'[124] The former part of the *śruti* has contradiction with this latter part which deals clearly with difference.

Reply: The cited latter part of the *śruti* also analyses the *Devas* and men who are awakened and states that 'he indeed became *Brahman*' whereby it is clear that non-difference is the subject-matter. It cannot be said that the context is that of pure *Brahman* and therefore, non-difference of *jīva* and *Brahman* cannot be the subject-matter because the context is that of *Brahman* in the form of effect.

Objection: In such words as 'I became Manu and sun',[125] 'I' has been used in the sense of the inner self of *jīva*. It is also clear that 'I' is a *sarvanāma* and not *sarvasyarūpa*.

Reply: It is not correct. Bādarāyaṇa's aphorism is as follows: 'But the instruction proceeds from a seer's vision agreeing with scriptures, as in the case of Vāmadeva'.[126] There it is clearly stated that Vāmadeva's words, 'I became Manu and Sun', are in the sense of 'I am *Brahman*'.[127] Therefore, the *śruti* is concerned with non-difference.

Objection: The word *Brahman* is used in the sense of that which patronises and therefore, non-difference cannot be the sense of 'I am *Brahman*'. Moreover, if it is taken in that sense it will be of no use because the former part of the same *śruti*[128] makes the same sense.

Reply: The former part 'that *Brahman* knew only itself'[129] restates *jīva* and then the *Brahmatva* of *jīva* is stated. Therefore, the *śruti* is invariably in the sense of non-difference.

In the *Muṇḍakopaniṣad* it is said: 'He who knows that highest *Brahman*, becomes *Brahman* itself'.[130] This sentence also is in the meaning of non-difference of *jīva* and *Brahman*.

Objection: Here the second word *Brahman* is in the sence of *jīva* because the word *Brahman* has many meanings such as the *Brahmin* caste, *jīva* and the *Brahmā* of the trinity. The usage 'two Brahmans' etc., makes it clear that the word *Brahman* can be in the sense of *jīva*. Therefore, the meaning of the *śruti* is that 'one who knows the great *Brahman* is *jīva* alone and not the great *Brahman*'. In fact, that is why the first word Brahman is qualified by the word 'highest'.

Reply: It is true that the word *Brahman* has many meanings and it can therefore, mean *jīva*. However, in the *śruti* the word *Brahman* is in the sense of the supreme self because the state of *jīva* which is not

Brahman is there even before the realisation of *Brahman*. It need not be achieved by the knowledge of *Brahman*. Thus the second word *Brahman* also is in the sense of highest *Brahman*.

The *śruti* 'being *Brahman* he goes to *Brahman*'[131] also denotes non-difference.

Objection: In this *śruti* the first *Brahman* word means *jiva*. The meaning of the *śruti* is that *jīva* goes to *Brahman*. *Jīva* is the agent of going and *Brahman* his destination. Thus the *śruti* deals with difference and not non-difference.

Reply: It is not correct. The first word *Brahman* is also in the meaning of the supreme *Brahman* itself. It is used taking into consideration the difference of *Brahman* caused by extraneous adjuncts and that is how the relation of agent and object in the *śruti* suits too. Tnus this *śruti* also should be taken in the meaning of non-difference itself.

Śrutis such as 'in the supreme indestructible *Brahman* all become one',[132] 'there is no other seer but he'[133] 'there is nothing that sees but it',[134] 'if he makes the smallest distinction in it, there is fear for him',[135] 'he is the one God hidden in all beings'[136] etc., also deal with non-difference. Smṛtis also can be cited in evidence of non-difference. *Bhagavadgītā* says: 'I am the knower of the body in all the bodies'.[137]

Objection: Here the word knower is used in the sense of the omniscient and not in the sense of *jīva*. All the bodies including conscious and material are considered to be the body of *Īśvara*.

Reply: *Īśvara* who is in all bodies and who is all-governing is omniscient and therefore, he need not be dealt with here. What is said here is the non-difference of *Īśvara* from *jīva* who dwells in the bodies of all.

Objection: Jaimini says: 'The signification sanctioned by the *Vedas* is to be regarded as more authoritative, because the *Vedas* are the sole means of knowing dharma'.[138] In the *Vedas* the knower is *Brahman*.

Reply: Where there is contradiction between the signification sanctioned by *Vedas* and that obtained otherwise, the former will be more authoritative. Here no contradiction is there. In fact, all the *Vedas* proclaim the non-difference of *Ātman* and *jīvas*.

32. *Inference on the non-difference of jīva and Brahman*

Inference also is evidence for the non-difference of *jīva* and *Ātman*.

Jīvas are not really different from *Brahman* because they are *Ātman* like *Paramātman*.

Objection: The generality of *Ātman* is the probans here. If the unity of *Ātman* is accepted there will be no generality of it. Consequently there will be no probans and the inference will be invalidated by non-favourable counter argument.

Reply: Even though non-difference is eternal reality, generality of *Ātman* can be admitted for all practical usages. In the present inference cognisership also is probans. It is there in *jīva*. The same is indiscriminately superimposed on *Ātman* and therefore, there is no absence of probans in the said inference. Unsublatedness also is probans in the same inference.

Objection: Unsublatedness is not there in the material world. Therefore, the probans is inconstant.

Reply: It is true, unsublatedness is not there in the material world. What is there is sublatedness. Therefore, there is no inconstancy too. In fact, real difference is nowhere and for the same reason there is no question of inconstancy at all.

Objection: In the very same manner as non-difference is established, difference also can be established based on inference.

Reply: Such inference will be sublated by the contradiction with perception itself. *Śrutis* also negate the validity of such inference. Therefore, inference such as 'the *jīvas* under dispute differ from *Brahman* because they are *Ātman* like the known *Ātman*' has no locus standi. It is a pseudo inference. It has no similarity with such inferences as the '*jīvas* under dispute are not really different from *Brahman* because they are substances like *Brahman*'.

There is also inference for the unity of *jīva* in all the bodies. The bodies under dispute are dependent on Caitra since they are bodies like the known bodies.

Objection: This inference does not establish unity of *jīva* because a body dependent on Caitra can also be dependent on others. If it is said that it is dependent on Caitra alone then, since the supreme self also is there, the probandum will be defective.

Reply: What is meant is dependence of Caitra who is worldly. Then there is no defect for probandum too.

Another inference can be coined for establishing the unity of *jīva*. *Ātman* is not many based on the generality which is the pervaded to substancehood because he is all-pervasive like ether.

Objection: In each *kalpa* ether is different and therefore, the probandum is defective there. Since ether is limited there is defect of probanshood also. Though *Ātmatva* has no generality as atomness, difference can be established and therefore, there is the fallacy of *arthāntara* also.

Reply: What is meant by the inference is that the locus *Ātman* is not many at the very same time of having the generality that is pervaded with substancehood because it is related to grossness of the same time like ether. Since the subject is qualified, there is no *arthāntara*.

Falsity of difference also can be inferred. The difference under dispute is false or superimposed at some place because it is a difference or because it is superimposed like the difference of moon. Falsity was dealt within detail earlier.[139] Just like difference, the knowledge of difference also is false. Inference is evidence. The knowledge of difference under dispute is false because it is a knowledge of difference like the knowledge of difference of moon. Similarly, inferences like '*Ātmatva* is pervaded with unity because it exists in *Ātman* alone like *Caitratva*' etc., also can be cited. Thus inference is valid evidence for the non-difference of *jīva* and *Ātman*.

33. *Unity based on being part of Brahman*

Jiva and *Brahman* are one and the same because the former is described as a part of the latter in the *śrutis* and *smṛtis*. *Śruti* says: 'His feet are all the beings'.[140] Similarly, *smrti* says: 'The eternal *jīva* in the world of *jivas* is a ray of myself'.[141] *Jiva's* partness of *Brahman* is not in the sense that he constitutes *Brahman* because *Brahman* has no beginning at all.[142] It is also not in the sense that he is a piece of *Brahman* because *Brahman* cannot be cut.[143] It is also not in the sense of being collective because collection is not different from the collective and therefore, during wordly experience also it will have to be said that there is no pure *Brahman* different from the worldly *jīva*. It is also not in the sense of being different at the same time because we do not accept such a state. It is also not like a portion of cloth to the cloth because *Brahman* has no limitation by area at all. Therefore, *jīva's* partness of *Brahman* is in the sense of superimposed one just like the partness of ether limited by jar in the great ether. This is with reference to the view that *jīva* is qualified per proprium. Eventhough *Brahman* is partless there can be part in it based on extraneous adjuncts. Partness is not similarity and being the pervaded at the same time because in that case, a subtle cloth will have to be considered part of a gross one. The word part is mainly in the sense of a portion of the substance. It can be used in the sense of superimposed portion also. It is in the sense mentioned here that Bādarāyaṇa's *sūtras* also fit in.

Bādarāyaṇa says that *jīvas* are parts of *Brahman* because of the mention that they are different and also because some read otherwise of its identity with fishermen, slaves, gamblers and others.[144] The *srutis* involved in the *sūtra* also reveal the fact that difference between *jīva* and *Brahman* is accepted in practical usage though non-difference is the ultimate reality. *Śrutis* such as 'it is that which we must search out, it is that which we must try to understand',[145] 'knowing it alone one becomes a sage',[146] 'he who dwells in the soul and controls the soul from within'[147] etc., are evidence for the same. Some followers of the *Atharvaveda* read in their hymn to *Brahman* of the identity of it with the *dāśās*, *dāsās* and *kitavās*.[148] Therefore, it is only in fitness of things to say that non-difference is the ultimate reality whereas partness of *jīva* with *Brahman* is practical.

At another place it is illustrated: 'You are a woman, you are a man, you are a younger man or a maid; you are old tottering about with the help of a stick, having taken birth you have your face everywhere'.[149] It is also said: 'After having known all the forms and names, the wise man goes on uttering them'.[150] All such *śrutis* reveal the non-difference of *jīva* and *Brahman*. However, for explaining the difference of the cogniser and the cognisable difference is assumed in many *śrutis*. There is no justification in trying to establish difference as the ultimate reality based on those *śrutis*. *Śrutis* and *smṛtis* that deal with non-difference are more powerful than them and therefore, there is no harm for the unity of *Brahman*.

34. *Unity based on the law of object and its reflection*

Unity of *jīva* and *Brahman* can be established based on the law of the object and its reflection. As in the case of a face and its reflection, *Brahman* and *jīva* are the reality and its reflection respectively.

Objection: In the case of an object and its reflection unity is not apprehended. Let us take the example of Caitra. Caitra and his reflection are known separately as Caitra and his reflection themselves by those who are around him. Caitra himself knows his hand and its reflection as entirely different.

Reply: In the case of an object and its reflection, prima facie, there is a feeling of difference. However, on rational verification it can be perceived that there is no difference between the object and its reflection. The same law can be applied in the case of *Brahman* and *jīva* also. It can be explained. One sees Caitra outside his house. Later he sees him inside of the house. Even if one is perplexed at the sight of Caitra inside the house, as to the unity of Caitra whom he saw outside and whom he sees inside, on verification of the essential peculiarities of Caitra one understands him to be Caitra himself. Similarly, one sees one's own face on the mirror and at first takes that reflection as if different and later, on verification, finds that there is nothing different from one's own face on one's neck. Similar is the case of one's own hand and the sort. In fact, the object and its reflection are not different. Therefore, *Brahman* and *jiva* are also not different.

Objection: If the reflection of the object is on a copper plate or such unclear medium how can there be *primafacie* feeling of difference? Then, how can there be knowledge of non-difference later on verification?

Reply: Why should we go in for unclear reflections as example? If the medium is clear the reflection also will be clear and there non-difference can be perceived too.

Inference also is evidence for the unity of object and its reflection. Reflection is non-different from its object since it has the general properties its object has, since it is not locus for properties quite opposite to those its object has and since it is not born of that from which its object is not born. It cannot be said that this inference is inconstant in the right and left hands of one and the same person, which are very similar because there also there is difference of the two hands and not non-difference. It cannot also be said that the second probans in the inference is non-established since the face and its reflection are face to face and therefore contradictory because that contradiction is a creation only of the medium. In fact, the face and its reflection are not loci for contradictory properties. It cannot also be said that the third probans in the inference is non-established in the reflection born just after the object because as far as those who advocate non-difference are concerned, there is nothing in between the just born object and its reflection.

Objection: Unity of *jīva* and *Brahman* has to be inferred as follows: *Jīva* is not different from *Brahman* since it is a reflection of *Brahman*. Here the probans should be 'since it is dependent on it and similar to it' and not 'the reflection *jīva* is dependent on the medium' because *jīva* is beginningless. And the probans 'since, it is dependent on it and similar to it' is pervaded with difference and is therefore contradictory. Bādarāyaṇa also vouchsafes the same by the *sūtra* 'hence also are the illustrations of the sun's reflection etc.'[151]

Reply: Dependence on extraneous adjunct means to be present along with the extraneous adjunct only. It is not contradictory to being beginningless. Beginningless *jīva* also can be dependent on extraneous adjunct. Therefore, it is not correct to allege contradiction in the probans after taking the word reflection in the sense of different and similar at the same time. In short, it is established that reflection is non-different from the object, of which it is reflection. Since all *jivas* are reflections of *Brahman jīva* and *Brahman* are one and the same.

35. *Refutation of the minuteness of jīva*

Objection: How can there be unity of *jīva* and *Īśvara* since the former is minute and the latter omnipresent?

Reply: *Jīva* is not minute. There are *śrutis* and inference to this effect. *Śrutis* say 'he is everlasting, all pervading'[152] and 'he is that great unborn *Ātman*'.[153] Inference is as follows: *Jīva* is not minute since he is locus for properties that are perceptible and since he is possible to be perceived like a jar. Another inference: *Jīva* is not minute since he is *Ātman* and since he is not material like *Īśvara*. There are also reasonings which refute the minuteness of *jīva*. If *jīva* were minute it will not be possible for him to enjoy knowledge, pleasure etc., that pervade all over the body.

Objection: There are *śrutis* which establish the minuteness of *jīva*. *Muṇḍaka* says: 'This *Ātman* is minute'.[154] Another *śruti* says: 'that living soul is to be known as a part of the hundredth part of the point of a hair, devided a hundred times and yet it is infinite'.[155] Therefore, *jīva* is minute.

Reply: *Śrutis* dealing with the all-pervading nature of *jīva* are larger in number. When there is contradiction between the minority and majority of *śrutis* the latter prevails over the former and the former ones are to be explained in the light of the latter. Moreover, perception of pleasure etc., as pervading all over the body cannot be otherwise explained. Therefore, all arguments in favour of the minuteness of jiva are to be discarded.

Objection: Jīva is not pervader because he departs from this body. *Śruti* says: 'He departs from this body; he goes upwards and reaches that world; from that world he comes to this world'.[156] *Smṛti* also says: 'The *yogin* attains that lunar light and then returns'.[157]

Reply: The act of departure and the sort are of the mind and the same are dealt with in the *srutis* as if those of the consciousness qualified per accidens by the mind.

Objection: The *śruti*, 'they having enjoyed the fruits of deeds on the heights of heaven that are the abodes of pleasure, enter this world or an inferior one',[158] says that it is *jīva* himself who departs. *Jīva's* path of journey has been described in the *śruti* beginning with 'he leads them to Brahman'[159] and also in the *smṛti* 'the departing men who know *Brahman* reach *Brahman*'.[160]

Reply: *Atman's* enjoyment of pleasure etc., is through extraneous adjuncts. It is quite natural that the experience and departure of the mind can be imposed on *Ātman* since the locus of both mind and *Ātman* is the same. Only a pervaded can go to pervaded. *Brahman* is the pervader and therefore, *jiva* cannot go to *Brahman.* And for the same reason the *śrutis* and *smṛtis* deal with the journey of *jīva* in the sense that the going and liberation are in the very same substratum.

Objection: There are any number of inferences for the minuteness of *jīva*. *Ātmatva* is minute since it is a generality directly pervaded with substanceness like earthhood. *Jīva* is not pervading since he is not material, not substratum for the non-inherent cause of remoteness and not omnscient, at the same time. *Jīva* is not pervading since he is substratum for particular non-eternal qualities that are different from sound and is the abode of mental impressions, like mat. *Jīva* is minute since he is locus for contact that is non-inherent cause of knowledge, like mind.

Reply: All these inferenees are invalid. In the first inference the probans has extraneous adjunct. 'Not to be pervading' is the same. In the second and third inferences also the probans has the same defect. *Anātmatva* is the extraneous adjunct. In the fourth inference there is lack of example.

In short, *jīva* is not minute. He is pervading in nature. The *śruti* says: With the quality of mind and the quality of body that lower one is seen small even like the point of a goad.'[161] It is clear from this that the minuteness of *jīva* is created by the mind and not natural to him. *Jiva* in fact, is all pervading.

As in the case of other *paricchedas*, Madhusūdana concludes the second *pariccheda* also of *Advattasiddhi* with some verses. He says that what he has presented in the book are the gems he collected from the authoritative texts of the system and also from the words of his gurus. His own intellectual role in the composition of the book is in combining the *śrutis*, reasonings and words of his *gurus*.

REFERENCES

[1]Vide, PS, II, 3, 46.
[2]Vide, PP, p. 322.
[3]Vide, TP, p. 192.
[4]Vide, TU, II, 1, 1.
[5]Vide, BU, IV, 3, 7.
[6]Vide, IS, p. 25.
[7]Vide, CU, VI, 8, 7.
[8]Vide, SS, I, 178.
[9]Ibid., I, 169.
[10]Ibid., I, 384.
[11]Ibid., I, 167.
[12]Vide, SU, VI, 11.
[13]Vide, ASU, 4.
[14]Vide, TU, II, 6, 1.
[15]Vide, BU, IV, 4, 23.
[16]Vide, MS, III, 3, 14.
[17]Vide, BRS, I, 1, 27 etc.
[18]Vide, BU, II, 3, 6.
[19]Vide, SU, I, 6.
[20]Vide, BG, V, 29.
[21]Vide, BUBV, p. 60.
[22]Vide, SU, III, 8.
[23]Vide, MU, III, 1, 3.
[24]Vide, BG, XI, 5.
[25]Ibid., XIII, 13.
[26]Vide, CU, I, 6, 6.
[27]Vide, BRS, II, 1, 31.
[28]Vide, BU, II, 3, 6.
[29]Vide, SU, III, 19.
[30]Vide, TU, II, 1, 1.
[31]Vide, PS, V, 2, 91.
[32]Vide, CU, VI, 3, 2.
[33]Vide, BRS, I, 1, 2.
[34]Ibid., I, 1, 3.
[35]Vide, TU, III, 1, 1.
[36]Vide, Āpadeva, MNP, ed., Eng., Tr., Edgerton, Franklin (New Haven, 1929), Paras 88-181.
[37]Vide, PS, I, 4, 30.
[38]Ibid., II, 3, 28.

[39]Vide, MNP, paras 88-181.
[40]Vide, TU, III, 1, 1.
[41]Vide, CU, VI, 2, 3.
[42]Vide, Jayāditya and Vāmana, *Kāśikā* on PS, I, 4, 30.
[43]Vide, Jinendrabuddhi. *Nyāsa* on *Kāśikā* on PS, I, 4, 30.
[44]Vide, Patañjali, *Mahābhāṣya* on PS, I, 4, 30.
[45]Vide, Kaiyaṭa, *Pradīpa* on *Mahābhāṣya* on PS, I, 4, 30.
[46]loc. cit.
[47]Vide, TU, II, 6, 1.
[48]Ibid.
[49]loc. cit.
[50]Vide, BU, III, 7, 23.
[51]Vide, Vidyāsāgara, NC, ed., Anantakṛṣṇaśāstri, N.S. and Rāmasvāmiśāstri (Madras, 1959), p. 468.
[52]Vide, BU, IV. 3, 9.
[53]Ibid., IV, 3, 6.
[54]Ibid.
[55]Ibid, IV, 3, 5.
[56]Vide, PPV, p. 610.
[57]Vide, TU, II, 4. The Sanskrit word for 'turns away' is *nivartante*.
[58]Vide, KU, III, 15.
[59]Uide, TU, II, 1, 1.
[60]Vide, BU, IV, 3, 7.
[61]Ibid., III, 9, 28.
[62]Ibid., IV, 4, 20.
[63]Viee, KU, IV, 14.
[64]Ibid.
[65]Vide, BG, IV, 5.
[66]Ibid., XV, 17.
[67]Vide, SU, IV, 6.
[68]Vide, SPB, XIV, 5, 30.
[69]Vide, KU, V, 13.
[70]Vide, SU, IV, 5.
[71]Vide, BG, XIV, 2.
[72]Vide, MU, II, 1, 10.
[73]Vide, CU, VIII, 1, 6.
[74]Vide, BRS, IV, 4, 17.
[75]Ibid., IV, 4, 8.
[76]Ibid., IV. 4, 21.
[77]Vide, MS, II, 2, 1.
[78]Vide, MU, III, 1, 1.
[79]Ibid., III, 1, 3.
[80]Ibid., III, 1, 1.
[81]Ibid.
[82]Ibid., III, 1, 3.
[83]Ibid.
[84]Ibid., III, 1, 2.

[85]Vide, MK, I, 17.
[86]Vide, MU, I, 1, 3.
[87]Ibid., I, 1, 4.
[88]Ibid., I, 1, 5; 6.
[89]Ibid., II, 1, 10.
[90]Ibid., II, 2, 11.
[91]Ibid., III, 2, 7.
[92]Ibid., III, 2, 9.
[93]Vide, BU, III, 7, 1.
[94]Ibid., III, 7, 3
[95]Ibid., III, 7, 1.
[96]Ibid.
[97]Ibid., III, 7, 3.
[98]Ibid., I, 4, 7.
[99]Ibid., I, 4, 10,
[100]Ibid., I, 4, 7.
[101]In different editions of *Advaitasiddhi* it is wrongly mentioned as sixth chapter. *Maitreyibrāhmaṇa* is in the fourth chapter of *Bṛahadāraṇyakopaniṣad*.
[102]Ibid., IV, 6, 15.
[103]Vide, BRS. I, 2, 20.
[104]Vide, CU, VI, 8, 7.
[105]Vide, BU, IV, 4, 24.
[106]Vide, TU, II, 7, 1.
[107]Vide, CU, III, 14, 1.
[108]Vide, *Bhāmati* on BRS, I, 1, 1.
[109]loc. cit.
[110]Vide, MU, III, 1, 1.
[111]Vide, PS, IV, 2, 63.
[112]Vide, *Mahābhāṣya*, on PS, IV 2, 63.
[113]Vide, CU, VI, 8, 4.
[114]Vide, PS, II, 1, 1.
[115]Vide, *Mahābhāṣya* on PS, II, 1, 1.
[116]Vide, MS, I, 4, 25.
[117]Vide, BRS, II, 3, 29.
[118]Vide, Patañjali, *Mahābhāṣya* on PS, I, 1, 23.
[119]Vide, CU, VI, 2, 1.
[120]Ibid., VI, 8, 7.
[121]Ibid, VI, 14, 2.
[122]Ibid., VI, 1, 3.
[123]Vide, BU, I, 4, 10.
[124]Ibid.
[125]Ibid.
[126]Vide, BRS, I, 1, 30.
[127]Vide, Saṅkara, Commentary on BRS, I, 1, 30.
[128]Vide, BU, I, 4, 10.
[129]Ibid.
[130]Vide, MU, III, 2, 9.
[131]Vide, BU, IV, 4, 6.

[132]Vide, MU, III, 2, 7.
[133]Vide, BU, III, 7, 23.
[134]Ibid., III, 8, 11.
[135]Vide, TU, II, 7.
[136]Vide, SU, VI, 11.
[137]Vide, BG, XIII, 2.
[138]Vide, MS, I, 3, 9.
[139]Vide, supra, chapter V, 5—35.
[140]Vide, Cu, III. 12. 6.
[141]Vide, BG, XV, 7.
[142]Ibid, II, 20.
[143]Ibid, II, 23, 24.
[144]Vide, BRS, II, 3, 43.
[145]Vide, CU, VIII, 7, 1.
[146]Vide, BU V, 4, 22.
[147]Vide, SPB, XIV, 6, 7.
[148]Vide, Saṅkara, Commentary on BRS, II, 3, 43.
[149]Vide, SU, IV, 4,3.
[150]Vide, TA, III, 12, 16.
[151]Vide, BRS, III, 2, 18.
[152]Vide, JU, X, 2.
[153]Vide, BU, IV, 4, 22.
[154]Vide, MU, III, 1, 9.
[155]Vide, SU, V, 9.
[156]Vide, CU, VIII, 6, 5.
[157]Vide, BG, VIII, 25.
[158]Vide, MU, I, 2, 10.
[159]Vide, CU, IV, 15, 16.
[160]Vide, BG, VIII, 24.
[161]Vide, SU, V, 8.

CHAPTER VII

Pariccheda—3

In the fiirst *pariccheda* false bondage beginning from ignorance was dealt with. Then the author intended to deal with the means for severing that false bondage, in the second *pariccheda*. Impartite knowledge of *Brahman* is the means. However, objections arose against the very assumption of impartite knowledge, on the ground that *Ātman* is not non-dual. Hence the second *pariccheda* was devoted to the discussion of the unity of *Ātman*. Now, in the third *pariccheda*, Madhusūdana deals with the means proper whereby realisation of *Brahman* can be attained and the false bondage severed.

1. *Subsidiary position of thinking and meditation in relation to hearing*

Those who are desirous of severing bondage should realise *Brahman*. And for realisation hearing is the principal means and thinking and meditation are subsidiaries to it. It is said in the *Pañcapādikāvivaraṇa* that hearing is the principal means since it is direct and has no obstruction for the realisation of *Brahman* and that thinking and meditation become means of realisation of *Brahman* by way of creating concentration of mind which is possible as a result of the mental impression regarding *Brahman*.[1]

Objection: Hearing which is in the form of discussion cannot be considered as the peculiar cause of the knowledge of unity produced by verbal testimony because as in the knowledge of *dharma*, in the knowledge of *Brahman* also discussion has got the function of only revealing the proper way of doing things. It is just like the role of argument in inference.

Reply: Discussion is the determination of the purport of the significative potency of words. The peculiar cause of knowledge derived from verbal testimony is words, the purport of which is to be determined. Therefore, discussion can be included in the peculiar cause of knowledge. Its function is not revealing the proper way of doing things alone.

Objection: The peculiar cause of verbal knowledge is the knowledge of words having expectancy etc. Therefore, the knowledge of purport which has served its function by eradicating false knowledge regarding the purport, cannot be included in the peculiar cause. If it is included, thinking etc., also will have to be included in the same.

Reply: If the knowledge of purport is not included in the peculiar cause then expectancy etc., also need not be included because they have served their function by eradicating the false knowledge of the lack of expectancy etc. Therefore, knowledge of the purport is peculiar cause of knowledge and for deciding the purport discussion is necessary whereby it also has to be included in the peculiar cause.

There is differenec between the causality of hearing and that of thinking and meditation. Hearing directly produces verbal testimony whereas thinking and meditation co-operate with hearing in the same.

Objection: As far as the resultant knowledge is concerned all the three, hearing, thinking and meditation, are equally important. Even then if hearing is considered as the principal one, in the case of *hīṣ*, *ūrg* and *ū* which are prescribed to be spelt in connection with the *sāman* for rain[2] also there will be this state of being the principal and the subsidiaries.

Reply: There is no such problem. Hearing is the peculiar cause of verbal testimony and thinking and meditation are subsidiaries since they only co-operate with it. That is not the case with the provision of spelling *hīṣ*, *ūrg* and *ū* which have equal status of causality. Therefore, there is no state of one being the principal and others being subsidiaries there.

The śruti says: 'Verily *Ātman* is to be seen, to be heard, to be perceived, to be marked in mind'.[3] In fact, thinking and meditation are possible only after hearing. If meditation is supposed to be the principal means, then the realisation of *Brahman* will be something like the realisation of one's own fiancee and thus it will lose its seriousness. It cannot be said that since meditation is prescribed by the *Vedas* there is no such problem because better let us take the *Vedas* themselves as valid proof. Why should we go in for meditation leaving aside the *Vedas*? Hearing of *Vedas* is therefore, the principal means for realisation and thinking and meditation are its subsidiaries.

2. *Fitness of the necessary arrangement explained in the Vivaraṇa*

Positive and negative reasonings reveal that hearing etc., are the means for realisation of *Brahman*. And for the same reason injunction which prescribes hearing etc., is not one originated as an *apūrvavidhi* but it is an injunction of necessary arrangement.

Objection: Hearing is the means of direct realisation. It is not known from any other source. Therefore, the injunction which prescribes hearing is an *apūrvavidhi.*

Reply: It is not correct to say tnat hearing, as a means of realisation, is quite unknown. In the study of the science of music we know that hearing is the means for the direct realisation of primary notations like *ṣaḍja*. Therefore, injunction on hearing is not an *apūrvavidhi.*

Objection: Simple study of *śāstras* is not the cause of realisation of things dealt with therein. The *dharmaśāstras* deal with heaven and the sort which are to be attained hereafter. No one can attain them by the simple study of the *dharmaśāstras.*

Reply: What is said is with regard to *śāstras* which deal with things which are perceptible. *Ātman* is perceptible like *ṣaḍja* etc., but it is not the case with *dharma.*

Objection: If *Ātman* is subject to perception the study of *Śāstras* is of no use. Moreover, there is no rule that only things which are perceptible need be studied.

Reply: Of course, there in no such rule. There is also no rule that things which are perceptible only need be studied through the *śāstras. Ṣadja* etc., which are perceptible are studied in the science of music. In fact, what necessitates study are doubt and fruitfulness. Eventhough *Ātman* is generally known as 'I am', there is doubt regarding its specific nature. The specific knowledge of *Ātman* is fruittul too. Therefore, it cannot be said that the study of *śāṣtras* dealing with *Ātman* is useless.[4]

Objection: An injunction becomes an injunction of necessary arrangement when it prescribes one of the two alternatives applicable. That means there should be another means too. In the case of *Ātman* which has not colour etc., there is no other means for the realisation of it. Therefore, the injunction which prescribes the means of realisation of *Ātman* cannot be one of necessary arrangement.

Reply: Eventhough there is no other means in the case of *Ātman* which is devoid of any particularity, there is a generality of means for the realisation of *Ātman*. Therefore, there can be a quest regarding the particular means and for the same reason the injunction which prescribes that particular means can be one of necessary arrangement also. It is like the injunction 'he is to beat the rice grains'. Freeing of the grains from the husks can be effected by other means such as that with finger-nails etc. Freeing the rice grains is there in the case of all means as a generality. Therefore, the injunction which prescribes beating as the means for freeing grains from husks and which has its specific purpose also, is an injunction of necessary arrangement whereby the particular beating is stipulated.

Objection: There is difference between the example cited and the present case. In the case of the beating of rice grains, there is specific purpose of attaining the *adṛṣṭa* attached therein. In the case of hearing of *Vedas* there is other alternative. The knowledge of reality can be effected from *itihāsas*, *purāṇās* etc., which contain all the knowledge contained in the *Vedas*.

Reply: The *śruti* says: 'Brahmins seek to know him by the study of the *Vedas*, by sacrifice, by gifts, by penance, by fasting'.[5] It is clear from this that the *adṛṣṭa* born from each of these acts and also the necessary arrangement have direct use in the purification of mind and making it to seek *Brahman*. It is the mind purified by *adṛṣṭa* that realises *Brahman* and severs bondage. Therefore, *vivaraṇakāra's* view that hearing is prescribed by necessary arrangement is correct. The sayings of other *ācāryās* in this regard also can be substantiated in the same way.

3. *Fitness of hearing etc., being subject to injunction*

Objection: What do you mean by this hearing? Is it understanding the purport by significative potency? Or is it understanding the word which is qualified by the said potency? Or is it understanding the principles that reveal the purport? Or is it knowledge born from the advice of the *ācāryas* and the *śāstras*? It cannot be the first because there is no significative potency of words in the case of *Brahman* which is beyond the target of words. For the same reason no word qualified by the said potency applies to *Brahman* too. The other options also cannot be accepted for the reasons already mentioned. It cannot be said that hearing is the enjoining of the *Vedāntas* in *Brahman* as per the *acārya's* oration because as said in the first case, *Brahman* is not subject to words. Hearing cannot also be said to be *vādakathā* using particular sentences because nowhere hearing is used in that sense. Since there is no injunction of hearing there can be no injunction of thinking or meditation also.

Reply: There is no harm for the first sense. It cannot be said that there is no significative potency of words in the case of *Brahman* because eventhough there is no such significative potency in pure *Brahman* there can be the same useful for the knowledge of *Brahman*, in the case of qualified *Brahman*. And the purport is possible in unqualified *Brahman*. Therefore, discussion is not at all useless. It cannot be said that the impartite sense will be lost because as dealt with earlier, it indicates the essential nature only. Therefore, there is no obstruction for hearing being subject of injunction. And for the same reason thinking and meditation also can be prescribed by injunction. It cannot be said that hearing, being a knowledge, is not subject to injunction because in fact, it is reasoning. It is a mental state different from the class of knowledge. That is why Sureśvara has used the term hearing in the sense of deeds.[6]

Objection: Since the sense of the purport is born from the evidence like beginning and conclusion etc., it is not proper to exclude it from the class of knowledge. In the propitiation of word as cow etc., there is no such dependence on evidences.

Reply: *Advaitins* do not consider beginning and conclusion etc., as evidences. Thus, since hearing etc., are not knowledge but actions of the mind, they can be subject to injunction.

Madhusūdana has dealt with the same in his *Siddhāntabindu* and *Vedāntakalpalatikā*. Vācaspatimiśra considers hearing etc., as only restatements.

4. *Fitness of discussion being caused by injunction on hearing*

It is the injunction on hearing which provides for discussion. And it has necessitated the origin of the *jijñāsāsūtra* of the *Brahmasūtras*.[7]

Objection: There is the defect of mutual dependency in the injunction of discussion. Desire for the realisation of *Brahman* is a pre-requisite for the competent candidate for the study of *Vedānta*. This desire originates from hearing. Thus, hearing is necessary for the origin of desire for the realisation of *Brahman* and the same desire is necessary for hearing whereby presents the mutual dependency.

Reply: For one who has studied the *Vedas* there arises an indirect knowledge about *Brahman*. From that knowledge arises the desire for the realisation of *Brahman*. This is the pre-requisite included among those required for the candidate who wants to study *Vedānta*. Therefore, there is no defect of mutual dependency or so.

Objection: The discussion dealt within the *jijñāsāsūtra* is in the form of reasonings which are useful for finalising the ultimate reality. Otherwise, the prescription of the same for the initiation of the *śāstra* which is the combination of reasonings will not be fit. Hearing is not that type of reasoning because if it is so, it will have no difference from thinking. Therefore, there is no cause-effect relation between the injunction on hearing and the *jijñāsāsūtra*.

Reply: Since both the *jijñāsāsūtra* and the injunction on hearing have the same subject, there is no cause-effect relation between them. However since the *jijñāsāsūtra* deals with the discussion of the six principles that determine the purport which is in the form of knowing the significative potency subject to the injunction on hearing, both can be considered to be having the same subject. Thinking is subjecting the facts heard, to reasoning and therefore, there is no non-difference between hearing and thinking.

Objection: If thinking is subjecting the facts heard, to reasoning or remembering the word subjecting that fact or recognition or a mental impression in the form of hearing which creates the fruit of emphasising the impression, then the same is obtained by hearing itself and thererfore, injunction on thinking will be useless.

Reply: Since thinking is the reasoning useful for clearing doubts regarding fitness or unfitness of the facts heard, there is no such defect as you allege.

Objection: In that case the first *sūtra* of *Bādarāyaṇa* which prescribes the necessity of discussion should be said to be caused by the injunction on thinking and not by the same on hearing.

Reply: The discussion on the principles which determine the purport presented by hearing, is more important than that which clears doubts regarding the fitness or unfitness of the purport. Therefore, it is better to consider injunction of hearing as the cause of the former. Discussion on the fitness or unfitness is casual.

Hearing and thinking can be defined in another way also. Hearing is reasoning of the principles such as beginning and conclusion etc., which determine the purport and which have been dealt with in the *samanvayādhyāya* of the *Brahmasūtras*. Thinking is the understanding of reasons which discard doubts regarding lack of meaning etc., and which have been dealt with in the second chapter of the *Brahmasūtras*.

Objection: If thinking is of the sort said, a person who has ascertained the validity of the *Vedas* will have no necessity of it

Madhusūdana replies to the opponent in the affirmative. As far as such persons are concerned there is no necessity of thinking at all. Thus, it is established that hearing is understanding the purport. And the same is dependent on discussion on the principles for the same. Therefore, the *jijñāsāsūtra* which establishes the necessity of discussion is cause by the injunction on hearing and not by that on thinking.

Objection: *Edvaitins* consider the discussion on *karmakāṇḍa* as that which is necessitated by the injunction on sacrifices. Similarly, let the discussion on *brahmakāṇḍa* also be that which is necessitated by the injunction on knowledge. Discussion on the sacrifices ends in the determination of sacrifices which are to be performed. Similarly, discussion on *Vedānta* is intended for determining the realisation of *Ātman* as the means for overcoming grief, as evidenced by such *śrutis* as 'he who knows *Ātman* overcomes grief'.[8] It is better to assume necessitation on one injunction of knowledge than on many injunctions of sacrifices.

Reply: It is true that the effect presupposes cause. However, so as to make it injunctive its necessitation by injunction has to be invariably declared. Otherwise, injunction on knowledge can be applied in the case of sacrifices and then injunctions on the study of the *Vedas* as well as performance of sacrifice, will be futile. Even if it is held that discussion is necessitated by the injunction on thinking, the same problem is there. Therefore, injunction on hearing is that which necessitates discussion which is envisaged in the *jijñāsāsūtra.*

5. *Fitness of Vācaspati's view*

Vācaspatimiśra holds that the injunction on the study of the *Vedas*, since it ends in the knowledge of meaning, is that which necessitates discussion both in the cases of *karmakāṇḍa* and *jñānakāṇḍa.* According to him there is no injunction on hearing etc., for hearing etc., are the cause of realisation evidenced by positive and negative reasonings.[9]

Objection: It is not correct to say that the study of *Vedas* ends in the knowledge of meaning becauae study of the *Vedas* is everlasting. In its non-performance harm has been prescribed too.

Reply: Injunction on the study of *Vedas* is for the knowledge of meaning. It has to be admitted that one does *Vedic* rites as per the Vedic portions studied and understood by him. Thus, one performs rites only after knowing the meaning of *Vedic* prescriptions. And study of the same is the result of the study of the *Vedas*. In the absence of the *Vedas* performance of the rites is not possible. Since eternal rites are there, harm prescribed in the absence of performance of such rites, is fit too.

Some hold that study of the *Vedas*, the result of which is knowledge of meaning, is an everlasting rite. Others hold that the study has the seen result of knowledge of meaning as well as unseen result of doing away with the harm that will be caused by the non-performance of the same, as in the case of the non-performance of the daily rites such as *sandhyāvandana*. The opponent's view that the injunction on the study of the Vedas is eternal and is cause of discussion in *karmakāṇḍa* and *brahmakāṇḍa* alike, is not correct because he holds that the *jijñāsāsūtra* is necessitated by the injunction on thinking. Infact, discussion in the form of thinking which expiates further discussion by clearing doubts regarding unfitness, also is necessitated by the injunction on the study of the *Vedas*. Therefore, the *jijñāsāsūtra* is not caused by the injunction on thinking.

6. *Refutation of knowledge being dependent on man*

The argument that the original form of knowledge born from scriptures, is the subject of injunction is not correct because even in the absence of such knowledge a general knowledge can be there.

Objection: The *śruti* 'that which is done by knowledge'[10] etc., deals with knowledge as a subsidiary. That which is not subject to injunction cannot be subsidiary.[11]

Reply: The *śruti* cited occurs in the context of propitiation of *udgītha* and there the meaning of knowledge which is subject to injunction is propitiation which, being a subsidiary, is not at all impossible. Bādarāyaṇa also has said that there is no obligatory rule about propitiation, for, that is obvious from the *Upaniṣad* in as much as propitiation has a separate result consisting in the elimination of hindrance to a rite[12] whereby it is clear that being subsidiary and subject of injunction are not concomitant.

Objection: No one aspires for knowledge of bad odour and the sort; but the knowledge of *Brahman* is not so. And in the knowledge of *Brahman* which is very minute, willful action is necessary.

Reply: It is not so. Willful action is necessary for the means of knowledge and not in the case of knowledge of *Brahman*.

Objection: The knowledge of the meaning of *śāstra* is concomitantly dependent on man. *Brahman* is the meaning of *śāstras*. Therefore, the knowledge of *Brahman* rests with man.

Reply: It is only the instrument of knowledge that rests with man. It cannot be said that good knowledge is prescribed and bad prohibited since they are dependent on man because there also the prescription and prohibition apply only to instruments.

Objection: If injunction is not direct, the knowledge of *Brahman* in name etc., prescribed for propitiation will contradict. There also it will have to be said that the propitiation does not rest with man.

Reply: It is not the case everywhere. The defects mentioned in the case of knowledge being subject of injunction and being dependent on man are not present in the case of injunction on propitiation.

Objection: Let the instrument of knowledge be dependent on man. However, why should dependence of knowledge on man be denied? Donation depends on the giver and the recipient alike. The same is the case of knowledge also.

Reply: We do not deny being the subject of injunction solely on the ground of being dependent on something else. What is meant by the refutation of the dependence of knowledge on man is the lack of option for him to know or not to know according to his wish. Thus knowledge is not dependent on man.

7. *Refutation of injunction on knowledge*

If knowledge is subject to injunction there arises a number of questions. Of what type is this knowledge revealed by injunction? Is it verbal testimony? Or is it simple repetition? Or is it meditation on the object superimposed without regard to reality? Or is it some other knowledge which ends in direct perception of reality? It cannot be the first because as in *karmakāṇḍa* knowledge born of verbal testimony is self-established and it cannot be something which is to be executed and which is subject to injunction. It cannot be the second also because then arise further questions. Is it for release? Or is it for realisation? It cannot be for release because since it is born of *apūrva* it will be non-eternal like heaven. It cannot be otherwise because in your view, unlike in ours, release is not the cessation of bondage but the reach of other world. It cannot be said that the *śruti* 'he does not take birth again'[13] reveals eternality because other *śrutis* establish the non-eternality of heaven achieved by deeds. Here is the *śruti*: 'Therefore, just as the enjoyment here acquired by deeds is consumed so enjoyment in other worlds acquired by merit also is consumed'.[14] Reasoning also is there to the effect that whatever is born is non-eternal. It cannot be for realisation because then whether it is with seen result or unseen? It cannot be with seen result because realisation of the eternal truth by repetition of perceptible knowledge is not possible. It cannot be with unseen result because realisation is born of valid evidence and not of *adṛṣṭa*. For the reasons already mentioned the third view that knowledge is meditation on the object superimposed without ragard for reality also cannot stand. Meditation is, in fact, not in the form of knowledge. The fourth view also cannot be accepted because then verbal testimony will fall invalid. Therefore. knowledge of *Brahman* is not subject to injunction.

If hearing is in the form of knowledge, it cannot be subject to injunction as we have seen in the foregoing paragraph. It is because of this that hearing is accepted as something that does not belong to the class of knowledge. Hearing which is in the form of discussion, is like the mode of performance known through verbal testimony. It is capable of creating perceptible knowledge. Thinking and meditation are the subsidiaries of hearing which is the principal means of realisation of *Brahman* revealed by injunction.

8. *Fitness of perception being born from verbal testimony*

Objection: How can verbal testimony create perception? There is no evidence for that.

Reply: There are ample evidences. The *śruti* says: 'He perceived what he said'.[15] Another *śruti* makes mention of 'those who have well perceived the object of knowledge of *Vedānta*'.[16] The first *śruti* evidences that teaching alone can create perception of *Ātman* and the second one reveals the fact that knowledge born of *Vedānta* is perception.

Inference also is evidence for the capability of words to create perception. Knowledge born from such sentences as 'that thou art' is perception since it is not counter-correlate of the eternal negation existing in perceptive knowledge like the generality of knowledge. If the knowledge born from the sentence 'that thou art' is not perception the false perception will not be sublated. It cannot be said that intellect is that which creates perception because intellect does not exist as the peculiar cause of perception anywhere. In fact, *Ātman* is self-luminous and pleasure etc., are known by *sākṣin*.

Objection: The said inference is defective since there is favourable counter for the same. The verbal testimony under dispute is not cause of perception since it is verbal testimony.

Reply: The counter argument is inconstant in such perceptions as 'you are the tenth'. It cannot be said that there also organs are peculiar cause and that words are only co-operative because even for one who has no eyes and who is in utter darkness, the false perception is sublated by the said sentence. Even if there are eyes they are needed no more in the perception born from that sentence.

Objection: Is this nature of creating perception inherent in words? Or is it created by the object which is perceptible? It cannot be the first because of prolixity. The second also cannot be correct because then the rule that perception of non-difference is possible only by hearing *Vedānta* will be violated.

Reply: Where perception is born from verbal testimony, there the knower and the object perceived are non-different. Therefore, there is no trouble of the sort alleged.

Objection: If knowledge born from words is perception, words also will have to be considered as the means of perception.

Reply: The determinant of the means of perception is to be the peculiar cause of perceptual knowledge and to be different from words at the same time.

Objection: The *śruti* says: 'It is to be perceived by the mind alone'.[17] Therefore, mind alone is the means of perception and not words.

Reply: Here is another *śruti*: 'I ask thee about that *aupaniṣada puruṣa*'.[18] Here the *taddhitapratyaya* in the word *aupaniṣada* is used as a direct statement in the sense of 'excellent in regard thereto'.[19] Therefore, *Upaniṣads* are the only means of realisation of *Ātman*. The argument that mind alone is the means of perception is prolix. Therefore, it is proper to consider words also as the valid means of perception. Sentences like 'that thou art' create perceptual knowledge of *Brahman*. Release from bondage in the form of severing ignorance is to be attained by the knowledge of *Brahman*. For the knowledge of *Brahman* hearing is the principal means and thinking and meditation are subsidiaries. Hearing is imparted through the injunction of necessary arrangement.

Madhusūdana concludes the third *pariccheda* with a few epilogic lines which proclaim the superb scholastic purpose the book serves. He requests the scholars to examine his work without unwanted prejudices and to accept whatever is palpable to them.

REFERENCES

[1]Vide, PPV, p. 411.
[2]Vide, TB, VIII, 8, 18.

[3]Vide, BU, II, 4, 5.
[4]Vide, Vācaspatimiśra, *Bhāmati*, on BRS, I, 1, 1.
[5]Vide, BU, IV, 4, 22.
[6]Vide, BUBV, p. 1069.
[7]Vide, BRS, I, 1, 1.
[8]Vide, CU, VII, 1, 3.
[9]Vide, *Bhāmati* on BRS, I, 1, 1.
[10]Vide, CU, I, 1, 10.
[11]Vide, Jaimini, MS, I, 4, 6.
[12]Vide, BRS, III, 3, 42.
[13]Vide, CU, VIII, 15, 1.
[14]Ibid., VIII, 1, 6.
[15]Ibid., V., 16, 3.
[16]Vide, MU, III, 2, 6.
[17]Vide, BU, IV, 4, 19.
[18]Ibid., III, 9, 26.
[19]Vide, PS, IV, 4, 18.

CHAPTER VIII

Pariccheda—4

The third *pariccheda* dealt with the means for attaining the final goal of man. The fourth and concluding *pariccheda* of the book deals, in general, with the final goal itself. Release from bondage is the finale of all *Vedāntic* thought. It is to be achieved by knowledge of *Brahman* alone.

1. *Eradication of ignorance*

Objection: Release cannot be eradication of ignorance. If it is so, is it non-different from *Ātman* or different? If it is non-different it will be eternal and therefore, it cannot be a target to be achieved. If it is different, further questions arise: Whether it is true or false? If it is true *Advaita* will be in danger. If it is false it will also have to be considered either ignorance itself or some effect of it.

Reply: *Ātman* indicated by the final mental state is itself in the form of eradication of ignorance. Thus, release becomes the target on account of the final mental state being the target. It cannot be said that by the eradication of the final mental state, release also will be eradicated because we know that the cook is a cook even after his cooking. Citsukha has said the same thing: 'Eradication of ignorance is *Ātman* known as indicated by the final mental state. Even after the destruction of that mental state release can be there like the cook etc.'[1]

Objection: If *Ātman* is indicated by the final mental state it will have to be accepted that final release can be attained even in the state of *jīvanmukti*.

Reply: Do you mean release, in general, in the state of *jīvanmukti* or release for ever? If it is the first we accept it because release, in general, is there even in the state of *jīvanmukti*. It cannot be the second because release for ever is not there in *jīvanmukti*. Final release, as said earlier, is *Ātman* itself indicated by the final mental state.

Attainment of release is in the same manner as one searches for his necklace while wearing it on his neck and finally finds it out. Release is already attained by every one. However, ignorance has created a veil on it. What is done by realisation is eradication of that veil of ignorance. Eradication of ignorance is the essential nature of *Ātman* itself or a mental state in that form. Some hold the eradication of ignorance to be of a special type.[2] It is only to explain things easily so as to be understood by those who are poor in calibre.

2. *Eradicator of ignorance*

The realisation of the self-luminous *Brahman* cannot be the eradicator of ignorance because it is, infact, by realisation that ignorance comes to be known to be. However, *Brahman* realised through the perceptual mental state attained by hearing etc., cannot but be the eradicator of ignorance.

Objection: Is it the self-luminous consciousness that eradicates ignorance? Or is it the perceptual mental state? It cannot be the first because self-luminous consciousness is there even now and therefore, eradication of ignorance also should be there. It cannot be the second because mental state is false and it cannot eradicate ignorance or realise *Brahman*.

Reply: It is not the ordinary mental state that eradicates ignorance, but consciousness in the form of mental state or mental state which holds the reflection of consciousness. There is no harm in the false mental state eradicating ignorance and realising *Brahman*. It is like negation creating that which is existing. That which is only apparent causes joy etc., of practical reality too.

Objection: What is it that eradicates the final mental state of knowledge which eradicates ignorance? Is it that it eradicates itself or is there anything other than that which eradicates it? It cannot be the first because then it will have to be considered as momentary. That which causes its own loss without depending on anything else is momentary. It cannot be the second also because in that case it should be either *Ātman* itself or something else. *Ātman* is not cause to anything. Everything other than *Ātman* is that which is to be eradicated too.

Reply: We see that loss of the yarns creates loss of cloth. Similarly, the loss of ignorance which is the material cause of mental state causes the loss of the mental state too. Even if consciousness is considered as that which causes loss of the final mental state, there is no harm for the pure consciousness. Momentariness is the loss of something on its own, in its own form, without depending on anything else. When there is dependence on itself in some other form there is no momentariness. In fact, eradication of ignorance is itself in the form of a mental state. Therefore, there is no question of eradication of the eradicator. Eradication of the mental state is *Ātman* itself. Therefore, there is no problem of eradication of that which creates the eradication.

3. *Release, being in the form of pleasure, is the goal of man*

Objection: In your view, release is not only the eradication of pain but also the glittering of unsurpassed pleasure. And to be pleasure is not the goal of any man because everybody wants only to have pleasure and not to be pleasure. Otherwise, the self-destruction accepted by the Buddhists also will have to be considered to be the goal of man. It cannot be said that to be pleasure, not of others, is the goal of man because no one wishes to be so. Moreover, it is prolix too. It is known through positive and negative reasonings that everyone aspires pleasure of one's own.

Reply: Pleasure etc., being the goal of man, do not depend on not being other's. Nor do they depend on being one's own. They are the goal of man because they can be realised. Their being one's own or other's is unavaoidable just like the non-eternality or dependence on cause, of objects.

Objection: If capability of being realised is the factor that decides the goal, pleasure of man will be the goal of *Īśvara* too because he is capable of realising our pleasure etc., since he is omniscient.

Reply: Simple realisability is not that which makes pleasure etc., the goal of man. The goal should be that which is not known as something to be discarded. *Īśvara* knows our pleasure etc., as something to be discarded and therefore, they cannot be the goal of *Īśvara*. In the case of pleasure which is in the essential nature of *Īśvara*, we have no objection in its being the goal. There is no prolixity because so as to avoid unknown pleasure being goal, it will have to be said so. Pleasure realisable is the goal of man.

Objection: Since Ānandabodha has said that pleasure in the form of utmost illumination is the goal of man,[3] it is not correct to say that pleasure realisable is the goal of man.

Reply: What is meant by Ānandabodha is realisation of pleasure in the form of utmost illumination.

Objection: Pleasure known in the form of pleasure alone is the goal of man. *Advaitins* do not admit pleasure in the form of pleasure but do admit it in the form of *Ātman.*

Reply: Realisability will explain everything else. Therefore, anything said in addition to it will cause prolixity.

4. *Fitness of release for consciousness alone*

Objection: For whom is this release the goal? Is it for *ahamartha*? Or is it for consciousness alone? It cannot be the first because in your system release cannot apply to *ahamartha*. It cannot be the second because there is no experience such as 'let consciousness alone be released' like that we have: 'let me be released'.

Reply: Consciousness in *ahamartha* which is there at the time of release, is the goal of man.

Objection: If pleasure is the absence of pain only, then it will not be the goal of man as the release conceived by the *vaiśeṣikas*. If it is something beyond that, duality will be present.

Reply: Even though it is beyond the absence of pain, it is not beyond *Ātman*. And therefore, there is no problem of the sort alleged too.

Objection: Pleasure and its knowledge are different. If pleasure alone is *Ātman*, it will not be the goal of man since its knowledge is not there. If *Ātman* is both pleasure and its knowledge, impartiteness will be lost.

Reply: Pleasure and its knowledge are one and the same *Ātman*. Therefore, there is no relevance for duality. If there is no difference between pleasure and its knowledge how is the usage 'knowledge of pleasure'? In such cases, 'pleasure' is used so as to distinguish *Ātman* from the pain created by ignorance and knowledge is used so as to distinguish it from the material.

Objection: If the absence of pain and pleasure are really different from pain there will present *apasiddhānta*. If they are not different, it will not be possible to say that pleasure is the goal of man.

Reply: Pain is superimposed and for the same reason its difference also cannot but be so. Therefore, there is no scope for *apasiddhānta*.

Objection: Even though pleasure is known, since it is self-luminous, the absence of pain cannot be so known and therefore, it will not be the goal of man.

Reply: Absence of pain is not different from *Ātman*. Therefore, when pleasure which is not different from *Ātman* is known, absence of pain also can be known. Thus it is established that pleasure which is not different from self-luminous consciousness is the goal of man.

5. *Fitness of jīvanmukti*

The pleasure of *Ātman* is experienced by *jīvanmukta*. *Jīvanmukta* is one who has eradicated his ignorance by the realisation of *Brahman* and at the same time continues to have his body. On realisation of *Brahman*, though one's ignorance is expunged, one's body does not collapse immediatety because the mental impression of ignorance still follows as in the case of one who trembles even after the destruction of one's illusion of the serpent or as in the case of the wheel that runs even after the loss of its connection with the rod. It cannot be argued that mental impression follows only a deed or knowledge because we know that the good smell of flowers follows even after the removal of flowers from the casket. Inference also can be put forward for the same. The loss under dispute is concomitant with mental impression since it is a loss and at the same time different from the loss of mental impression like the loss of knowledge. Mental impression has no material cause though it is an effect. It is like destruction. Since it is dependent on pure *Brahman*, like ignorance, it has no dependence on ignorance too.

Objection: How can there be an existent effect without a material cause?

Reply: Even after the destruction of yarns which are the material cause of cloth the cloth exists for a moment.

Objection: There, destruction of the yarns is the cause and that of the cloth is the effect. Both do not exist at the same time. Similarly, ignorance is cause and the body effect. On the destruction of ignorance body should not exist, but *jivanmukta* bears his body even for years after the destruction of ignorance.

Reply: There is difference between the two cases. In the case of the example there is no obstruction. In the case of *jivanmukta* there is the obstruction caused by *prārabdha*.

Jivanmukta continues to have a part of his ignorance. It cannot be said that there is no part and whole with regard to ignorance because eventhough there is no part and whole there are different forms of ignorance. The *Bṛhadāraṇyaka* says: 'Indra appears in many forms through ignorance.'[4]

Objection: What is meant by the form of ignorance? Is it generality? Or is it a property in the form of significative potency or so? Or is it a particular state like ear-rings to gold? It cannot be the first or second because then that ignorance cannot be the material cause of body. It cannot be the third too because how can there be a state without that which has the state?

Reply: Ignorance has more than one power. In the case of *jīvanmukta* the power of concealment is lost. However, the power of projection remains. It will be lost only at the end of his *prārabdha*. The *śruti* says: 'By meditating on him, by joining him, by becoming one with him there is further cessation of all ignorance in the end'.[5]

It can also be said that the minute forms of ignorance are its parts. Even after the destruction of ignorance its minute particles which are competent to keep the body, continue to exist. Therefore, there is no harm in saying that there is the state of *jīvanmukti*.

6. *Refutation of grades in release*

Dvaitins hold *jīvanmukti* and final release as follows: Even after realisation, as long as one has not the supreme reverance which gives the supreme pleasure, one will not get the benediction of *Īśvara* and so one will have to rear the result of one's *prārabdha* in the world. He is *jīvanmukta*. When one achieves the supreme reverance, benediction of *Īśvara* will be obtained and the final release attained. Final release has different grades.

Madhusūdana discards the view of *dvaitins*. One who has realised *Brahman* needs to wait only until his *prārabdha* is exhausted so as to attain emancipation. The *śruti* says: 'For him there is only so much delay as he is not delivered; then he will attain perfection'.[6] Therefore, there is no need of the benediction of *Īśvara*. Any *śruti* or *smṛti* or *purāṇa* which goes against this, need not be adhered to, for, they are meant only to vouchsafe the *śruti* cited and similar ones. In fact, *smṛtis* and *purāṇas* are to be interpreted so as not to go against the *śrutis*. The *Muṇḍaka* says: 'By the very fact that he seeks for it, does it become attainable; of him this *Ātman* reveals its own nature'.[7] It is clear from this that benediction is for realisation and therefore, *smṛtis* etc., should be explained accordingly. It cannot be said that benediction is useful in the exhaustion of *prārabdha* because it exhausts only by enjoyment.

There are also no comparative degrees in release because the question of degrees arises only in duality and there is no duality in release. Moreover, the *śruti* 'he attains absolute equality'[8] discards degrees whatsoever in release. If grades are accepted in release it will become non-eternal like heaven etc. Moreover, one who has release of a lower grade will feel pain and will take envy of another who has a higher grade of release.

Objection: Do you discard grades in release owing to the lack of difference there? Or is it because all the differences there are the same? It cannot be the first because *śrutis* reveal difference there. It cannot be the second because then arise further questions. Does it mean that *jīva* and *Īśvara* are the same or jivas? It cannot be the first because *jīva* and *Īśvara* are different since both have diverse properties such as minuteness and omnipresence, partness and wholity and dependence and independence. If all the *jivas* are *Īśvara*, *Īśvara* himself will be many whereby the whole seheme of universe will collapse. *Smṛtis* also reveal the fact that *jīva* and *Īśvara* are different. Bādarāyaṇa also says that the released soul gets all the divine powers except that of running the universe as is known from the context which deals with *Īśvara* and from the non-proximity of *jīvas*.[9] Here it is clearly said that running the universe is only within the power of *Īśvara* and not of *jīva* whereby the difference between the two is established. Inference also can be coined for the same. It cannot also be said that *jīvas* are the same because some *jīvas* are superior, whereas some others are inferior. Equality of all *jivas* is contrary to what all the *śrutis*, *smṛtis*, *sūtras* and inferences reveal.

Reply: There is no difference at all in release and for the same reason no grade in release can be established. As already stated *śrutis* establish the non-difference of *jīva* and *Brahman*. Difference and unity are quite opposite and therefore, there is no scope for allegations based on the second option presented earlier. If grades are accepted in release there arise further questions. Whether these grades are in final release or in the release in the form of uplift to the world of *Brahmā* etc.? It cannot be the first because grades in release have been refuted by *Bādarāyaṇa*. He deals, is detail, with the question of grades in release and concludes that there is no grade there.[10] In the second case we have no objection.

In fact, there is no superiority or inferiority or difference of any kind with regard to *Brahman*, *jīva* or pleasure. Attainment of pleasure in its essential form in the self-luminous *Ātman* is release. It is unique and there is no question of grades whatsoever.

Madhusūdana concludes his Advaitasiddhi with the ten epilogic verses. The last verse reveals the fact that *Advaitasiddhi* is the fourth among the *siddhis*, the other three being *Iṣṭasiddhi*, *Naiṣkarmyasiddhi* and *Brahmasiddhi*.

REFERENCES

[1]Vide, TP, IV, 8.
[2]Vide, Vimuktātman, IS, chapter VIII.

[3]Vide, Ānandabodha, NM, Fasciculus III, (CSS No. 87) p. 288.
[4]Vide, BU, II, 5, 19.
[5]Vide, SU, I, 10.
[6]Vide, CU, VI, 14, 2.
[7]Vide, MU, III, 2, 3.
[8]Ibid., III, 1, 3.
[9]Vide, BRS, IV, 4, 17.
[10]Ibid., III, 4, 51, 52.

PART THREE

OBSERVATIONS

CHAPTER IX

General Observations

On the basis of the general study and also of the textual examination of *Advaitasiddhi* undertaken in the foregoing chapters some observations are made here. Observations made by Madhusūdana in in the course of his theoretical elaboration also are incorporated. Illustrations are avoided. A careful perusal of *Advaitasiddhi* will account for what has been said so far and what will be said hereafter.

Type to which Advaitasiddhi belongs

Generally two types of works have originated in the vast philosophical literature of Sanskrit. One type is called *adhikaraṇaprasthāna* and the other *vādaprasthāna*. An *adhikaraṇa* is a complete argument treating one subject in all its details. It consists of five limbs, namely, subject, doubt arising on the subject, view of the opponent, conclusion and relevancy. Some *ācāryas* add a sixth limb too, namely, fruitfulness. In the *Brahmasūtrabhāṣya* of Saṅkara we can see *adhikaraṇa*-wise treatment of the topics concerned. The *bhāṣya* was embellished by a number of commentaries and subcommentaries which also go by the name of *adhikaraṇaprasthāna. Vāda* is polemical discussion proper.[1] It is infact, syllogism adopted in accordance with the accepted policy of the philosophy concerned. *Vāda* also has got its own limbs. *Naiyāyikas* accept five limbs namely, proposition, reason, example, application and conclusion. *Mīmāṁsakas* accept the first or last three of these limbs. Madhusūdana also has upheld this tradition of *Mīmāṁsā*.

Vāda aims at the ascertainment of truth. This can be done by way of discarding the opponents' views and establishing one's own.[2] *Khaṇḍanakhaṇḍakhādya* of Śrīharṣa is a poineer work in the *Vādaprasthāna* of the *Advaitavedānta* school. *Tattvapradīpikā* of Citsukha also ranks on the same line with *Khaṇḍanakhaṇḍakhādya* in the *vādaprasthāna* of the *Advaitavedānta* school. *Advaitasiddhi* of Madhusūdanasarasvati also has an equal position. It is aptly said that *Khaṇḍana-Advaitasiddhi-Citsukhī* constitute the tripple hard nut of neo-vedantism.[3]

Nyāyāmṛta and Advaitasiddhi—a short camparison

Thanks are due to Vyāsatīrtha for having started the argument which necessitated the origin of *Advaitasiddhi*. Both *Nyāyāmṛta* and *Advaitasiddhi* together constitute the fountain-head of a series of highly polemical works in *Vedānta.*

The task undertaken by Vyāsatīrtha is worthy to be appreciated by his opponents too. He collected from the voluminous literature on *Advaita* the most crucial points for discussion, systematically arranged them and criticised them with a keen mind. Madhusūdana only had to follow suit though to refute Vyāsatīrtha. As far as the method of argument is concerned Madhusūdana has fully adopted the path opened by his opponent. And the indebtedness of both Vyāsatīrtha and Madhusūdana to *Navya Nyāya* is none the less.

Mainly there are two kinds of philosophical disputation. One is called *sandhāyasaṁbhāṣa* and the other is called *vigṛhyasaṁbhāṣa.*[4] The former is friendly discussion while the latter is aggressive. Madhusūdana has adopted the former style while Vyāsatīrtha has adopted the latter. *Dvaitins* may not agree to the proposition that Vyāsatīrtha's style is aggressive. However, it is a fact. There is no point in questioning the profundity of Vyāsatīrtha's thought. He was an able defender of the *dvaita* polemics. And it was for the same reason that his style became aggressive. It is only in tune with the requirements of *Vāda* to discard the opponent's views. Vyāsatīrtha did the very same thing so as only to be followed suit by Madhusūdana. However, Madhusūdana has maintained a friendly chord throughout his *Advaitasiddhi.*

There is an opinion that the policy of Vyāsatirtha was destructive while that of Madhusūdana was constructive.[5] This is correct only when viewed from the standpoint of *Advaitins.* Of course, Vyāsa tīrtha tried to shatter into pieces the well-built doctrines of *Advaita.* This was done by him with the good intention of constructing the edifice of *Dvaitavedānta* on the foundation already laid by Madhva. If this policy of Vyāsatīrtha is viewed as purely destructive the same logic can be applied to that of Madhusūdana also. Madhusūdana's intention also was to refute *Dvaita* so as to establish *Advaita.* He has plainly admitted the fact that *Advaita* can be established only by discarding *Dvaita.*[6]

In fact, destruction and construction need not be posed as two entirely different things which cannot co-exist. Both can co-exist in time and place. Really speaking, construction presupposes destruction because it is one of the basic principles of the dialectics of motion. When we view *Nyāyāmṛta* and *Advaitasiddhi* as separate single units we can see both destructive and constructive policies on the part of each author. Take for example the problem of the reality of the world. Vyāsatīrtha endeavours to establish the reality of the world by discarding the *advaita* view of the falsity of the world. Similarly, Madhusūdana also tries to establish the falsity of the world by discarding the *dvaita* view of the reality of the world. Viewed from a dialectical angle, both *Nyāyāmṛta* and *Advaitasiddhi* can be seen to constitute a coherent whole with its own internal contradictions.

Employment of Navya-Nyāya dialectics

The well known Sanskrit saying 'Kāṇādaṁ pāṇinīyaṁ ca sarvaśāstropakarakam' can be fully illustrated in *Advaitasiddhi*. No argument can proceed without the help of language. And for the correct use of language grammer is inevitable. In addition to the general use of the principles of grammar Madhusūdana has relied on the specific rules laid down by Pāṇini so as to substantiate his own position.

Madhusūdana's employment of the dialectics of *Navya Nyāya* in *Advaitasiddhi* is the most striking. This was necessitated by the same action of Vyāsatīrtha in his *Nyāyāmṛta*. One thing should be borne in mind in this connection: Though Vyāsatīrtha and Madhusūdana adopt the dialectics of *Navya Nyāya* they have no agreement with the views of the *naiyāyikas*. The attitude of both, towards the specific methods of *Navya-Nyāya* dialectics, is evident in their respective works. We can take for instance the dispute between Vyāsatīrtha and Madhusūdana on the use of the doubt arising out of a diversity of opinions.[7]

Vyāsatīrtha accuses that *Advaita* has introduced such innovations as the exhibition of the doubt arising from a diversity of opinions in imitation of the method of *Nyāya*. *Advaitins* really have ho hesitation to admit the same. In fact, what Vyāsatīrtha himself does is the same. One thing has to be accepted by both *dvaitins* and *advaitins*: The employment of *Navya-Nyāya* dialectics has contributed much to the theoretical perfection of both the schools of thought.

Navya Nyāya reaches its consummation in the works of Gaṅgeśopādhyāya. His famous work *Tattvacintāmaṇi* concentrates mainly on *Navya Nyāya* logic and epistemology. The *Navya Nyāya* schools of Mithila and Navadvīpa represent methodological perfection. Madhusūdana employed *Navya Nyāya* dialectics in his works, especially

Advaitasiddhi, not simply as a sequel to the use of the same by Vyāsatīrtha. Madhusūdana could realise the fact that the technique of *Navya Nyāya* is useful for the most perfect and unambigious expression of philosophical principles. That is why all the systems of Indian philosophy depend on it in one way or other.[8] As far as any study relating to the scholastic period of Indian philosophy is concerned, a smattering over *Navya Nyāya* is indispensable.

Madhusūdana's scholarship in *Navya Nyāya* is inestimable. He was a student of the Navadvīpa school of *Navya Nyāya*. He mastered the works of great *naiyāyikas* beginning from Udayana and reaching to Gaṅgeśa. It is verily said:

> navadvīpaṁ samāyāte madhusūdanavākpatau
> cakampe tarkavāgīśaḥ kātarobhūt gadādharaḥ.[9]

The whole of *Advaitasiddhi* is evidence for Madhusūdana's mastery over *Navya Nyāya* and its fruitful application in polemical discussion. All the technicalities of *Navya Nyāya* dialectics, especially those pertaining to logic, epistemology and semantics can be seen in *Advaitasiddhi*. Going through the pages of *Advaitasiddhi* one will frequently confront with such expressions as *avacchedakatā*, *pratiyogitā*, *viṣayatā*, *viṣayitā*. *prakāratā*, *viśeṣyatā*, *vidheyatā*, *koṭikatā* etc., which are peculiar to *Navya Nyāya*. The technique of the insertion of *paryāpti*, the use of double negative etc., which are also peculiar to *Navya Nyāya* can be seen in plenty in *Advaitasiddhi*.[10] It is in the first and second *paricchedas* of *Advaitasiddhi* that we come across the use of *Navya Nyāya* to the optimum level. One without any knowledge of *Navya Nyāya* will be perplexed to go through the pages of *Advaitasiddhi*.

It was Śrīharṣa who first introduced nyāya dialectics into *Vedānta* for the refutation of *Dvaita*. In his *Khaṇḍanakhaṇḍakhādya* he criticised the views of *dvaitins* including *naiyāyikas* and established the sole reality of pure self-luminous consciousness, *Brahman*. Later, Citsukha in his *Tattvapradīpikā* also did the same thing. However, the credit of producing a wholesome verbatim retort to any single work of *Dvaita* goes to Madhusūdana. Such wholesome use of *Navya Nyāya* as is there in *Advaitasiddhi*, cannot be seen elewhere in *Advaita*.

Style, in general, of Advaitasiddhi

In polemical literature linguistic precision of a high order is inevitable for the successful presentation of facts. Madhusūdana has adhered to be matter of fact and precise throughout his *Advaitasiddhi*. It has to be noticed that he has exhibited exemplary skill in this matter. He has paid equal attention to avoid aphoristic style in the name of precision. At times Madhusūdana has resorted to a highly scholastic style so as only to suit that of his opponent. As a result, the language of *Advaitasiddhi* has become far removed from ordinary Sanskrit; sometimes. However, it has never degenerated into ambiguous jargon in *Advaitasiddhi*.

It is quite surprising that even while engaging in a rough theoretical warfare, Madhusūdana maintains a form of language profound in poetic beauty. The clarity of his expressions also owes much to this poetic language. *Advaitasiddhi* may seem to be tough and unaccessible to an ordinary reader. However, once we got acquainted with the style of Madhusūdana, there would be no difficulty at all. The rythm of language as well as thought we obtain in *Advaitasiddhi*, is of a peculiar type.

Madhusūdana speaks to his opponent in a very friendly manner. Here is an example: Madhusūdana concludes the topic, the denial of the particular, with a verse as follows:

> tasmādevam viśeṣoyam na mānaviṣayaḥ sakhe
> viṣādam jahi matsiddhāvidyayā sarvasaṅgatiḥ.[11]

Madhusūdana coins such couplets to conclude his contentions.[12] Only a writer of Madhusūdana's calibre will be able to address his opponent in such a magnanimous way and at the same time without losing an inch in theoretical confrontation.

It is a common nature of all *advaitins* to ascribe, whatever they say, to their predecessors. Finally all such assertions will reach in the supreme authority of *Vedānta*, namely, the *Upaniṣads*. Madhusūdana also has not deviated from this line. Concluding the second *pariccheda* of *Advaitasiddhi* he says that whatever he has presented in *Advaitasiddhi* is obtained from his teachers.[13] However, he has presented everything he borrowed from his teachers only after putting it to the test of his intellect.[14]

Standard of polemics in Advaitasiddhi

Madhusūdana has kept the high standard of polemics throughout *Advaitasiddhi*. One of the ill-effects of the methodology of *Navya*

Nyāya in due course has been the degeneration of philosophical disputation into linguistic barrenness or simple logomachy. Some authors intentionally introduced in their texts a style which is quite unintelligible. We can never see such tendencies on the part of the author of *Advaitasiddhi*. *Advaitasiddhi* maintains so high a standard that for an appreciation of it, a very systematic study is necessary.

The reason for the high standard of polemics in *Advaitasiddhi* is *Madhusūdana's* strict adherence to the *Vādakathā*. This is in accordance with the traditional line of *Vedānta* also. *Bhagavadgīta* mentions *Vāda* as the highest order of disputation.[15] Only dispassionate and matter of fact persons can engage in *vāda*. Madhusūdana, as he himself claims, was a *muni*.[16] His approach, as a result, is factual rather than personal.

The original source of the highly polemical standard of *Advaitasiddhi* is that of the Buddhist *śūnyavāda*. Discussion on the status of the world in *Advaitasiddhi* bears testimony to this. It is the *śūnyavādin's* polemical fervour which is designed to demolish all vestiges of reality of the material world that is adopted by *Advaita*.[17]

Reliance on smṛtis and purāṇas

The infallible authority of the *Upaniṣads* is of prime concern for the *ācāryas* of *Advaita*. *Brahman* is known from the *Upaniṣads* alone. In all the *Upaniṣads* the texts become fully reconciled when they are accepted as establishing *Brahman* as their fullest import. Bādarāyaṇa has discussed the matter in detail.[18] Śaṅkara has gone one step further and stated that the aphorisms of Bādarāyaṇa are meant for stringing together the flowers of the sentences of the *Upaniṣads*.[19] Madhusūdana also has upheld the idea of the great old *ācāryas*. He has coronated the *Upaniṣads* as the king of the *pramāṇas* accepted by *vedāntins*.[20] However, Madhusūdana has made a personal contribution by elevating the authority of *smṛtis* and *purāṇas*. And it is not in supercession of the authority of *Upaniṣads* too.

Madhusūdana's reliance on *smṛtis* and *purāṇas*; is not so evident in his *Advaitasiddhi* as it is in his other works such as *Gītāgūḍhārthadipikā*, *Bhāgavatapurāṇaprathamaślokavyākhyā* etc. However, he quotes frequently from various *smṛtis*, *purāṇas* and *itihāsas*, in the course of his arguments, in *Advaitasiddhi* also. *Saṅkarṣaṇasūtra*, *Mahābhārata*, *Mīmāṁsāsūtra*, *Yogasūtra*, *Mahābhāṣya*, *Pāṇinīyam*, *Carakasaṁhitā*, *Skandapurāṇa*, *Yogavāsiṣtha*, *Rāmāyaṇa*, *Mitākṣarā*, *Viṣṇupurāṇa*, *Kūrmapurāṇa*, *Brahmavaivartapurāṇa*, *Manusmṛti*, *Hari-*

vaṁśa, *Brahmāṇḍapurāṇa* etc., have been depended upon by Madhusūdana, apart from the *Prasthānatraya* and other authoritative texts of former acaryas of *Advaita*. The reason behind Madhusūdana's reliance on *smṛtis* and *purāṇas* is his emphasis on *bhakti* as a means of emancipation. More about this will be dealt with later.[21]

Madhusudana's school as evidenced by Advaitasiddhi

Madhusūdana's contribution to system building, within the reference of *Advaita*, is a subject suitable for detailed study. What is intended here is to answer the question whether Madhusūdana has contributed so much material of his own through *Advaitasiddhi* for the formation of an *Advaita* school of Madhusūdana or not? If, not in what school of *Advaita* he can be assigned a place? This also has to be examined.

In the course of development of *Advaitavedānta* there arose a number of differences of opinion with regard to the minute details of philosophical principles. These differences led to the origin of different schools within the broad framework of theoretical *Advaita*.[22] Five such schools can be discerned in the history of *Advaita*. These are *Ekajīvavāda*, or *Dṛṣṭisṛṣṭivāda*, *Ābhasavada*, *Pratibiṁbavāda*, *Avacchedavāda* and *Sṛṣṭidṛṣṭivāda*. Madhusūdana subscribes to the first of these schools, namely *Ekajīvavāda* or *Dṛṣṭisṛṣṭivāda*. He deals with the same elaborately in *Advaitasiddhi*.[23] In his *Siddhāntabindu* also Madhusūdana examines all the principal schools of thought within *Advaita* and concludes that *Ekajīvavāda* or *Dṛṣṭisṛṣṭivāda* is the final *advaita* position.[24]

According to *Ekajīvavāda* pure consciousness is *Īśvara* and consciousness qualified per accidens is *jīva*. As regards the authorship of this theory and also its supporters there is difference of opinion among scholars. The reason for this is the leniency shown by the *ācāryas* to more than one school at the same time. The same is the case with Madhusūdana also. While being an ardent supporter of the school of *Ekajīvavāda*, Madhusūdana shows adherance to Sureśvara who is supposed to be the propounder of *Abhāsavāda*, to Vācaspatimiśra who is the propounder of *Avacchedavāda* and also to other *ācāryas*. In fact, within each of the schools mentioned above, there arose further deviations of views.

Judged from the attitudes taken by Madhusūdana in his *Advaitasiddhi* he can be placed in the school of *Vivaraṇa*. This does not mean that he has no contribution of his own in *Advaitavedānta*. Madhusūdana was an *advaitin* who could cope with the social necessities of his time to some extent. His emphasis on *bhakti* had several social implications. This shall be dealt with later.[25] For the time belng, let us conclude with the ascertainment of the school of Madhusūdana.

An analysis of the philosophical standpoints taken by Madhusūdana in his *Advaitasiddhi* shows that he cannot be considered to have initiated a fresh school of his own in *Advaita*. He belongs to the *Vivaaaṇa* school subscribed to by Padmapāda, Prakāśātman and Sarvajñātman. At the same time, Madhusūdana has his own eontribution in the matter of combining *bhakti* with theoretical *Advaita*. It can be aptly said that Madhusūdana initiated a branch of monistic theism within the school of *Vivaraṇa* in *Advaita*.

Place of Advaitasiddhi in Advaitavedānta literature

Advaitasiddhi occupies an important place in the history of *Advaitavedānta* literature. It originated at a particular critical juncture whereby its importance is multiplied. *Advaita* has grown ever since its origin in fierce resistance of pluralism of all kinds. Vyāsatīrtha composed his *Nyāyamṛta* completely demolishing the foundations of *Advaita*. His claim for assigning the same status of reality as *Brahman* has, to world also, put *Advaita* to a hard test. In fact, *Advaita* was at stake as a result of the origin of *Nyāyāmṛta*. It was *Advaitasiddhi* which saved *Advaita* in such a hard time. The place of it in the whole of *Advaitavedānta* literature is governed by this historical fact.

The dialectical and exegetical perfection of *Advaita* reached its highest peak in *Advaitasiddhi*. It should also be noted that no work of the gigantic dimension of *Advaitasiddhi* originated in *Advaita* after Madhusūdana. Thus *Advaitasiddhi* is not only a work of supreme importance in the history of *Advaita* but it is also the last great work of its type.[26]

It cannot be said that Madhusūdana simply saved the position of *Advaita* from the attack of *Dvaita*. In fact, Madhusūdana could strengthen the position of *Advaita*, theoretically and practically, a lot. *Advaitasiddhi* envisages a wholesome scheme in *Advaita* about which more will be said in the next chapter.

For a fair appreciation of *Advaitasiddhi* a knowledge of *Nyāyāmṛta* is necessary. These two works, along with their commentaries and subcommentaries, constitute the basis of *Neo-Vedānta*. Without a thorough study of these two works no student of Indian philosophy can profess to have specialised in *Vedānta*.[27] And the very same fact reveals the important place the two works occupy in Indian philosophical literature. It can also be said that without studying *Advaitasiddhi* no student of *Advaita* can profess to have mastered *Advaita*. The place *Advaitasiddhi* occupies in the *Advaitavedānta* literature also is evident from this.

REFERENCES

[1]Vide, supra, chapters IV; V, 2.

[2]Ibid., Chapter V, 2.

[3]Vide, Gaṅgānāthjhā, Eng. Tr., AS, Vol. I (Indian Thought Series No. 10, Allahabad, 1910), p. 18.

[4]Vide, *Carakasaṃhitā*, *vimānasthāna*, VIII.

[5]Vide, Anantakṛṣṇaśāstri, N.S., NAAS, Vol. I (Calcutta, 1934), p. 37.

[6]Vide, supra, chapter V, 2.

[7]Vide, supra chapter V, 3.

[8]Vide, Dinescandraguha, NNSL, (Varanasi, 1968), p. 1.

[9]Vide, AS, p. 11.

[10]For more about the technicalities of *Navya Nyāya* see, NNSL by Dinescandraguha. In fact, the employment of *Navya Nyaya* in *Advaitasiddhi* is a topic for detailed study.

[11]Vide, AS, p. 809. see for the English version, supra, chapter VI, 17.

[12]Vide, AS, pp. 814, 837, 851, 865 etc.

[13]Vide, AS, p. 854.

[14]Ibid.

[15]Vide, BG, X, 32.

[16]Vide, supra, chapter I.

[17]Vide, Chattopādhyāya, D.P., WLWDIP (Delhi, 1977), p. 31.

[18]Vide, BRS, I, 1, 4.

[19]Vide, Commentary on ARS, I, 1, 2.

[20]Vide, SB, p. 21.

[21]Vide, infra, chapter XI.

[22]Vide, Agnihotri, Chunilal; AIOC, Vol. III (1961), pp. 86—91.

[23]Vide, supra, chapter V, 39, 40

[24]Vide, SB, pp. 42—51.

[25]Vide, infra, chapter XI.

[26]Vide, Dasgupta, S.N., HIP, Vol. I, pp. 419-20.

[27]Vide, Anantakṛṣṇaśāstri, N.S., NAAS Pt. I (Calcutta, 1934), Introduction p. 4.

CHAPTER X

Observations On Schematism

Schematism

Advaita as a philosophy has a full-fledged schematism of its own. *Brahman* is the principle at the head of the schemata. Even though the world is illusory according to *Advaita*, in the broadest schematism of *Advaita*, the world also has an appropriate place. Without elaborating upon the schematism of *Advaita* let us examine the same in *Advaitasiddhi*, because it will save time and energy since both are not at variance.

Since *Advaitasiddhi* orginated as a verbatim retort to *Nāyāmṛta* the author had no option to include in it the schematism of *Advaita* according to his own intentions. It might be because of this that Madusūdana wrote his *Siddhāntabindu* exclusively dealing with the whole perceptual process of *Advaita* wherein is involved essentially the schematism of *Advaita*. However, this does not mean that there is no schematism at all in his *Advaitasiddhi*. In fact, a schematism is involved in it; the only thing is that we have to reconstruct it in an orderly manner. The whole of the schemata of *Advaita* as well as of *Advaitasiddhi* can be summed up in six heads namely, *Brahman*, ignorance, superimposition, *jīveśvaravibhāgavyavasthā*, *mānameyapratikarmavyavasthā* and liberation.

Brahman

Madusūdana's observations on *Brahman* come mainly in the second pariccheda of *Advaitasiddhi*.[1] *Brahman* is the absolute reality. It is the one without a second. Within itself also there is no multitude. *Brahman* is impartite. Accordingly the cognition of *Brahman* also is impartite. *Śrutis* deal with *Brahman*. Such sentences as 'that thou art'[2] have the impartite sense of *Brahman*. All the *śrutis* finally end in *Brahman*.

Brahman has no quality at all because *śrutis* deal with the qualitylessness of *Brahman*. *Brahman* is formless too. In fact, *Brahman* is consciousness, existence, bliss etc. Everything other than *Brahman* that seems to be is superimposed on *Brahman*. Madhusudana has indicated this in the very first salutational verse of *Advaitasiddhi*.[3]

Brahman is the material as well as efficient cause of the world.

Brahman is self-luminous. It is not the express sense of words. There is no difference whatsoever in *Brahman*. There is no particularity also in *Brahman*. Since *Brahman* is self-luminous the realisation of it also is self-luminous. In short, *Brahman* is unique.

Though *Brahman* is the ultimate reality Madhusudana accommodates everything other than *Brahman* which seems to be also in a scheme of reality. For this he introduces the principle of three-fold existence.[4] Everything other than *Brahman* which seems to exist up to the realisation of *Brahman*, has practical reality. Everything that seems to be for the time being and is subject to sublation now itself, has only apparent reality. It is, in fact, this three-fold concept of reality that substantiates the whole schematism of *Advaita* as well as *Advaitasiddhi*. Otherwise, there will be no relevance for anything other than *Brahman* whereby *Advaita* philosophy itself will be futile.

Ignorance

Madhusūdana deals with ignorance towards the second half of the first *pariccheda* of *Advaitasiddhi*. It is ignorance which combines *Brahman* and everything other than *Brahman* which seems to be. Ignorance is at the root of all dualities. Madhusūdana indicates the same also in the first salutational verse of *Advaitasiddhi*.[5] He says that everything, beginning right from *pramātṛtva*, is superimposed by ignorance.[6]

Brahman runs this world by way of ignorance. A fairly long discussion is made by Madhusūdana on the definition as well as fitness of the existence of ignorance. Ignorance is beginningless because of its dependence on beginningless consciousness. Ignorance is that which is beginngless, existent and at the same time subject to negation by knowledge. It can also be defined as that which is the material cause of false. The false world is superimposed on *Brahman* as a result of ignorance. Ignorance is negated directly by knowledge being knowledge.

Perception is evidence for the existence of ignorance. Every one perceives: 'I am ignorant, I don't know me and others'. Particularly, there is the perception: 'I don't know what you have said'. The well known reference of perception concerning *suṣupti* also is evidence for ignorance. It is as follows: 'So far, I had been in pleasant sleep; I did not know anything'.

Ignorance can be inferred also.[7] *Śrutis* and presumption are also there as evidence for ignorance.[8] Madhusūdana discards all arguments of opponents against ignorance being subject to knowledge, it existing in consiousness, *Brahman* being locus of ignorance, *jīva* being locus of ignorance and also fitness of the object of ignorance.[9]

A general misunderstanding regarding ignorance is that it is purely negative. Madhusūdana clears this misunderstanding. Ignorance has a positive aspect. In fact, it is existent and has practical reality. The whole schematism of *Advaita* will be collapsed in case ignorance is not admitted as a positive reality. This does not in any way, hamper with the sublation of ignorance by knowledge. Otherwise, the knowledge of *Brahman* will not be competent enough to do away with ignorance.

Superimposition

Madhusūdana's observations on superimposition go hand in hand with those on ignorance. The long discussion on falsity, which we come across in the beginning of *Advaitasiddhi*, presupposes superimposition. The falsity of the world is established on the basis of its being superimposed. The definition of falsity also involves in itself superimposition. For instance, the definition of falsity given by *Vivaraṇakāra* plainly states that it is the state of being discarded by cognition.[10] It is evident that only something which is superimposed can be dircarded by cognition.

Brahman and everything other than it beginning from ignorance, are related through superimposition. Madhusūdana indicates this also in the first salutational verse of *Advaitasiddhi*. The word used by him there is *kalpita*.[11] In fact, what Madhusūdana does by depicting *pramātātva* and the sort as *kalpita* in the very first verse, is reserving the chance to sublate the *kalpita* later. And he deals with the fact that the false world is subject to sublation. The substantiation of indefinability and denial of *asatkhyāti* and *anyathākhyāti*[12] etc., are to be cited in this connection.

The system of *Advaita* can never be explained without the phenomenon of superimposition. The metaphysical concept of the perpetual oneness of ultimate reality does not accept any historical evolution. At the same time the practical reality of the mutlifarious universe has to be substantiated too. Superimposition explains the arbitrary mixing up of reality and unreality by man. Once superimposition is accepted *Advaita* can contradict ultimately real representation of everything other than *Brahman*. That is the importance of superimposition in the schematism of *Advaita*. That is why Śaṅkara devotes the whol of his introduction to the commentary on *Brahmasūtras* for the dise-cussion of superimposition.[13]

Jīveśvaravibhāgavyavasthā

Madusūdana's observations on *jīveśvaravibhāgavyavasthā* are found scattered in *Advaitasiddhi*. The very *jīveśvaravibhāgavyavasthā* is of pratical reality and is of so much validity. In fitness of things dealt with in *Advaitasiddhi* in retort to *Nyāyāmṛta*, Madhusūdana had no scope to elaborate upon *jīveśvaravibhāgavyavasthā*. On the contrary, he had to defend the non-difference of *jīva* and *Brahman*.

In ultimate reality *jīva* and *Brahman* are not separate entities. Madhusūdana discards the validity of inference on the difference between *jīva* and *Brahman* put forward by his opponents.[14] However, he joins hands with his opponent in accepting the practical reality of difference. Elaborate discussion regarding the unity of *jīva* and *Ātman* follows.[15]

Mānameyapratikarmavyavasthā

Discussion on the *mānameyapratikarmavyavasthā* has been occasio-ned in *Advaitasiddhi* by the arguments of the opponents themselves. Madhusūdana deals with the superimposition of the world on *Brahman*. *Dvaitins* put a number of questions. Madhusūdana answers them and presents a number of reasonings in support of the falsity of the world on account of its being superimposed.[16] *Dvaitins* argue that if the world is superimposed the *pratikarmavyavasthā* accepted by *advaitins* will go against it because *pratikarmavyavasthā* is dependent on the relation between subject and object and *advaitins* consider the relation also superimposed. Madhusūdana discards the argument and establi-shes the *mānameyapratikarmavyavasthā* of *Advaita*.[17]

Liberation

The last two paricchedas of *Advaitasiddhi* are devoted to the discus-sion on the means and form of the summum bonum of *Advaita*. The third *pariccheda* deals with the means of liberation and the fourth *pariccheda* deals with liberation proper.[18]

Realisation is the means of liberation. Hearing is the direct means for realisation. Thinking and meditation are subsidiaries to hearing. Realisation and liberation are non-different. And realisation alias liberation is for consciousness alone. Liberation, being in the form of pleasure, is the final goal of man.

Realisation can be attained by the eradication of ignorance. This can be attained in this life itself. One who has achieved this end in this life and is still alive is called *jīvanmukta.* On the extinction of *prārabdha,* final liberation is attained. Others hold that there are different grades in liberation. *Advaitins* do not accept any grade in liberation. Liberation is, in fact, sole supreme blissful *Brahman* itself.

All the residuary categories which we come across in *Advaita* have to be accommodated in the six schemata mentioned above. The fact that Madhusūdana had an integral idea of the whole schematism of *Advaita* is evident from *Advaitasiddhi.* As evidenced by *Advaitasiddhi* the schematism of *Advaita* is in strict accordance with the basic trend of pure idealism.

REFERENCES

[1]Vide, supra, chapter VI.
[2]Vide, CU, VI, 8, 7.
[3]Vide, supra, Chapter V, 1.
[4]Vide, supra, chapter V, 63.
[5]Vide, supra, chapter V, 1.
[6]Ibid.
[7]Vide, supra, chapter V, 43.
[8]Ibid., V, 44; 45.
[9]Ibid., V, 46-50.
[10]Ibid., V, 8.
[11]Ibid., V, 1.
[12]Ibid., V, 54-62.
[13]Vide, Śaṅkara, commentary on BRS, Introduction.
[14]Vide, supra, Chapter VI, 19.
[15]Ibid., VI, 20-34.
[16]Vide, supra, Chapter V, 32.
[17]Ibid., V, 33.
[18]Vide, supra, chapters VII, VIII.

CHAPTER XI

Philosophical and Other Observations

In the last chapter the stress was on restating the schematism of *Advaita* as evidenced by *Advaitasiddhi*. It can be considered a *samāsabhāṣaṇam*. The traditional way of this *samāsabhāṣaṇam* is more precise since everything is reduced into two basic categories called *dṛk* and *dṛśya*. What is intended in this chapter is a *vyāsabhāṣaṇam* highlighting the philosophical and other positions of *Advaita* as evidenced by *Advaitasiddhi*.

Ontological

In the course of the controversy between Vyāsatīrtha and Madhusūdana, ontological problems of being and reality, quality and quantity and cause and effect have come up for discussion. Being in its essential form is sole supreme blissful *Brahman*. It is the absolute reality. However, the superimposed world and things like shell-silver have to be explained in terms of some sort of reality. Therefore, Madhusūdana introduces the three-fold theory of reality.[1] Realities are absolute, practical and apparent. The world has practical reality and things like shell-silver have only apparent-reality. It is a paradox that *Advaita* assigns reality of one kind or other to each and every thing and phenomenon.

The opponents argue that the three-fold reality is enough to explain everything. They plead for admitting the existence of realities lower in status than apparent and higher than practical but lower than absolute. Madhusūdana discards their argument and skillfully combines all realities within the three-fold division.[2]

The falsity of the world elaborately dealt with by Madhusūdana in the first half of the first *pariccheda* of *Advaitasiddhi*, does not go against the practical reality of the world. Falsity is defined accordingly.[3] Falsity and reality next to that of *Brahman* go together.

Quality is dependent on objectivity while quantity is dependent on not only objectivity but also spatiality and temporality. *Brahman* is independent of all these.[4] Therefore, quality and quantity are only in things other than *Brahman*. In other words, they depend on practical and apparent realities alone and not on absolute reality.

Cause-effect relation of *Brahman* and everything other than *Brahman* is fairly elaborately dealt with by Madhusūdana.[5] *Brahman* is the non different material and efficient cause of the world. However, this is not in a direct manner. Ignorance and its resultant super-imposition are there as intermediaries. Causality of *Brahman* is by way of being the substratum for superimposition.

The ontological position envisaged in *Advaitasiddhi* is in strict consonance with the traditional view of *Advaita*. Right from the days of *Gauḍapāda Advaita* upholds the absolute reality of *Brahman* and the falsity of everything other than it. This is diametrically opposite to the view of *dvaitins*. And for the same reason much heated discussion between Vyāsatīrtha and Madhusūdana centered round this ontological point.

Cosmological

In a philosophy which holds the whole world to be false what relevance is there for the genesis of the world? *Advaita* does not accept the real origin or development of the world. But this denial of reality is with regard to ultimate reality alone and not practical. Within the scheme of *mānameyapratikarmavyavasthā* the genesis of the world can be well explained.

It is against this background that the cosmology of *Advaita* attains a peculiar importance. Cosmology of *Advaita* as well as of *Advaitasiddhi* cannot be reduced to simple creationism. It cannot also be called evolutionism. It is infact, *vivarta* by which is meant transfiguration rather than transformation. The concept of *dṛṣṭisṛṣṭi* accepted by Madhusūdana[6] is in complete attunement with the *vivartavāda* of *Advaita*.

Brahman which is the material as well as efficient cause of the world[7] is qualityless, formless and nameless.[8] Origination means *Brahman's* taking name and form. The very same process is called *vivarta*. It is entirely different from *parināma*. *Vivarta* is an unreal modification while *pariṇāma* is actual evolution.

Advaita cosmology bases on the *vācāraṁbhaṇa śruti* of *Chandogya Upaniṣad*. 'All things made of clay are known when a lump of clay is known, since a modification has speech as its origin and exists only in name.'[9] Bādarāyaṇa deals in detail with the cosmology of *Vedānta* in the *araṁbhaṇādhikaraṇa* of *Brahmasūtras*.[10] Madhusūdana also deals with the same in detail twice in his *Advaitasiddhi*.[11] It is the keynote of the cosmology of *Advaita* as well as of *Advaitasiddhi*.

The principle by which the origin and development of the world is explained in *Advaita* is called *anirvacanīyakhyāti.* Madhusūdana elaborately deals with the same.[12] He also discards the *asatkhyāti, anyathākhyāti* etc., held by others so as to explain the origin etc., of the world as well as of object that become the predicate of knowledge.[13] *Asatkhyāti* upholds creationism whereby the origin of everything from non-existence is explained. The *śruti* that non-existent was there in the beginning,[14] is put forward in evidence of *asatkhyāti.* Madhusūdana puts forward a number of *śrutis* dealing with the undistinguished nature of unique *Brahman* in the beginning. Similarly *anyathākhyāti* which upholds simple apprehension of one thing at some other place also has no locus standi according to Madhusūdana.

Origin, existence and dissolution of the world are conceived as a continuum by *Advaita.* Since it is in the very same locus which is single, unique and absolutely real the theory of evolution of *Sāṅkhyas* also has no rationale for approval. The *naiyāyika* view of placing a God as the creator at the head also has no sanctity. The sequence of the origin of worldly objects has only secondary place in *Advaitasiddhi* since it is of concern only for the ignorant.

Epistemological

Theory of knowledge of *Advaita* is found applied in *Advaitasiddhi* rather than the elaboration of it. The *pramāṇas* accepted by *Advaita* as well as by *Advaitasiddhi* are six namely, perception, inference, comparison, verbal testimony, presumption and non-cognition. In tune with the views of the great old *ācāryas* Madhusūdana accepts the supreme validity of verbal testimony.[15] However, If we analyse quantitatively the dependence on *pramāṇas* in *Advaitasiddhi* we can see that the same on inference is not so bad. This might be because of the employment of *Navya Nyāya* methodology. And in that, Vyāsatīrtha is more responsible than *Madhusūdana*. Since Vyāsatīrtha employed the same throughout his *Nyāyāmṛta,* Madhusūdana who encountered him had no option but to follow suit. In the first *pariccheda* of *Advaitasiddhi*, especially in dealing with falsity, the stress on inferencetis in the excess. However, Madhusūdana has shown no reservation to make it clear that verbal testimony is superior in validity when compared with other *prāmāṇas.*[16]

One may ask: What is the relevance of a theory of knowledge in *Advaita* according to which there is nothing other than *Brahman*? This question proceeds from a colossal misunderstanding of the epistemological position of *Advaita*. *Advaita* never denies the cognisability of things other than *Brahman*. On the contrary it is committed to establish the cognisability whereby falsity can also be established.[17] In this respect epistemology of *Advaita* is closely connected with its cosomology and both come under the broad scheme of *mānameyapratikarmavyavasthā*.[18] Falsity and perceptibility go hand in hand in *Advaita* as well as *Advaitasiddhi*. This is with regard to the world. What is fully perceptible and perceptual everywhere actually is *Brahman*.Even though *Brahman* is absolute non-dual reality we superimpose on it a world of fleeting duality. Madhusūdana establishes the fitness of omniscient *Brahman* being the locus of ignorance[19] wherefrom proceeds all duality. The ground which substantiates the theory of knowledge of *Advaita* is the reality of duality for all practical purposes.

Two more things have to be stated in connection with the theory of knowledge of *Advaita*. One is the co-existence of the validity of verbal testimony and perception. Validity of perception is not independent and for the same reason it has to admit the superiority in validity of verbal testimony. At the same time there is no harm in perception being born from verbal testimony.[20] The other thing is the self-luminousness of *Brahman*. *Brahman* is self-luminous.[21] The most important thing is that the realisation of *Brahman* also is self-luminous.[22] It is upto realisation and not inclusive of it that the theory of knowledge is relevant. Any discussion beyond that level is futile also. That is why the method of presentation of '*neti neti*'[23] has become prominent in *Advaita*. Right from the first salutational verse to the last topic of *Advaitasiddhi* Madhusūdana has maintained this basic approach even while waging terse word war against Vyāsatīrtha.

Teleological

Teleological conceptions of *Advaitasiddhi* are in consonance with its own ontological, cosmological and epistemological conceptions. Prominence of extra human purposes and expediency is the prime concern for teleology and *Advaitasiddi* upholds the same. *Advaita* agrees to the teleological argument of *naiyāyikas* so far as it does not assert to prove the existence of God.

Advaitasiddhi does not conceive of a God beyond or equal to *Brahman*. Such divisions as *jīva* and *Īśvara* have only practical reality. Ultimately *jīva* and *Ātman* are non-different.[24] Transhuman purpose is not to be misunderstood as something of a serious nature. In fact, it is only a *līla* of the sole supreme reality to transfigure itself. *Ad-*

vaitasiddhi considers the whole universe and its intricacies as an organic entity regulated by *Brahman*. And the expediency peculiar to *Advaita* teleolagy is also involved in it.

Eschatological

The fourth *pariccheda* of *Advaitasiddhi* is concerned mainly with eschatological problems. *Advaita* has a complete eschatology built with the materials from the *Upaniṣads*, *Brahmasūtras* and *Bhagavadgīta*. The theory of *karma* and also of rebirth are relevant here. Transmigration is an unending process except for those who have attained release. And the relevance of release also is the same. *Chāndogyopaṇiṣad* says: 'he does not take birth again.'[25] Lord Kṛśṇa says to Arjuna- 'Having attained to me they do not take birth again'.[26] This is with regard to the *parāvidya*. Release is attained by the eradication of ignorance.[27] Release being in the form of pleasure supreme is the final goal of man.[28]

Advaita maintains that those who have fulfilled their duties but have not yet reached the highest goal have two paths of journey after death.[29] *Advaitasiddhi* makes mention of the same but does not elaborate upon it.[30] It is quite natural for a highly polemical text like *Advaitasiddhi*. Max Muller was correct when he said that the adoption of this eschatology by *Vedānta* simply on the authority of the *Upaniṣads* is strange to be believed.[31] *Advaitasiddhi* is concerned with the final goal and not with the so-called paths. *Advaitasiddhi* elaborates upon the fitness of *jīvanmukti* as well as the absence of grades in release.[32]

Ethical

Ethics of *Advaita* lies in *Advaitasiddhi* embedded with its general organisation. And this is a common feature of Indian philosophical tradition. In strict accordance with the ontological position of *Advaita*, there is not much scope for talking of good, evil and morality. However, ethical problems are dealt with in *Advaita* in relation to the practical reality of the world. The theory of *karma* and also of rebirth is relevant in this connection also. It is in fact this theory that paves the way for ethics to proceed in *Advaita*.

There prevails an opinion that *Vedānta* is opposed to ethical theism. This has been subjected to severe criticism by several scholars.[33] The importance of ethics in *Advaitasiddhi* is to be guessed from the reliance of the author on *smṛtis* and *purāṇas*.[34] Madhusūdana frequently quotes from *Bhagavadgīta* which is generally accepted to be the science of ethics.

Theistic

The evolution of theism in Indian philosophy is a vast subject for detailed study. From what Max Muller calls henotheism,[35] it developed into monism through centuries. *Advaita* with its stress on *Brahman* often takes a pantheistic approach. It refuses to admit God who is the creator and the governor of the world as the summum bonum.[36] It was under this pretext that the rival schools of *Viśiṣṭādvaita* and *Dvaita* could flourish and win the support of the masses. A personal God of supreme position is of the prime concern for devotees. Madhusūdana's greatest contribution to *Advaita* philosophy is the theistic modification of it.

Madhusūdana was an ardent devotee of Śrīkṛṣṇa. It is a wonder as to how the learned *muni* who established the supremacy of *Advaita* by writing one of the accepted masterpieces of *Vedānta*, *Advaitasiddhi*, could proclaim Lord Kṛṣṇa as the ultimate reality.[37] Madhusūdana's emphasis on *bhakti* as a means for emancipation also goes in tune witn his devotion to Kṛṣṇa. One thing has to be borne in mind in this connection: Madhusūdana's soft corner towards theism never amounted to tend him corrupt the fundamental tenets of *Advaita*. *Advaitasiddhi* bears evidence for this. The discussion on the problem of grades in release can be cited as an instance.[38] In fact, Madhusūdana did not meddle with *bhakti* in his *Advaitasiddhi*. He wrote separate works for elaborating up on his views as an ardent devotee.

Methodological

The aggregate of ways of investigation and interpretation used by Madhusudana in *Advaitasiddhi* shows his dialectical approach. The principal tenets of Advaita are presented through the means of *pūrvapakṣa* and *siddhānta*. This method, in opposition to that of presenting facts through simple statements, is dialectical in the original sense of the term. The dialectical method in *Advaita* is not an invention of Madhusūdana. His predecessors beginning from Śaṅkara have profoundly used it. However, profuse use of the dialectical method to counter the arguments of a rival book in full was something new.

One should not be misled by the use of the term dialectical method. It is not used in the modern sense. It is a parodox that the dialectics of *Advaitasiddi* is essentially directed against the reality of the world absolutely. In the modern sense dialectics is the science of the general laws governing the development of nature, society and thought. And the same has no relevance in *Advaita* for which everything other than *Brahman* is superimposed. The theory of *dṛṣṭisṛṣṭi*[39] accepted by Madhusūdana is just contrary to the conceptions of modern dialectics. Therefore, the approach of Madhusūdana is dialectical with regard to only the methodology and not to the content part of *Advaitasiddhi*.

Historical

There is an opinion that history describes certain unique events in time and space and that it sticks to the particular and the personal and cannot explain the eternal truths of *Vedānta*.[40] This has originated from an outmoded view of history. Modern studies in the fields of philosophy and history have proved the contrary. A new branch of human knowledge known as historico-philosophical study itself has evolved.[41] History is not concerned with unique events alone. There are definite and regular laws which govern history. Viewed from this angle *Advaitasiddhi* also can be historically approached.

Madhusūdana is often accused of joining hands with Rāmānuja in accepting the importance of bhakti.[42] There is truth in it. The very ashes of Śaṅkara could have risen in protest against such a bold compromise by one of his followers with his opponents as Madhusūdana attempted.[43] However, Madhusūdana's act had a psychological effect of social relevance. A serious philosophical situation had arisen in the history of *Advaita* as a result of the strong theistic sentiment popularised by the other schools of *Vedānta* as well as the *Nyāya* system. Śaṅkara's emphasis on the *nirguṇaśrutis* could easily be depicted as completely unwarranted and even a matter of his idiosyncracy. What was needed was a genuinely philosophical retort to the opposing schools and systems as well as the supply of material for quenching the theistic thirst of the followers of *Advaita*. What Madhusūdana did was actually the same.

It is a matter of importance that a scholar like Madhusūdana also could play his role in the Bhakti movement of the day. And for the same reason the movement itself was elevated to the level of one which served the intellectual circles as well as the common people.

The historical mission undertaken by Madhusūdana had far reaching results in Indian life. Madhusūdana could add to the philosophical heritage of India a gem like *Advaitasiddhi*. The theoretical repairs done by Madhusūdana on the foundations of *Advaita* which was at stake, have ever been of immense value. The historical importance of the controversy between Madhusūdana and Vyāsatīrtha represented by *Advaitasiddhi* and *Nyāyāmṛta* respectively, is so much that a historian of Indian philosophy like Dasgupta, S.N., devoted two complete chapters for the discussion of it.[44]

Since Madhusūdana patched up the theoretical foundations of *Advaita*, later practical *advaitins* such as Svāmi Vivekānanda and Śrīnārāyaṇaguru could devote more time for working for the uplift of the down-trodden. This does not mean that they did nothing in the matter of theoretical enrichment. What is intended is that as a result of the composition of *Advaitasiddhi* by Madhusūdana, *Advaita* could exist intact so that it could be utilised by Vivekānanda and Śrīnārāyaṇa. The healthy trend of the *Vādakatha* found applied in *Advaitasiddhi* is of practical relevance even today. It is a pity that ideological struggle of the present day not only lacks often in profundity of argument but also diminishes to the levels of incredibility. And hence is the relevance of the study of *Advaitasiddhi*.

REFERENCES

[1]Vide, supra, chapter V, 63.
[2]Ibid.
[3]Ibid., chapter V, 7.
[4]Vide, supra, chapter VI, 4—7.
[5]Ibid., VI, 8—10.
[6]Vide, supra, chapter V, 39.
[7]Viee, supra, chapter VI, 8—10
[8]Ibid., VI, 4—6.
[9]Vide, CU, VI, 1, 4.
[10]Vide, BRS, II, 1, 14.
[11]Vide, AS, pp. 323; 503. See also supra, chapter V, 15; 34.
[12]Vide, supra, chapter V, 54—57.
[13]Ibid., V, 59—60.
[14]Vide, TU, II, 7.
[15]Vide, SB, p. 21.
[16]Vide, supra, V, 19—20.
[17]Ibid., V, 33.
[18]Ibid., V, 33.
[11]Ibid., V, 48.
[20]Vide, supra, chapter VII, 8.
[21]Vide: supra, chapter VI, 11.

[22]Ibid., VI, 12.
[23]Vide, BU, II, 3, 6.
[24]Vide, supra, chapter VI, 27—28.
[2] Vide, CU, VII), 15, 1 See also AS, p. 824.
[26]Vide, BG, VIII, 15.
[27]Vide, supra, chapter VIII, 1.
[28]Ibid., VIII, 3.
[29]Vide, KAU, I, 2. See also BRS, III, 1, 12; 13.
[30]Vide, AS, pp. 851-58.
[31]Vide, Max Muller, SSIP (Varanasi, 1971), p. 175.
[32]Vide, supra, chapter VIII, 5; 6.
[33]Vide, Kokileśvaraśāstri, IAP (Varanasi, 1979), chapter IV.
[34]Vide, supra, chapter IX.
[35]Vide, Max Muller, OGR (Varanasi, 1964), p. 260.
[36]Vide, Chattopadhyāya, D.P., Indian Atheism (New Delhi. 1983), p. 25.
[37]Vide, Rajagopalan, V, PA, p. 254.
[38]Vide, supra, chapter VIII, 6.
[39]Vide, suptra, chapter V, 39.
[40]Vide, Srīnivasāchari, P.N., PV, p. XXXIV.
[41]Vide, Oizerman, Theodor, PHP (Moscow, 1973), p. 5.
[42]Vide, Mainkar, T G., CSCB (Delhi, 1969), p. 16.
[43]Vide, Zimmerman, R., Foreword, Eng. Tr. of SB by Modi, P.M. (Bombay, 1929), p. I.
[44]Vide, Dasgupta, S.N., HIP, Vol. IV (Delhi, 1975), pp. 204-319.

CHAPTER XII

Conclusion

Vedāntic thought has assumed a new importance in the present-day world which is in an unprecedented crisis. However, the modern synthetic approach to *Vedānta* and science is often at the risk of objectivity. When viewed objectively, one can understand that diversity and contradictions have always constituted the dynamic force in Indian philosophy as well as in *Vedānta*. *Advaitasiddhi* bears evidence for the same. It is one of the best products of the terse theoretical fight that ensued between *dvaitins* and *advaitins*. The fight has been continuing for the last seven hundred years.

Madhusūdanasarasvati, the author of *Advaitasiddhi*, lived during the second half of the sixteenth and the first half of the seventeenth centuries A.D. He lived in Bengal. He led an ascetic life throughout. He produced a school of his disciples. More than twenty works have been ascribed to him. His authorship of ten of them is beyond doubt. *Advaitasiddhi* is one among them.

The *siddhi*-literature of Sanskrit is vast. The same of *Vedānta* also is fairly extensive. Of the sixteen works of the *siddhi*-literature, *Advaitasiddhi* stands first in importance.

Controversy between *dvaitins* and *advaitins* occupies an important position in the history of Indian philosophy. In his masterpiece *Nyāyāmṛta*, Vyāsatīrtha tore into pieces the well built theories of *Advaita*. In his masterpiece *Advaitasiddhi*, Madhusūdanasarasvati retorted *Nyāyāmṛta verbatim-et-litteratim*. The controversy continued between the followers of *Dvaita* and *Advaita*. An objective analysis of the controversy against its historical setting is relevant today.

Advaitasiddhi is a highly polemical text belonging to the *vādaprasithāna* of Indian philosophy. It stands on a par with *Khaṇḍanakhaṇḍakhādya* of Śrīharṣa and *Tattvapradīpika* of Citsukha. *Advaitasiddhi* consists of four *paricchedas*. There are one hundred and twelve topics in all. The principal commentaries on *Advaitasiddhi* are *Siddhivyākhyā* of Balabhadra, *Gauḍabrahmānadīyam* of Brahmānandasarasvati, *Saralavyākhyā* of Rameśvaradatta and *Bālabodhini* of Bāgchi, Yogendranāth. Besides these, sub-commentaries, translations, adaptations etc., are also there.

In the very beginning of *Advaitasiddhi*, the author pays tributes to Viṣṇu who is truth, consciousness and bliss. In order to establish *Advaita*, falsity of the world has to be established. And it is to be done through any of the three *kathās* namely, *vāda*, *jalpa* and *vitaṇḍā*. Since doubt arising from a diversity of opinions is the forepart of discussion, first of all, the diversity of opinions has to be presented. Whether falsity is, that which cannot be contradicted by any true knowledge other than that of *Brahman*, which is fit to be perceived as existent, which is different from consciousness and which is the counter-correlate of non-existence of all the three periods of time in its locus, or not? Whether ether is false or not? Whether earth is false or not and so on.

Ānandabodha has coined inference on the falsity of the world. The world under dispute is false because it is cognisable, material and finite like shell-silver. Falsity can be defined in five ways: Padmapāda's definition is that falsity is not being the locus of either reality or unreality like shell-silver. Prakāśātman defines it in two ways: Falsity is being the counter correlate of negation for all the three periods of time in the very some locus where it appears to be. It is the state of being discarded by cognition. Citsukha defines falsity to be the counter-correlate of the absolute negation existing in the locus where it appears to be. Ānandbodha's definition is that falsity is being something different from existence.

Falsity also is false. It will not result in the reality of the world bscause it happens so only when both have different metaphysical status. Here, both have the same status.

Cognisability can be defined in many ways. It has a formal content. Materiality is the character of non-cognition or of non-self. Finiteness means limitedness by time, space or object.

Citsukha presents another inference on falsity. The cloth is the counter-correlate of the absolute negation in the yarns because it is a composite whole like other composite things. There is no presence of extraneous adjuncts in the proof of this inference. The inference has no similarity with pseudo-inferences also. It cannot be contradicted by perception. Perception has no superior validity than that of inference or verbal testimony. In fact, inference contradicts and negates perception. Verbal testimony also does so. This is evidenced by the *apacchedādhikaraṇa* of *Mīmāṁsā*.

The inference is not similar to that which tries to establish fire to be cool. It cannot be argued that perception has non-contradiction because it is subject to rejection by inference and verbal testimony. Perception cannot be taken to be valid because there is no surety to its non-contradiction in future.

Though opponents counter-pose inference on the reality of the world, it has no locus standi. There can be particular inferences also on the falsity of the world. Madhusūdana presents twenty six such inferences. Inference on the falisty of the wold has no contradiction with scriptures, because all the *śrutis* establish the falsity of the world and the sole reality of *Brahman.*

It is a fact that the probans of the inference is non-existent. However, there is no harm for the inference because the non-existent also can be probans. In the absence of probanshood for the non-existen-it will sublate many inferences and perceptions of our practical ext perience. There is no cogniser-cognisable relation also. There are enough of reasonings in support of the falsity of the world.

Even if the world is false there is no harm for the *pratikarma-vyavasthā* accepted in *Advaita.* All reasoaings against the falsity of the world can be easily denied. In fact, the *śrutis* are fit to establish the falsity of the world. Though opponents try to exhibit sublation of the *śruti* dealing with non-duality, Madhusūdana ably refutes the same.

The meaning of the *śruti* 'one only' etc., clearly mentions the sole reality of *Brahman* as well as the falsity of the world. Otherwise, the state of being discarded by cognition will not be fit. In fact, the world has come into seeming being through the process of *dṛṣṭisṛṣṭi.* The *draṣṭā* of the process is only one *jīva* and not many. It is his ignorance that causes superimposition of the world.

Ignorance as defined by Citsukha is beginningless, existent and at the same time negated by knowledge. It can also be defined as the state of being negated directly by knowledte being knowledge. Ignorance is perceptible. It can also be inferred. *Ṣrutis* also reveal the existence of ignorance. Presumption also is evidence for the same. Ignorance is known through *sākṣin* and not through pure consciousness. However, ignorance can be there in pure consciousness. There is nothing unfit in the omniscient *Brahman* being the locus of ignorance *Jīva* also can be the locus. Pure consciousness is the object of ignorance.

It is as a result of ignorance that *ahaṁkāra* etc., originate. *Śrutis* reveal by implication that pure consciousness is without any *ahaṁkāra.* Agency etc., are properties of non-self. Even if *ahamartha* is non-self, it seems to be as that of *Ātman*. It is as a result of the superimposition of the unity of *Ātman* and the body.

Ignorance is indefinable. Perception, inference, verbal testimony and presumption are evidences for the same. Indefinability is the state of being sublated.

In superimposition the objects are non-existent. Therefore, *asatkhyāti* is not relevant. *Anyāthākhyāti* also is not correct. Infact, the superimposed objects originate from ignorance. They are evolutes of ignorance. In the knowledge of such illusory things there are two *vṛttis*; the *vṛtti* of the mind and that of ignorance. Existence is of three kinds: absolute, practical and apparent. *Brahman* is absolutely existent, the world practically and objects like shell-silver apparently.

In the second pariccheda of *Advaitasiddhi* the means of severing the false bondage is dealt with. Impartite cognition of *Brahman* is the means. The sentence beginning with 'reality' has impartite sense. *Māhavākyas* like 'that thou art' reveal the impartite sense of *Brahman*. *Brahman* has no quality or form. Consciousness etc., are the essential nature of *Brahman*. *Brahman* is the material as well as efficient cause of the world. *Brahman* is self-luminous. The realisation of *Brahman* also is self-luminous. *Brahman* is not the express sense of words. *Brahman* has no particularity. There is no difference, whatsoever, in *Brahman*. Perception, inference and other evidences trying to establish difference in *Brahman*, in *jīva* between *Brahman* and among *jīvas*, are invalid.

There are certain *śrutis* dealing with the difference of the practically real world. There is no harm in that. In fact, *śrutis* dealing with difference are restatements. Difference in words etc., is not evidence for difference in *Ātman*. *Śrutis* dealing with difference have not the six principles that determine purport in their support. Unity is the essential nature of *Ātman*. *Jīva* and *Ātman* are one and the same. The *śrutis* that deal with unity have no contradiction with any other evidence. In fact, *śrutis*, inference and other evidences establish unity. Unity of *jīva* and *Brahman* can be established based on the law of the object and its reflection also. Since reflection is non-different from the object, *Brahman* and *jīva* are non-different.

Jīva is all pervading and is not minute. There are *śrutis* and inference as evidence to this effect. 'He is everlasting, all-pervading' etc. are *śrutis*. Inference is that *Jīva* is not minute since he is locus for properties that are perceptible and since he is subject to perception like a jar.

In the third pariccheda of *Advaitasiddhi* the means of severing bondage alone is dealt with. Realisation of *Brahman* is the means. Hearing is the principal means for realisation and thinking and meditation are subsidiary means. The injuction which prescribes hearing is one of necessary arrangement. It is quite possible for hearing etc., to be subject to injunction. Discussion can be caused by injunction on hearing. Vācaspatimiśra holds that the injunction on the study of the *Vedas* is that which necessitates discussion in the case of both the *karmakāṇḍa* and the *jñānakāṇḍa*.

Knowledge is not dependent on man. There can be no injunction on knowledge. Hearing is not knowledge but is a particular mental state.

Verbal testimony can produce perception. *Śrutis* and inference are there as evidence for the same. Knowledge born from such *śrutis* as 'that thou art' is perception since it is not counter-correlate of the eternal negation existing in perceptual knowledge like the generality of knowledge. *Upaniṣads* which are verbal testimony are the valid means of perception of *Brahman*.

The fourth and last *parricheda* of *Advaitasiddhi* deals with the final goal of man. Release from bondage is the final goal. It can be achieved by eradication of ignorance. Ignorance can be eradicated by the realisation of *Brahman*. *Brahman* indicated by the final mental state eradicates ignorance. The problem of eradication of the final mental state does not arise because it is *Brahman* itself.

Release is in the form of pleasure. Therefore, it can be the final goal of man. Release is for consciousness alone. Since pleasure and its knowledge are non-different there is no question of the known or unknown nature of release. The pleasure of *Ātman* is realised by *jīvanmukta* who has eradicated his ignorance by the realisation of *Ātman*.

In the final release there are no grades at all. The question of grades arises only in difference. In release there is no difference of any sort. Release attained through the realisation of non-dual *Brahman* is unique. All the *śrutis*, *smṛtis*, *purāṇas*, *śutras* and all other evidences are to be explained in this sense.

Madhusūdana concludes his *Advaitasiddhi* with ten epilogic verses. *Advaitasiddhi* is the fourth among the *siddhis*. The other three are *Iṣṭasiddhi*, *Naiskarmyasiddhi* and *Brahmasiddhi*.

The credit of having caused the origin of *Advaitasiddhi* goes to Vyāsatīrtha. *Nyāyāmṛta* of *Vyāsatīrtha* presents us with an aggressive discussion while *Advaitasiddi* does a friendly one. Both have employed the *Navya Nyāya* dialectics. And both *Nyāyāmṛta* and *Advaitasiddhi* belong to the *vādaprasthāna.*

Madusūdana's style, in general in his *Advaitasiddhi,* is matter of fact and precise. The language of *Advaitasiddhi* shows poetic beauty and profundity at the same time. The author has kept a high standard of polemics throughout *Advaitasiddhi.* The infallible authority of the *Upaniṣads* has been accepted by Madhusūdana. However, he relies on *smṛtis* and *purāṇas* also.

Madhusūdana belongs to the school of *Ekajīvavāda* of *Advaita.* This is in tune with the *Vivaraṇa* school as well. The school of Madhusūdana can better be called that of monistic theism.

Advaitasiddhi occupies an important position in the literature of *Advaita.* Without a study of *Advaitasiddhi* no student of *Advaita* can profess to have mastered *Advaita.*

Advaitasiddhi envisages a wholesome scheme of *Advaita.* The whole schematism of *Advaita* as well as of *Advaitasiddhi* can be summed up in six heads namely, *Brahman*, ignorance, superimposition, *jīveśvaravibhāgavyavasthā, mānameyapratikarmavyavasthā* and liberation. Madhusūdana's observations on *Brahman* come mainly in the second *pariccheda* of *Avaitasiddhi.* Ignorance is dealt with mainly in the second half of the first *pariccheda.* Along with it come observations on superimposition also. *Jīveśvaravibhāgavyavasthā* is found scattered in *Advaitasiddhi. Mānameyapratikarma vyavasthā* is explicitly dealt with in the first *pariccheda.* The last two *parichedas* deal with the means of liberation and liberation proper. The fact that the author had an integral idea of the whole schematism of *Advaita* is evident in the works of Madhusūdana especially in *Advaitasiddhi.*

Ontological problems of being and reality, quality and quantity and cause and effect have been presented by Madhusūdana in *Advaitasiddhi. Brahman* is the essence of all being. It is absolutely real. *Brahman* is the material as well as efficient cause of the universe. Cosmology of *Advaita* proceeds from this fact. Origination means in *Advaita* only *Brahman's* taking name and form. It is comprised in the *anirvacanīyakhyāti.*

The theory of knowledge of *Advaita* is found applied in *Advaitasiddhi.* As usual, *pramaṇas* are six, namely, perception, inference, camparison, verbal testimony, presumption and non-cognition. *Pramāṇas* are valid only upto realisation not inclusive of it. That is why in *Advaita* the method of *neti neti* is accepted. Madhusūdana has also upheld the method in *Advaitasiddhi.*

Teleological conceptions of *Advaitasiddhi* are in consonance with its own ontological, cosmological and epistemological ones. Madhusūdana does not conceive of a personal God of paramount importance over and above *Brahman.* However, within the scheme of his *Advaita* Madhusūdana finds a place for a personal God. He was a great devotee of Lord Kṛṣṇa. His greatest contribution to *Advaita* was the theistic modification of it.

The methodological approach, in total, of *Advaitasiddhi* is dialectical. This cannot be applied to its content. By the composition of *Advaitasiddhi* also Madhusūdana was catering to the social needs of the day. He could save the theoretical position of *Advaita* from a grave philosophical situation. At the same time he could do justice to the theistic sentiments of the people. He joined hands with the leaders of the Bhakti Movement of the day.

Advaitasiddhi is a gem of the philosophical heritage of India. Even today the healthy trend of the *vādakathā* found applied in *Advaitasiddhi* is relevant. The present day needs of ideological struggle warrant the same. The relevance of the study of *Advaitasiddhi* also is to be found in the very same fact.

Select Bibliography

I. Sanskrit

Advaitatattvaśuddhi of Anantakṛṣṇasastri, N.S., Madras, 1958.

Advaitatattvasudhā of Anantakṛṣṇaśāstri, N.S., Pt. I, Varanasi, 1960.

Advaitadīpikā of Anantakṛṣṇaśāstri, N.S., Nurani, year not seen.

Advaitadīpikā of Nṛsiṁhāśrama with the commentary of Nārāyanāśrama, Ed., Pathak, M.M. and Nene, G.S., Benares, 1919.

Advaitabrahmasiddhi of Sadānandayati, Ed., Tarkadarśanatīrtha, Gurucaran and Tarkavāgish, Pancānan, Calcutta, 1932.

Advaitaratnarakṣaṇa of Madhusūdanasarasvati, Ed., Anantakṛṣṇaśāstri, N.S., Bombay, 1917.

Advaitavedāntabindu of Anantakṛṣṇaśāstri, N.S., Benares, Samvat 2021.

Advaitasiddhāntavidyotana of Gauḍabrahmānandasarasvati with *Nṛsiṁhavījñāpana* of Nṛsiṁhāśrama, Ed., Sūryanārāyaṇaśukla, Benares, 1934.

Advaitasiddhi of Madhusūdanasarasvati with *Gurucandrikā* of Gauḍabrahmānandasarasvati, Ed., Srinivasachar, D., and Veṅkaṭanarasiṁhaśāstri, G., Mysore, 1933.

Advaitasiddhi of Madhusudanasarasvati with *Gauḍabrahmānandīyam*, *Viṭṭhaleśopādhyāyī*, *Siddhivyākhyā* and *Caturgranthī*, Ed. Anantakṛṣṇaśāstri, N.S., Revised Ed., Śivarāmaśāstri, Bombay, 1937.

——of Madhusūdanasarasvati with *Gauḍabrahmānandīyam*, *Vitthaleśopādhyāyī*, *Siddhivyākhyā* and *Caturgranthi* Ed., Anantakṛṣṇaśāstri, N.S., Parimal Sanskrit Series No. 7, Delhi, 1982.

——of Madhusudanasarasvati with *Bālabodhini* of Bāgchi, Dr. Yogīndranāth, Ed., Bāgchi, Dr. Sitansusekhar, 2 Vols. Varanasi, 1971.

——of Madhusūdanasarasvati Eng. Tr. of Jha, Pandit Gangānāth, incomplete, Allahabad, 1917.

——of Madhusūdanasarasvati with *Saralavyākhyā* of Kāmeśvaradatta, 2 vols., Bombay, 1923—24.

Advaitasiddhisiddhāantasāra of Sadānandavyāsa, 2 Pts., Benares, 1903.

Advaitāmoda of Abhyañkar, V.S., Ed., Apte, H.N., Poona, 1918.

Anuvyākhyāna of Madhvācārya with *Nyāyasudhā* of Jayatīrtha, Ed., Savanur, G.R., Dharwar, 1932.

Apohasiddhi, Kṣaṇabhaṅgasiddhi, Citrādvaitasiddhi, Sarvajñasiddhi etc., of Ratnakīrti in one book, Ed., Thakkur, Anantalal, Patna, 1975.

Arthaśāstra of Kauṭilya, Ed., Shamasastri, Benares, 1961.

Arthasaṅgraha of Laugākṣibhāskara, Ed. with Eng. Tr., Thibaut, Dr. G., Varanasi, 1974.

Aṣṭādhyāyī of Pāṇini, Ed. with Eng. Tr., Vasu, Śrīśachandra, 2 Vols., Delhi, Vol. I, 1062, Vol. II, 1980.

Ātmatattvaviveka of Udayana, Ed., Ḍhuṇḍhirājaśāstri, Benares, 1940.

Ātmabodha of Śaṅkārācārya with Ṭīkā of Madhusūdanasarasvati, Ed., Bhattācārya, D.C., Calcutta, 1961.

Iṣṭasiddhi of Vimuktāman, Ed., Hiriyanna, M., Baroda, 1933.

Īśvarapratipatttiprakāśa of Madhusūdanasarasvati, Ed. Gaṇapatiśāstri, T. Trivandrum, 1921.

Īśādidaśopaniṣadaḥ with commentary of Śaṅkārācārya, J., Motilal Benarsidas, Delhi, 1978.

Upaniṣadsaṅgrahaḥ Ed., Śāstri, J.L., 2 Pts., Delhi, 1980.

Ṛgveda with commentary of Sāyaṇa, Ed., Muller, F. Max, 4 Vols., Varanasi, 1966.

——Eng. Tr., Wilson, H.H., 7 Vols., Delhi, 1977.

Kāśikā of Jayāditya and Vāmana with *Prakash* Hindi commentary, Ed., Śrīnārāyaṇamiśra, 2 Vols. Benares, 1969.

Kiraṇāvali of Udayana, Ed., Dube, Vindhyeśvarīprasād, Benares, 1885-1919.

Khaṇḍanakhaṇḍakhādya of Śrīharṣa, Ed. with Skt. and Hindi commentaries, Jha, Dr. Navikāntha, Varanasi, 1970.

Gādādharī of Gadādharabhaṭṭa, Ed., Dube, Vindhyaśvarīprasād, C.S.S. No. 187, Benares, year not mentioned.

Candrikākhaṇḍanam of Rāmasubrahmaṇyaśāstri, Madras, 1927.

Candrikāprakāśaprasara of Venkaṭaramaṇācārya, Gauḍagiri, with *Advaitataraṇi* of Naṭeśārya, Madras, 1926.

Candrikābhūṣaṇam of Raṅgappācārya, Cochi, Ed. Madhvarāyācārya, Cochi, Kumbakonam, 1905.

Candrikāmaṇḍanam of Satyadhyānatīrtha, Tirupati, 1916.

Carakasaṁhitā of Āgniveśa, Ed., Ācārya, Jadavaji Trikaṁji, Varanasi, 1941.

Tattvacintāmaṇi of Gaṅgeśopādhyāya with *Dīdhiti* of Raghunathaśiromani, Ed., Tarkālaṅkāra, M. Chandrakanta, *Anumānakhaṇḍa* only, Calcutta, 1849.

——of Gaṅgeśopādhyāya Ed., Vidyāsāgara, Jīvānanda, *Upamānakhaṇḍa* only, Calcutta, 1972.

——of Gaṅgesopādhyāya with commentary of Tarkavāgīṣa, Mathurānatha, Ed., Tarkavāgiśa, Kāmākhyānātha, *Pratyakṣakhaṇḍa* only, Delhi, 1974.

——of Gaṅgeṣopādhyāya with *Prakāśa* of Rucidatta, Ed., Bālāśāstri, *Śabdakhaṇḍa*, incomplete, The Paṇḍit, Benares, 1871-74.

Tattvapradīpikā of Citsukha with commentary of Pratyaksvarūpa, Benares, 1884.

Tattvamuktākalāpa of Vedāntācārya, Ed., Śrīnivāsagopālācārya, T.T., Mysore, 1954.

Tattvāloka of Ānandajñāna, Ed., Dīkṣitar, T.A. Veṅkaṭeśvara, Bombay, 1969.

Tarkasaṅgraha of Annaṁbhaṭṭa, Ed., with Eng. Tr., Virūpakṣānanda, Svāmi, Madras, 1980.

Tāṇḍyamahābrāhmaṇa with commentary of Sāyaṇa, Ed., Vedāntavāgīsa, Ānandacandra, Calcutta, 1870,

Tātparyacandrikā of Vyāsatīrtha with Bhāṣya of Madhva, *Tattvaprakāśikā* of Jayatīrtha and *Prakāśa* of Rāghavendra, Ed., Rāghavendrācārya, R., Mysore, Vol. I, 1911, Vol. II, 1915, Vol. III, 1920, Vol. IV, 1922.

Taittirīyaraṇyaka with commentary of Sāyaṇa, Ed., Nārāyaṇaśāstri, Poona, 1934.

Daśaprakaraṇa of Madhvācārya with *Mandāramañjari* of Vyāsatīrtha etc., 4 Pts., Madras, 1969-72.

Nāṭyaśāstra of Bharatamuni with *Abhinavabhārati* of Abhinavagupta, Ed., Madhusudanaśāstri, Pt. I., Varanasi, 1971.

Naiṣkarmyasiddhi of Sureśvarācārya, Ed. Hiriyanna, M., Mysore, 1925.

——of Sureśvarācārya, with *Kleśāpahariṇi* of Saccidānandendrasarasvati, Svāmi. Holenarsipur, 1968.

Nyāyakusumañjalī of Udayana, Ed., Upādhyāyā, Padmaprasāda and Ḍhuṇḍhirājaśāstri, Benares, 1957.

Nyāyacandrikā of Vidyāsāgara, Ed., Anantakṛṣṇaśāstri, N.S. and Rāmasvāmiśāstri, Madras, 1959.

Nyāyadarśanam with *Bhāṣya* of Vātsyāyana and Hindi Tr., Dvārikādāsaśāstri, Svāmi, Benares, 1984.

Nyāyadīpavali of Ānandabodha with *Pramāṇamālā*, Ed., Bālarāmaudāseen mandalikā, Benares, 1907.

Nyāyamakaranda of Ānandabodha with commentary of Citsukha, Benares, Fasciculus I, 1901. Fasciculus II, 1903, Fasciculus III, 1905, Fasciculus IV, 1907.

Nyāyamanjari of Jayantabhaṭṭa, Eng. Tr., Bhaṭṭacārāya, Jānakī Vallabha, Delhi, Vol. I, 1978.

Nyāyaratna of Maṇikaṇṭha, Ed., Subrahmaṇyaśāstri, V., and Krishnamāchārya, V., Madras, 1953.

Nyāyavārtika of Udyotakara, Ed., Dube, Vindhyeśvarīprasād, Benares, 1915.

Nyāyasiddhāntamuktavali of Viśvanāthapañcānana, Benares, 1972.

Nyāyasūtra of Gotama, Ed., Basu, Major B.D., Allahabad, 1930.

Nyāyāmṛtādvaitasiddhī of Vyāsatīrtha and Madhusūdnasarasvati respectively with seven commentaries Ed., Anantakṛṣṇaśāstri, N.S., 1934.

Nyāyāmṛtādvaitasiddhī of Vyāsatīrtha and Madhusūdhanasarasvati respectively with Hindi commentary, Yogīndrānanda, Svāmi, 2 Vols., Varanasi, 1977.

Nyāsa of Jinendrabuddhi, Ed., Chakravarti, Sureshcandra, 3 Vols., Rajshahi, 1913-25.

Pañcadaśī of Vidyāraṇya Eng. Tr., Mahadevan, T.M.P., Madras, 1975.

Pañcapādikā of Padmapāda and Vivaraṇa of Prakāśātman with other commentaries, Madras Government Oriental Series, No. CLV, Madras, 1958.

Padārthadharmasaṅgraha of Praśastapada with commentary of Srīdhara, Vizianagaram, 1895.

Paratattvaprakāśikā of Vijayīndratīrtha, Nanjangud, 1972.

Paramārthabhūṣaṇam of Uttamur Vīrarāghavācārya, Madras, 1959.

Pratyabhijñāhrdayam of Kṣemarāja with Eng. Tr., Jaidevasingh, Delhi, 1963.

Praśastapādabhāṣya of Praśastadeva with commentary of Ḍhuṇḍhirājaśāstri, Ed., Nārāyaṇamiśra, Varanasi, 1980.

Prasthānabheda of Madhusūdanasarasvati, Śrīraṅgam, 1920.

Bṛhadāraṇyakopaniṣndbhāsya vārtika of Sureśvarācārya with Śāstraprakāśikā of Ānandagiri, Ed., Agase, K.S., Poona, 1992-94.

Bodhaikyasiddhi of Acyutarāya, Ed., Marulakara, S.S., Poona, 1951.

Brahmasiddhi of Maṇḍanamiśra, Ed., Kuppusvāmiśāstri, S., Madras, 1937.

Brahmasūtra of Bādarāyaṇa with Bhāṣya of Sankarācārya, Eng. Tr., Gambhīrānanda, Svāmi, Calcutta, 1965.

Brahmasūtrānugunyasīddhi of Kṛṣṇaśāstri, Ed., Hariharaśāstri, Kumbakonam, 1926.

Brahmānandīyabhāvaprakāśa of Pañcāpagesaśāstriar with *Tippaṇa* of

Subrahmaṇyaśāstri, V, Cochin, 1961.
Bhagavadgīta of Vyāsa with *Bhāṣya* of Madhvācārya, *Prameyadīpikā* of Jayatirtha and *Bhāvaprakāśa* of Śrīnivāsatīrtha, Ed., Janorikar, G.M., Bombay, 1887.
——of Vyāsa with commentary of Saṅkarācārya and Eng. Tr., Mahādevaśāstri, Allādi, Madras, 1977.
Bhāmatī of Vācaspatimiśra, Ed., Ḍhuṇḍhirājaśāstri, Benares, Pt. I, 1935, Pt. II, 1937.
Bhedajayaśrī of Venīdattācārya, Ed., Upādhyāya, Tribhuvan Prasād, Benares, 1933.
Bhedadhikkāra of Nṛsiṁhāśrama, Ed., Drāvida, Lakshmaṇaśāstri, Benares, 1904.
Bhedaratnam of Saṅkaramiśra, Ed., Sūryanārāyaṇaśukla, Benares, 1933.
Bhedasiddhi of Viśvanātha pañcānanabhattācārya, Ed. Suryanārayaṇaśukla, Benares, 1933.
Bhedojjīvana of Vyāsatīrtha with commentary of Śrīnivāsa, Ed., Krishnācārya, T.R., Bombay, 1901.
Mahabhārata of Vyāsa, Ed., Krishnācarya, T.R. and Vyāsācārya, T.R. 18 Vols., Bombay, 1906.
Mahābhāsya of Patañjali with *Pradīpa* of Kaiyaṭa, *Uddyota* of Nāgeśabhaṭṭa and *Chāyā* of Vaidyanātha Payaguṇḍe, 3 Vols. Delhi, 1967.
Māṇḍūkyakārika of Gauḍapāda, Ed. with Eng. Tr., Karmarkar, R.D., Poona, 1953.
Mādhovatantramukhamardana of Appayyadīkṣita with *Vidhvaṁsana*, Ed., Apte, V.G., Poona, 1940.
Mādhvamukhālaṅkāra of Vanamālimiśra, Ed., Varkhedkar, Narasimhācārya, Benares, 1936.
Mānameyodaya of Nārāyaṇa, Ed., with Eng., Tr., Kunhan Rājā, C. and Suryanārāyaṇaśāstri, S.S., Adyar, 1975.
Mīmāṁsānyāyaprakāśa of Āpadeva, Eng. Tr., Edgerton, Franklin, New Haven, 1929.
Mīmāṃsāsūtra of Jaimini, Eng. Tr., Thadani, N.V., Delhi, 1952.
Mokṣasiddhi of Kṣṣṇagiri, Benares, 1181.
Yatīndramatadīpikā of Srīnivāsadāsa, Ed., with Eng. Tr., Ādidevānanda, Svāmi, Madras, 1949.
Yuktimallikā of Vādirājatīrtha with commentary of Surottamatīrtha, Ed., Krishnācārya, T.R., Bombay, 1903.
Raghuvaṁśa of Kālidāsa, Ed., Kale, M.R., Bombay, 1925.

Vākyapadīyam of Bhartṛhari with trilingual commentary Ed., Varma, Dr. Satyakam, *Brahmakāṇḍam* only, Delhi, 1970.

Vādaratnāvali of Viṣṇudāsa, Ed., Govindācārya Bannanje, Manipal, 1968.

Vādāvali of Jayatīrtha with *Bhāvadīpikā* of Rāghavendra, Ed., Krishnācārya, T.R., Bombay, 1905.

Vijñaptimātratāsiddhi of Vasubandhu, Ed. with Hindi, Tr. Tiwari, Dr. Mahesh, Varanasi, 1967.

Vedāntakalpataruparimala of Appayyadīksita, Ed., Tailanga, Rāmaśāstri, Benares, 1985.

Vedāntakalpalatikā of Madhusudanasarasvati, Ed., with Eng. Tr., Karmarkar, R.D., Poona, 1962.

——of Madhusūdanasarasvati, Ed., Rāmājñaśarmapāṇdeya, Benares, 1920.

Vedāntaparibhāṣa of Dharmarājādhvarīndra, Ed. with Eng. Tr., Snryanārāyāṇaśāstri, S.S., Adyar, 1942.

Vedāantaprakriyāpratyabhijñā of Saccidānandendrasarasvati, Svāmi, Holenarsipur, 1964.

Vedāntasāra of Sadānandayogīndra, Ed., with Eng. Tr., Nikhilānanda, Svāmi, Calcutta, 1968.

Vedāntasiddhāntamuktāvalī of Prakāśānanda, Ed., with Eng. Tr., Venis, Arthur, Varanasi, 1975.

Vedāntasiddhāntasaṅgraha of Vanamālimiṣra, Ed., Kavi, Devīprasādasarma, Benares, 1913.

Śaṅkarapādabhūṣaṇam of Raghunāthasüri, Ed. Marulakar, S.B. and Kāśikar, D., Poona, 1932.

Śataḍūṣaṇī of Vedāntadeśika, Ed., Śrīvatsankachār, V., Madras, 1974.

Śatapathabrāhmaṇa, Ed., Weber, Dr. Albrecht, Varanasi, 1864.

Śatabhūṣaṇī of Anantakṛṣṇaśāstri, N.S., Madras, 1956.

Srautākhaṇḍārthasiddhi of Rāmānandasarasvati, Ed., Sāmiśāstri, Benares, 1961.

Saṁkṣepaśārīraka of Sarvajñātman, Critical Ed. with Eng. Tr., Veezhināthan, Dr. N., Madras, 1972.

Saṁkṣcpaśārīrakasārasaṅgraha of Madhusūdanasarasvati Ed., Gupta, Govindadas, Benares, 1887.

Sarvadarśanasaṅgraha of Mādhavācārya with *Prakāsh* Hindi commentary, Ṛṣi, Dr. Umāśaṅkaraśarma, Varanasi, 1978.

Sarvavedāntasiddhāntasārasaṅgraha of Saṅkarācarya, Ed. with Eng. Tr., Tattvānanda, Svāmi, Kalady, 1970.

Siddhāntabindu of Madhusūdanasarasvati, Ed., Triambakamśāstri, Benares, 1928.

——of Madhusūdanasarasvati, Ed., with Eng. Tr., Divanji, P.C. Baroda, 1933.

——of Madhusudanasarasvati, Eng. Tr., Modi, P.M., Bombay, 1929.

——of Madhusudanasarasvati, with Sanskrit commentary of Abhyaṅkar, K.V., Ed., Abhyaṅkar, V.S., Poona, 1962.

Siddhāntaleśasaṅgraha of Appayyadīkṣita, Ed. Śāstri P.P.S., Srirangam, 1935.

Siddhitraya of Yāmunācārya, Ed., Śāstri, Rāmamiśra, Benares, 1900.

Sphoṭasiddhi of Maṇḍanamisra, Ed., Rāmanāthaśāstri, S.K., Madras, 1931.

Svarajyasiddhi of Gaṅgādharendrasarasvati with *Kaivalyakalpadruma*, Ed., Chaudhuri, B.M., Benares, 1891.

II. English

Ballantyne, J.R. The Sāṅkhya Aphorisms of Kapila, Varanasi, 1963.

Baller, E. Communism and Cultural Heritage, Moscow, 1984.

Bandopadhyay, Nandita. The Concept of Logical Fallacies, Calcutta, 1977.

Bhandarkar, R.G. Vaisṇavism, Śaivism and other Minor Religious systems, Varanasi, 1965.

Bharati, Svami Agehananda, A Functional Analysis of Indian Thought and its Social Margins, Varanasi, 1964.

Bhattacarya. Ashutosh, Studies in Post-Śaṅkara Dialectics, Calcutta, 1936.

Bhattacarya, B.K. Causality in Science and Philosophy, Calcutta, 1969.

Bhattacarya, Dineshchandra: History of Navya-Nyāya in Mithila, Darbhanga, 1958.

Bhattacarya, Janaki Vallabha: Negation, Calcutta, 1965.

Brodov, V, Indian Philosophy in Modern Times, Moscow, 1984.

Cenkner, William: A Tradition of Teachers: Śaṅkara and the Jagadgurus Today, Delhi, 1984.

Chakraborty, Nirod Baran: The Advaita concept of Falsity—A Critical Stady, Calcutta, 1967.

Chatterjee, Satischandra: The Nyāya Theory of Knowledge, Calcutta, 1950.

Chattopadhyaya, Debiprasad: Indian Atheism—A Marxist Approach,

Delhi, 1983.
——: What is Living and What Is Dead in Indian Philosophy, Delhi, 1977.
——: Indian Philosophy—A Popular Introduction, Delhi, 1982.
Chemparathy, George: An Indian Rational Theology, Vienna, 1972.
Das, A.C.: Studies in Philosophy, Calcutta, 1962.
Dasgupta, Dr. Surendranath: A History of Indian Philosophy, 5 Vols., Delhi, 1975.
Deussen, Dr. Paul: Outlines of Indian Philosophy, Berlin, 1907.
Deutsch, Eliot and Buitenan, J.A.B. Van: A Source Book of Advaita-vedānta, Honolulu, 1971.
Engels, Frederick: Anti During, Moscow, 1977.
Fagnet, Emile: Invitation into Philosophy, London, 1912.
Fedoseyev, Pyotr: Philosophy and Scientific Cognition, Moscow, 1985.
Gambhirananda, Svami; Eight Upaniṣads with commentary of Śaṅkarācārya, 2 Vols, Calcutta, 1966.
Goreh, Nehemiah Nilakantha; A Rational Refutation of the Hindu Philosophical Systems, Vepery, 1897.
Guha, Dineschandra: Navya Nyāya System of Logic, Varanasi, 1968.
Gupta, Dr. Anima Sen: Sāṅkhya and Advaitavedānta A Comparative Study, Patna, 1973.
Gupta, Dr. Sanjukta: Studies in the Philosophy of Madhusudana-sarasvati, Calcutta, 1966.
Gupta, Sisirkumar: Madhusudanasarasvati on the Bhagavadgita, Delhi, 1977.
Hiriyanna, M.: Indian Philosophical Studies, Mysore, Vol. I, 1957, Vol. II, 1972.
——: Outlines of Indian Philosophy, London, 1951.
Hiriyanna, M.: The Mission of Philosophy, Mysore, 1960.
Ingalls, D.H.H.: Materials for the Study of Navya-Npāya Logic, London, 1951.
Joshi, R.V.: Studies in Indian Logic and Metaphysics, Delhi, 1979.
Kapra, Fritjof: The Tao of Physics, London, 1985.
Katre, S.M.: Introduction to Indian Textual Criticism, Poona, 1954.
Kattackal, Dr. Jacob: Religion and Ethics in Advaita, Kottayam, 1982.
Kharin, Yu, A.: Fundamentals of Dialectics, Moscow, 1981.
Lad, A.K.: A Comparative Study of the Concept of Liberation in Indian Philosophy, Burhanpur, 1967.

Macnicol, Nicol: Indian Theism, Delhi, 1968.

Mainkar, T.G.: A Comparative Study of the Commentaries on the Bhagvadgita, Delhi, 1969.

Malkani, G.R.: Metaphysics of Advaitavedānta, Amalner, 1961.

Matilal, B.K.: The Navya Nyāya Doctrine of Negation, Cambridge, 1968.

Mill, John Stuart: System of Logic Ratiocinative and Inductive, London, 1916.

Muller, F. Max: Lectures on the Origin and Growth of Religion, Varanasi, 1964.

——: Six Systems of Indian Philosophy, Varanasi, 1971.

——: The Upaniṣads, 2 Pts., Delhi, 1969.

Murty, Dr. K. Satchidananda: Revelation and Reason in Advaitavedānta, Delhi, 1974.

Narain, K.: An Outline of the Madhva Philosophy, Allahabad, 1968.

Oizerman, Theodor: Problems of the History of Philosophy, Moscow, 1973.

Pandeya, R.C.: A Panorama of Indian Philosophy, Delhi, 1966.

Pandit, W.N.: The Place of Bhakti in Advaita Philosophy, Nagpur, 1945.

Plekhanov, G.: The Development of the Monist View of History, Moscow, 1980.

Radhakrishnan, Dr. S.: Indian Philosophy, 2 Vols. Museum Street, W.C., 1941.

Rao, Alur Venkat: A Handbook of Sri Madhvācārya's Purnabrahma Philosophy, Dharwar, 1954.

Rao, Dr. K.B. Ramakrishna: Ontology of Advaita with special reference to Māya, Mulki, 1964.

Rao, Dr. P. Nagaraja: The Epistemology of Dvaitavedānta, Adyar, 1976.

Rogers, Arthur Kenyon: A Brief Introduction to Modern Philosophy, London, 1909.

——: A Students' History of Philosophy, London, 1908.

Roy, Raja Ram Mohan: Selected Works, Delhi, 1977.

Roychowdhury, Makhanlal: The Din Ilahi, Calcutta, 1941.

Safaya, Raghunath: Indian Psychology, Delhi, 1976.

Sahasrabudhe, M.T.: A survey of the Pre-Śaṇkara Advaitavedānta, Poona, 1968.

Sastri, Gaurinath: The Philosophy of Word and Meaning, Calcutta, 1959.

Sastri, Kokileswara: An Introduction to Advaita Philosophy, Varanasi, 1979.
Sastri, Manmathnath: Outlines of Hindu Metaphysics, Delhi, 1976.
Saxena, Dr. Lekshmi: NeoHegelian and Neo-Advaitic Monism, Delhi, 1980.
Sharma, B.N.K.: History of the Dvaita School of Vedānta and its literature, Delhi, 1981.
———: Lectures on Vedānta, Dharwar, 1973.
———: Philosophy of Sri Madhvācārya, Bombay, 1962.
Singh, Dr. Satyavrata: Vedāntadeśika: A Study, Varanasi, 1958.
Sinha, Ajitkumar: Vedānta and Modern Science, Bombay, 1978.
Sinha, Jadunath: Indian Realism, Delhi, 1972.
Sircar, Dr. Mahendranath: The System of Vedāntic Thought and Culture, Calcutta, 1925.
Solomon, Esther, A.: Avidyā: A Problem of Truth and Reality.
Solomon, Theodor, J. The Origin and Development of Early Indian Bhakti, Chicago, 1966.
Srinivasachari, P.N.: Philosophy of Viśiṣṭādvaita, Adyar, 1970.
Ui, H.: Vaiśesika Philosophy, Varanasi, 1962.
Varadachari, K.C.: Aspects of Bhakti, Mysore, 1966.
Verma, K.M.P.: Kant and the Gīta, New Delhi, 1980.
Vidyabhusana, Satischandra: History of Indian Logic, Calcutta, 1921.

III. Miscellaneous (Articles, Collections, Dictionaries, Journals etc.)

A Dictionary of Philosophy, Lacey, A.R., London, 1980.
A Dictionary of Philosophy, Frolov, I., Moscow, 1984.
Advaitagranthakośa, prepared by a disciple of Sri Iṣṭasiddhīndrasarasvati, Calcutta, year not mentioned.
Advaitākṣaramālikā, Kanchipuram, 1978.
Advaitavedānta Literature—Bibliographical Survey, Thankasvami, R., Madras, 1980.
'Advaitism in the Religious Experiences and Thoughts of the Bhaktas', Maitra, S.N., Vedāntakesari, No. 17, Madras, 1930.
Ain-I-Akbari of Abul Fazl in 3 Vols., Tr. Eng. Blochman, Delhi, Vol. I, 1977, Vols. II & III, 1978.
Annals of the Bhandarkar Oriental Research Institute, Vols. VIII, IX, XI, XIII, Poona, 1928-31.
———Diamond Jubilee Volume, Poona, 1978.
Brahmavādin 1895-1940, Combined Volume, Bangalore, 1981.
Catalogus Catalogorum, Aufrecht, Theodor, Wiesbaden, 1962.

Cultural Heritage of India, 4 Vols., Calcutta, 1975.
'Date of Madhusudanasarasvati', Nahane, A. Sulochana, A.B.O.R.I., Vol. XXX, Poona, 1949.
'Dialectics and its Place in Indian Thought', Shanbhag, D.N., Journal of Karnataka University, No. 17, Dharwar, 1973.
Dr. S. Radhakrishnan Souvenir Volume, Moradabad, 1964.
Einstein and the Philosophical Problems of Twentieth century Physics, Moscow, 1983.
Encyclopaedia of Indian Philosophy, Potter, Karl, H., Delhi, Vol. I, 1983 (Revised), Vol. II, 1977.
'Gangeśa on the Concept of Universal Property', Matilal, B.K., Philosophy East and West, No. XVIII, 1968.
Indian Historical Quarterly, Vol. XIII, 1937.
Jha Commemoration volume, Poona, 1937.
Journal of Royal Asiatic Society of Bengal, Vol. XXVIII, Calcutta, 1860.
Logic, Methodology and Philosophy of Science III, Ed., Rootselaar, B. Van and Staal, J.F., Amsterdam, 1968.
Madhva's commentaries on Aitareya, Bṛhadāraṇyaka, Chāndogya, Kena, Kaṭha, Muṇḍaka, Praśna, Yajnīyamantra, Ātharvaṇa and Taittirīya Upanisads, Udipi, 1969.
'My approach to Indian Philosophy', Staal, J.F., Indian Philosophical Annual, 1966.
Preceptors of Advaita, Ed., Mahadevan, T.M.P., Secundarabad, 1968.
Proceedings and Transactions of the All India Oriental Conference, 21st Session, Poona, 1968.
Śabdakalpadruma of Bahadur, Radhakantadev, 5 Vols. Delhi, 1961.
Studies in Indian Thought, Ed., Harold, G., Coward, Delhi, 1983.
'The Definition of Pervasion in Navya Nyāya', Mukherjee, A.K., Journal of Indian Philosophy, No. 4, 1976.
The Mysore Orientalist, Vol. III, 1973.
Vācaspatyam of Tarkavācaspati, Tārānāth, 6 Vols., Varanasi, 1962.
'Vedānta and Communism', Sharvananda, Prabuddhabhārata, No. 50, Calcutta, 1945.
'Viṣṇu the Pervader', Danielon, Alain, Adyar Library Bulletin, Vol. XVIII, 1954.

Cultural Heritage of India, 4 Vols., Calcutta, 1975.
'Date of Madhusūdanasarasvatī', Nabane, A. Sulochana, A.B.O.R.I., Vol. XXX, Poona, 1949.
'Dialectics and its Place in Indian Thought', Shanbhag, D.N., Journal of Karnataka University, No. 17, Dharwar, 1973.
Dr. S. Radhakrishnan Souvenir Volume, Moradabad, 1964.
Einstein and the Philosophical Problems of Twentieth-century Physics, Moscow, 1983.
Encyclopaedia of Indian Philosophy, Potter, Karl, H., Delhi, Vol. I, 1983 (Revised), Vol. II, 1977.
'Gaṅgeśa on the Concept of Universal Property', Matilal, B.K., Philosophy East and West, No. XVIII, 1968.
Indian Historical Quarterly, Vol. XIII, 1937.
Jha Commemoration volume, Poona, 1937.
Journal of Royal Asiatic Society of Bengal, Vol. XXVIII, Calcutta, 1860.
Logic, Methodology and Philosophy of Science III, Ed., Rootselaar, B. Van and Staal, J.F., Amsterdam, 1968.
Madhva's commentaries on Aitareya, Bṛhadāraṇyaka, Chāndogya, Kena, Kaṭha, Muṇḍaka, Praśna, Yājñyamantra, Ātharvaṇa and Taittirīya Upaniṣads, Udipi, 1969.
'My approach to Indian Philosophy', Staal, J.F., Indian Philosophical Annual, 1966.
Preceptors of Advaita, Ed., Mahadevan, T.M.P., Secundarabad, 1968.
Proceedings and Transactions of the All India Oriental Conference, 21st Session, Poona, 1968.
Śabdakalpadruma of Bahadur, Radhakantadev, 5 Vols, Delhi, 1961.
Studies in Indian Thought, Ed., Harold, G., Coward, Delhi, 1983.
'The Definition of Pervasion in Navya Nyāya', Mukherjee, A.K., Journal of Indian Philosophy, No. 4, 1976.
The Mysore Orientalist, Vol. III, 1973.
Vācaspatyam of Tarkavācaspati, Tārānāth, 6 Vols., Varanasi, 1962.
'Vedānta and Communism', Sharvananda, Prabuddhabhārata, No. 50, Calcutta, 1945.
'Viṣṇu the Pervader', Danielou, Alain, Adyar Library Bulletin, Vol. XVIII, 1954.

Index

O